TRAIL RUTS

OREGON'S CENTENNIAL WAGON TRAIN

Jim,
Enjoy!
Dick Carter
3/9/17

RICHARD LEWIS CARTER

SEATTLE, WASHINGTON

SEPTEMBER 11, 1976, JANUARY 2016

Printed in the United States of America

First Printing, 2016

ISBN: 978-1522726371

For orders, permissions, or requests, including special discounts for quantity purchases to schools and churches, please contact the author at dcart29@comcast.net.

The content written by the author or contributors in this book is the sole opinion of that section's creator and does not necessarily represent the opinions or policies of any other individuals or any of the other organizations or companies included.

Developmental Editor and Designer:
Kristin Carroccino, www.carroccinocollective.com

Manuscript typist: Karen Robinson

Proofreaders: Penny Reid and Beth Cockrel

Cover Photo: The author rides "Chief" ahead of the wagon train as it crosses the plains of Wyoming. Photo by Ivan Hoyer.

Any artwork not specifically credited is part of the public domain.

To our pioneer ancestors who suffered countless hardships to make us all that we are today.

TABLE OF CONTENTS

AUTHOR'S NOTE, 2016 .... - 1 -

INTRODUCTION, 1976 .... - 3 -

I. THE ORGANIZATION .... - 5 -

II. INDEPENDENCE CAMP ....- 17 -

III. POTTAWATOMI TERRITORY ....- 27 -

IV. RAIDERS AND OTHER RUCKUSES ....- 38 -

V. FAIRBURY OR BUST ....- 47 -

VI. THE LITTLE BLUE ....- 56 -

VII. THE PLATTE...- 66 -

VIII. THE NORTH PLATTE ....- 80 -

IX. FT. LARAMIE RELIVED ....- 94 -

X. THE UPPER NORTH PLATTE ....- 103 -

XI. ANTELOPE COUNTRY ....- 114 -

XII. THE SWEETWATER ....- 124 -

XIII. GREEN RIVER RENDEZVOUS ....- 139 -

XIV. WEDDINGS AND GRAVES...- 150 -

XV. FROM THE BEAR TO THE SNAKE ....- 161 -

XVI. THE SNAKE..- 175 -

XVII. HEAT AND HOT TEMPERS ....- 185 -

XVIII. EASTERN OREGON... 199 -

XIX. UMATILLA COUNTRY..- 212 -

XX. THE COLUMBIA ....- 224 -

XXI. THE WILLAMETTE...- 237 -

XXII. SETTLING IN OREGON..- 242 -

APPENDIX: *ON TO OREGON CAVALCADE* ....- 248 -

OREGON CAVALCADE ITINERARY ....- 254 -

OREGON CAVALCADE MAP........................- 255 -

REFERENCES ....- 256 -

ACKNOWLEDGEMENTS ....- 258 -

ABOUT THE AUTHOR........................- 259 -

Oregon Trail Ruts* near Guernsey, Wyoming. Public Commons photo by Phil Konstantin.

* "Trail ruts" are deep indentations in the earth made by the thousands of heavy wagons pioneers drove across the West during the 19th Century that can still be seen in some places of the original Oregon Trail.

AUTHOR'S NOTE, 2016

At age 86 I've been thinking of leaving some kind of legacy to my heirs and to the world. Lacking a financial fortune, I have decided to leave something more valuable: the rich memories of a great experience.

Trail Ruts retraces the pathway of one of mankind's greatest migrations: the nineteenth-century movement of people wanting a new start in the Oregon Territory. The celebration of Oregon's 100th year of statehood gave rise to the idea of honoring our pioneer forbearers with a wagon train in the late 1950s. This story relates what happened when that idea became reality.

I'm hoping my readers will feel personally ennobled as they read about the adventures of our ancestors: we Oregonians in the 20th Century who formed a group to retrace the path of the pioneers, as well as those future Oregonians in the 19th Century we were learning about. After all, reading is a way of feeling proud because of the exploits of others. Reading about the courage, struggles and victories of our predecessors also lends a fresh perspective to our own day-to-day living.

My life was changed greatly by my experience in 1959 of traveling in the footsteps—and *trail ruts*—of a generation of Americans who migrated west to settle in territory foreign and daunting to most of them. In addition to being an exploration of our nation's, and my own family's history, my experience on the Oregon Trail was transformative because of my fellow sojourners: a group of men and women who, like me, were eager to experience the past in order to shape the present and hopefully our futures.

I've written this account in part to share their stories and how living in a community of fellow travelers one summer in the mid-20th Century on an historic trail left most of us in awe of the tenacity and ingenuity of our forebears. Our struggles with personality differences in our own self-formed community, clashes with property owners along the Trail, illness, fatigue, disappointments, joys, new friendships, and much laughter surely paled in comparison to the Oregon Trail pioneers. During the 1800s people on this 2,100-mile trek suffered the rigors of covered wagon travel as well as personality conflicts and disagreements over how to manage a wagon train. The pioneer journals we read often spoke of the same kinds of problems.

I completed writing the manuscript of my account of the 1959 "Oregon Cavalcade" in 1976. After communicating with a few publishing houses, I decided to let this story rest until the time was ripe. Several decades have passed; I've raised a family and watched my grandchildren begin embarking on their own adventures, enjoyed a good career and fruitful retirement. The advent of digitalization and ability to self-publish, as well as my advancing age, informs me that this is the right time to publish my Oregon Trail memories. As technology, fast-paced living, and conflicts seem to be ever-increasing in the 21st Century, I think it's good to sit back and experience what life may have been like not all that long ago with those who came before us as we read and ponder their wealth of stories.

—Richard Carter,
January 2016, Seattle, Washington

INTRODUCTION, 1976

In 1959 a group of adventure-minded romantics, progeny of pioneers, set out to reenact the exodus of their ancestors to Oregon. They feigned some rigors of the trek; other hardships were genuine. The problems of group loyalty vs. self-interest were just as real in 1959 as in the 1840s and 50s. The twentieth-century group was not menaced by cholera or Indians, but instead they fought tourists and traffic. This book compares the adventures and hardships found along the Oregon Trail in two eras, the mid-nineteenth and the mid-twentieth centuries.

The "Oregon Trail" is more a name of function than of location. To those who used this overland route to come to Oregon, it was the "Oregon Trail." However, for those who were traveling to California, it was the "California Trail," and for Mormons going to Utah and Idaho, the same route was the "Mormon Trail." Some people compromise and call it the "Immigrant" or "Emigrant" trail. Either spelling is acceptable, depending on whether you're thought of as leaving the East or as arriving in the West. In view of the lack of an agreed-upon proper noun, I'll usually only call it by the word "trail" using a lowercase "t."

At times the pioneers seeking California gold, Utah religious freedom or Oregon land followed the same trace, and at other times there were several alternate routes. These different courses depended on the availability of water, pasture and fuel for campfires. The locations of these necessities varied from year to year and even from month to month. Basically the trail followed the routes of rivers and varied in width from 40 feet to 40 miles.

The use of the trail began when the first wagon was brought to the Oregon Territory in 1841, and tapered off after completion of the transcontinental railroad in 1866. Barbed-wire fences also discouraged the driving of covered wagons across the prairie. However, since the trail followed the smoothest terrain in the straightest line possible, many modern highways and railroads follow the same path. In this sense the trail is still in use.

Estimates of how many people came west over the Oregon Trail range from 50,000 to 500,000. Of those who began the trek, thousands died along the way. Most of these were cholera victims and were buried in unmarked graves. My own great-grandmother was among those who died that way. In Wyoming's Rocky Mountains where stone was available for headstones, graves can still be seen every few hundred feet. We counted an average of some 16 per mile. According to diaries written by survivors, just as many people died along other parts of the trail, but either the graves were left unmarked or the wooden markers disappeared.

Historians have been reluctant to say when a wagon train last came to Oregon via the Oregon Trail. Not only was the event unheralded, but semantical problems arise in defining "Oregon Trail," and "wagon train." If historians choose to call our route and our expedition authentic, they now have 1959 as a final date.

Besides telling about Oregon's Centennial Wagon Train and about the trail to Oregon, this book portrays instances of how the human animal can be sometimes petty and sometimes noble when subjected to the physical and psychological rigors of such a trek. Newspaper reporters who knew us well were kind and respectful in not writing about the friction and factions among wagon train members. Since time has settled the disputes and soothed the hurts, I feel secure in writing dispassionately and without malice about some of our conflicts.

I. The Organization

Chief Man-Afraid-of-His-Horse waved his lance and shouted defiance at the wagon train. We paralleled the hillcrest where the chief was riding and saw that ahead of us the raised ground ended in a slope down to the open prairie. We knew that any moment the Sioux warriors behind the crest might begin their attack. If they waited another three minutes we would be beyond the hill and they would have a broader expanse of open ground to charge across before reaching us. This would give us more time to circle up and defend ourselves before being overwhelmed. They had to attack soon or they would lose a strategic advantage. Our tension grew as we came closer to the open prairie.

Someone in the wagon train fired his revolver. The chief turned and shouted a command to his men. Suddenly at least 50 braves were silhouetted against the skyline where only the chief had been. Some were on foot; others rode horseback. All of them were wearing war paint and yelling fiercely. Without pausing on the hillcrest, they swept over it and charged towards us.

Our horses and mules started to gallop and our wagons bounced across the rough ground towards the flat where we could fort up. As I bounced along in Shorty Hilliard's wagon, I saw something ahead which made me feel betrayed and angry. Our pre-chosen battleground was filled with spectators! Thousands of them had gathered to watch the Indians wipe us out. Being unable to reach our chosen site, we were forced to circle where we were. Six of our seven wagons followed each other careening and tipping precariously as we crossed small gullies and hit boulders while attempting to form a circle. Meanwhile, the mules pulling the seventh wagon panicked and ran out of control up a swale away from the rest of us. Rudy Roudebaugh calmed them and got them back into our circle just as the Indians reached us.

Everything was confused. "My God," I thought angrily, "how could a person possibly get into such a mess in 1959?" The last battle with the Sioux had happened over 70 years before and here we were in another. As the Indians swept around us, I felt thankful that the whole episode was just an enactment. Our wagon train was only a replica of those of the 19th Century, and everyone was firing blanks. We and the Indians, beneath our costumes, were still real people.

The excitement had started back in Oregon in the mind of a Roseburg jeweler named Alan Knudtson. He began moving us towards this situation when he started thinking of ways to help Oregon celebrate its 100th anniversary as a state. Alan was the same man who in 1954 thought of racing horses against a southbound train to publicize the train's slow service. People along the 100-mile stretch of line still contend that the horses would have won had the train made all its regular stops.

Our wagon train's primary purpose was to enact a great phase of western history, and in doing this, to pay homage to the pioneers who used the Oregon Trail. Secondarily, the wagon train had a more commercial purpose: to let the country know Oregon was celebrating its State Centennial and to urge people to come visit. This commercial motive was primary in the minds of the people who financed the trip, but I found along the way that it made for better public relations if I reversed the priorities.

Along with Alan Knudtson there were several other young men from the Roseburg Jaycees: Verner Anderson, dentist; Dick Smith, hotel manager; Ivan Hoyer, radio announcer; and Eldon Caley, attorney. They formed a non-profit corporation called "On to Oregon Cavalcade, Inc." and planned a covered wagon trek from Independence, Missouri, to Independence, Oregon, a journey over 2,000 miles long.

Dick Smith, assistant manager of the Umpqua Hotel, was elected president of the corporation, and Alan Knudtson, the thinker, was vice president. Late in 1958 William Dawkins and Associates from Medford, Oregon, was retained to do the administration and publicity on the excursion. The firm also helped lobby $25,000 from the Oregon State Legislature to aid the trek.

I was 29 then and working for Bill Dawkins. Bill had been an English instructor of mine at Southern Oregon College. I remember him saying one time about those days, "I didn't worry much about planning a lecture when Carter was in class. All I did was pick some sort of intellectual argument with him and that took care of the hour." Bill quit teaching to form an advertising agency, and I transferred to the University of Oregon where I received my BA in journalism. From there I went to San Francisco where I worked in advertising for several large corporations. In October, 1958, I moved back to Oregon to work for Bill.

My life in San Francisco had caused me to lose touch with the kind of people I was to meet on the wagon train. My friends in California were Russian, Spanish or college educated, and I had been studying their languages. The people I would travel with along the Oregon Trail spoke a language that I knew from my childhood. It was not in the sounds, but in the choices of things to talk about. On the trail, I was once again with people whose main topics were weather, horses, nature, farming, and home-style food.

My Russian studies came about as a result of my feeling powerless while the wheels in Washington and the Kremlin made decisions affecting my life. To help me study the language I cultivated the friendship of Russian émigrés. I also came to know people like Tolstoy, Dostoevsky, Pasternak and Sholokhov through their writings. Then there was the Spanish side of my life. I studied flamenco guitar for two years and this brought me into contact with all sorts of people from Spain. I went beyond the two years of Spanish I'd had in college and learned to lament the Spanish Civil War as if I had lost it myself.

Upon returning to Medford, Oregon, my work for Bill Dawkins consisted mostly of helping to promote industrial development of our area. This was done under the direction of the local power company, our agency's main client.

One morning Bill and I were sitting in his office discussing the welfare of the firm. I remember the room was crammed full of mahogany, leather, carpets and drapes. A dim, cold February sun only served to let us know it was morning. Bill got on the subject of the wagon train he was helping plan "with that bunch in Roseburg."

"What we need to find now," Bill said, "is someone to go along to sort of be business manager and public relations man."

"There must be someone around you could snooker into that."

Bill ignored my facetious comment and went on. "The guys in Roseburg want to keep control of the operation, but I've let them know that if they want my help then I should handle all the money and business deals."

"And moving across the country like that, I guess they'll need a headquarters for banking and mailing."

"Yeah, well, they could handle mail, personnel and supply problems from Roseburg, but I want to be in on the financial decisions. After all, it was my help that got this through the State Centennial Commission and they are looking to me as being responsible."

The next day we returned to the same topic. "You know, Bill, that wagon train sounds interesting. I've got a week's vacation coming this summer. I was thinking last night it might be fun to go out and ride along with them a little ways."

Bill thought a moment, raised his left eyebrow and looked at me. "Come to think of it, you could go with them all the way if you wanted."

He gave me until the next day to think it over. I decided to do it. My mind had become filled with romantic clichés: struggling against nature, forging a path through the wilderness and developing bonds of friendship with my fellow pioneers.

I had been reading Boris Pasternak's <u>Dr. Zhivago</u> and was taken by his ideas on group loyalty. He wrote of accepting your fellow man as a victim of fate and coincidence like yourself, and that you should get along with him for mutual support. It may be impossible to him, but you can take it easy on him so he will go easy on you. You may even achieve something together.

The opportunity to be with a group of people dedicated to a common goal caused me to revel in dreams of camaraderie. My dream gave me a false idea about how the minds of my traveling companions would work. It was a great disappointment to discover later that no one but me had read <u>Dr. Zhivago</u>. Most of the people I was to be with had no idea of putting self-interest aside for the sake of the entire group. On the contrary, some of them kept us on edge with threats to destroy the group unless everything was managed to their personal satisfaction.

Bill Dawkins hired a wagon master for the expedition a month before I decided to go. Gordon R. Serpa, known as "Tex" to all his friends, had been on vacation from his ranch in Ashland, Oregon. He was spending time around the yacht harbor at Newport Beach, California. One day he came in from a fishing excursion and found a telephone message waiting for him. He returned the call and found it was Bill asking if he would accept the job as wagon master. Tex was interested enough to come back to Oregon and look into the situation. When he had met and spoken to the men in Roseburg, he accepted the job.

Tex had spent much of his 39 years around horses. His muscular frame had been pounded quite a few times in rodeo falls and in doing stunt work for movie studios. His curiosity and quick mind had done much to make up for his lack of any formal education beyond grade school. Among his many jobs, Tex had operated riding stables, trained horses, and had even run a wagon train taking tourists for rides around Truckee, Reno and Virginia City, Nevada.

After making my decision to go, I joined Tex in Roseburg where the "On to Oregon Cavalcade, Inc." had an office. We had to choose people to go with us, find wagon sponsors, buy and beg supplies, buy livestock, arrange for the wagons to be built, put together a motorized support section, plan our itinerary and arrange to have ourselves welcomed along the way. Probably the first wagon train member besides Tex and myself that we recruited was the wagon maker, Roy Brabham of Eugene, Oregon. We met Roy on his farm where he was building the wagons. He was dressed in denim overalls and had on a denim coat like some railroad workers wear. His well-worn felt hat had a sagging brim which kept the light out of his blue yes. The beard he was starting was coming out white. His teeth were clenched onto a small-bowled pipe, giving him an air of sternness which he turned out not to have at all.

Except for his calm and deliberate way of moving, Roy was like a hen counting her chicks as he clucked and scratched around his work shed showing us his treasures: a "Mitchell" axle here, over there a "Bain," on the wall some strips of Arkansas oak for bows, on the floor a form for bending them into shape. He picked up a heavy, iron-rimmed wagon wheel and showed us how it fit on an axle. Deftly he laid the reach and front axle into position on a rear axle to show us how the running gear looked when it was assembled. Our talk ranged into this year's cherry crop and the merits of logging with horses. Roy's tone and manner suggested patience and self-assurance in everything.

The six wagons that Roy built were similar to the original prairie schooners, but the top edge of the boxes didn't have the saucer-like curve of the Conestoga. The 16-foot boxes were new, but the running gear was gathered from old barns and sheds all over Oregon. Some of the wheels were at least 70 years old. Their iron rims turned out to be a discomfort suffered in the name of authenticity.

Weaver Clark built the seventh wagon. He came down from Hillsboro to meet us at Roy's place the day we were there. He said we should call him "Pop" since that was what he answered to in Hillsboro. His chin-whiskers and sideburns made him look all of his 66 years. We were a little concerned that he was that old, but his apparent strength and energy allayed our misgivings. His chatter made me think of a staccato cuckoo clock.

As we were looking at the wagons and other Americana around Roy's shed, Pop mentioned that when he was young he had lived around Gates, Oregon.

The name sounded familiar to me. "Did you know a family named Long there?"

He thought a minute. "Oh, yes. There was a Roy Long and he had a little sister named Nellie."

"Well," I told him, "Nellie Long is my mother."

Pop cocked his head and took a good look at me. "You mean that pretty little thing is *your* mother?"

I grinned and let it go at that. It didn't seem right to tell him that almost 45 more years of life had changed her considerably.

The next time we saw Roy and Pop was at a meeting of the entire expedition in Independence, Oregon. We were gathered to sign a wagon train charter. In the old days when people wanted to form a wagon train, they formed a company and signed a charter agreeing to pool their resources and efforts. They hired wagon masters out of joint funds and sometimes pooled their money to buy bulk supplies. They agreed to stand night watches, herd the livestock and hunt game, depending on each person's abilities and on the needs of the group. All of this was done to ensure a successful journey with a minimum of hardship to everyone. The charter seemed like a great idea, so we signed one too.

I met for the first time most of the people Tex had chosen to go. In choosing them he thought there would be long, boring days on the trail so he wanted people who would be interesting to each other. He also tried to choose Oregonians who would make favorable impressions on the people we met along the way. He preferred not to take anyone he considered an expert horseman because then there would be too many arguments about the best way to care for the animals. Later we realized that some sort of psychological testing would have helped to determine how well the members reacted to new situations and to stress. But there were lots of things we couldn't foresee at the Independence meeting.

Everyone there was jovial and friendly. They considered themselves lucky to have been chosen to go and were delighted to meet their fellow wagon train members. We had bought cowboy hats, buckskins, Levi's and boots, and had started growing sideburns and mustaches. The people of Independence seemed impressed with us and pleased at the honor which had come to them because of the name of their town. "Independence, Missouri, to Independence, Oregon" became a slogan to be repeated at every opportunity. The slogan would not have been bought, nor much less sold, on Madison Avenue, but it was something we lived with anyway. We heard it a lot at our first meeting.

Lowell Blair was there from Sheridan, Oregon. He had a feature article about the trek from his local newspaper and was chortling over it. Ben Griffith was there from Salem. He was telling everyone how he had grown up in Independence and was basking in the glow of "hometown boy makes good." Thyrza Pelling was there from Portland with her British accent. She was praising our wagon master and talking about the "jolly time" we would have. Others there besides Thyrza were helping create a misbegotten sense of optimism.

We posed for pictures and signed our charter. In that document we pledged "our lives, our fortunes, and our sacred honor to the end that" ... no, let's see, that's not it. I remember we signed a paper, but it was soon misplaced and what it said was soon forgotten.

At the meeting we also made plans for getting everyone back to Independence, Missouri. It seemed strange to start a journey on the Oregon Trail by going from west to east, but that direction does have precedence in history. In 1812 a group of John Jacob Astor's fur traders led by Robert Stuart walked east from Astoria on the Oregon Coast. They wandered around considerably, but by seeking out the path of least resistance they ended up traveling for the first time over the route that was later to be called the Oregon Trail.

In mapping our course we noticed that the trail was basically a trail of rivers. The rivers flowed through natural passes in the mountains and provided water and green grass for the travelers. Those rivers running north and south were both obstacles and necessary watering places, and those running east and west often had to be crossed several times in the quest for smoother roadways. In general, the rivers were sometimes a nuisance, but always a necessity.

Going from east to west, the first river on the trail was the Missouri. Most people travelled on it by riverboat to get to Independence or St. Joseph, where they organized their wagon trains. From Independence the trail crossed several creeks in a northwesterly direction to the Kansas River, then crossed it and followed the Little Blue into what is now Nebraska. From the headwaters of the Little Blue, it was a short overland journey to the Platte. The trail followed the Platte and then the North Platte into present-day Wyoming. From the North Platte the trail crossed the high country to the Sweetwater River. This river led the wagon trains almost as far as the Continental Divide near South Pass.

The trail then crossed a desert to the Green River and went over the mountains to the Bear River in southeastern Idaho. After the Bear River came the Portneuf. This led the pioneers to the Snake River near where Pocatello, Idaho, is now located. The trail paralleled the Snake over to what is now the Oregon-Idaho border. Here most pioneers left the Snake and went overland to cross the Grande Ronde, follow the Umatilla and reach the Columbia. The Columbia River led the pioneers into their promised land, the lush valley of the Willamette River.

The abovementioned Robert Stuart charted this route in 1812-13. He lost time running from Indians, looking for food, holed up for the winter and seeking an easy route. His trek took his party ten months. The pioneers in ox-drawn covered wagons were lucky to reach the Willamette Valley in six months. Our trek with horse-and mule-drawn wagons was to take four months. Welcoming committees along the route urged us to set up a time schedule so they would know when to expect us. We read books, studied maps and talked with historians to find out approximately which towns we would pass through. Tex then sat down and marked the trail off in 20-mile segments, figuring that that would be enough traveling for each day. We then published an itinerary based on the markings. This later was to cause us some grief, but it solved the problems of the moment. It gave our operation the appearance of being secure and businesslike. Had we been able to explain it to the horses and mules, we would have felt secure about it ourselves.

Lockwood Motors in Roseburg loaned us a station wagon that I was going to use for scouting the trail, finding campsites and doing advance public relations. At the Independence meeting it was decided that Tex, Roy Brabham, and Lowell and Edna Blair would drive with me back to Independence, Missouri. We loaded the dismantled wagons onto a Missouri-bound Consolidated Freightways truck on April 6. That same evening the group in my car left for Missouri to be there when the wagons arrived.

Gail and Pam Carnine and their children Gary, 12, and Cheryl, 14, were already in Missouri. They were living in a trailer house on what we came to call the Swope property. The Independence Jaycees had arranged for us to use the land as a campground and staging area until our April 19 starting date.

Tex and the Carnines had gone to Missouri in February to buy our livestock. When they started buying horses, people there inferred that they were itinerant horse traders. Consequently, they wouldn't cash even a certified check for Tex at the bank—which doesn't say much for Missouri horse traders. Finally, Tex made friends with several Jaycees in Independence and things improved. Men such as Bill Coil and Roger Bessmer were of such help that in two weeks the wagon train had a remuda of 10 mules and 12 horses.

With the Carnines already in Missouri, there were 16 more people besides us to come from Oregon. Most of them were coming by bus. Millard F. "Robbie" Roberts was bringing the semi-truck which was to be our barn on wheels. Pop Clark and his grandson, Bob Fineout, 21, were coming in the water truck and Ben Griffith was coming by train. Lyle Fenner, our publicity man, was flying partway then driving the rest of the way. He had to pick up a station wagon which the Plymouth people were loaning us.

The group in my station wagon arrived in Independence on the morning of April 9, with nine days ahead of us to get ready for the over 2,000-mile journey by wagon train.

The wagon train members pose for a group portrait at Burley, Idaho.

II. Independence Camp

They called the settlement "Independence Landing" in the early days because the steamboat "Independence" from St. Louis used to put in there. St. Louis was the political and financial headquarters of America's westward movement in the early 1800s, but Independence was the base for settlers in covered wagons. Here were the last blacksmith shops, stores, jails, saloons, brothels and churches that our forefathers would frequent before they set out for Oregon.

Psychologically the original pioneers were an adventuresome sort not much different from the people I was with in 1959. Some of them wanted to get away from something and others wanted to get to something. All of them, however, brought with them their troubles and good times wrapped in vague bundles labeled "character" and "personality." Inside these bundles were smaller boxes marked "temperament" and "intelligence." The quality of those contents determined how well the traveler would cope with life in general and wagon train treks in particular.

The day we arrived in Independence we set up tents and tarpaulin shelters on the Swope property around the Carnines' trailer house. An inch of snow fell that night. This put a chill on our idea of camping out, but we had no choice because there was no money in the budget for motels.

Except for my work in arranging starting ceremonies, most of our activity was the same as getting ready for any covered wagon journey. Shorty Hilliard had to shoe the horses and mules, Roy Brabham had to assemble the wagons, and all the drivers had to start breaking in their teams. The women bought supplies and put the chuck wagon in working condition. I drove people around on errands and Tex oversaw the whole operation.

The assembled wagons were beautiful with their bright orange running gear, green boxes and clean white canvas tops. Slogans painted on the canvas referred to the Oregon sponsors. Things like "On to the 100 valleys of the Umpqua" and "On to Drain, Ore." lacked catchiness but no one seemed to mind. Crowds gathered to watch the colorful chaos of our assembly area. Drivers with their new teams and wagons meandered around the green field of the Swope property and put on a good show.

Each of the seven drivers had arrived from Oregon by the time the wagons were put together. The men drew numbers from a hat for their teams. After the drawing, some men wanted to swap mules for horses or vice versa. After everyone was satisfied, they began preparing the animals for the trip. They adjusted the harnesses, hitched up the wagons and started toughening up the teams.

Except for a few motorized vehicles, the scene duplicated those of 100 years before. Of the vehicles, the most striking and prominent was the big semi-truck. The van part of it was useful for carrying hay and other supplies, and its sides served to advertise our presence. It was painted in brilliant green and gold bands with the words "On to Oregon Cavalcade" printed on the gold band in large black letters.

We also had a water wagon, a dual-wheeled truck with a 1,000-gallon water tank on its bed. This truck allowed us to not have to worry about always camping near water as the pioneers did. Tex's green pickup truck pulled an orange U-Haul trailer which served as our chuck wagon. More often, we chose to call it the "cook shack" or the "kitchen truck," depending on whether we were thinking of cooking in it or driving it. In Independence it was usually too drizzly and cold to eat outdoors, so we took our platefuls of food from the cook shack and crowded into the Carnines' trailer house.

One evening was especially smoky and steamy inside the crowded trailer. Shorty Hilliard was smoking roll-your-owns; Tex came in with a cigar clenched in his teeth and Roy Brabham sat placidly puffing his pipe. Our buckskins and Levi's drying out caused rivulets of condensation to flow down the windows. The noise of everyone talking and laughing made cacophonous crescendos and decrescendos and added a dimension of sound to the closeness of the room.

The three youngsters sometimes contributed with shouts and giggles. Besides Gary and Cheryl Carnine there was 11-year-old Janell Roudebaugh. Dark-eyed and dark-haired Janell had come to go along with her dad, Rudy, who drove the wagon sponsored by Drain, Oregon. The three of them sat squeezed together at the end of a couch and amused each other with pokes in the ribs and pops of their bubble gum. As their fatigue and the warmth overtook them, they alternately listened and dozed. Some of the grown-ups' sea stories roused them into wide-eyed wonder, but most of the talk was of little interest.

Shorty Hilliard had been having difficulties. Some of the horses and mules he was working with had never been shod. He and the men helping him tied the animals in "side hitches," "W hitches" and several other kinds of hitches, but the animals still struggled and fought when Shorty tried to shoe them.

I heard Roy ask Shorty, "What happened out there today, Shorty? I thought I saw you rolling around on that wet ground."

"Oh, that big bay mule—I thought he was going to stand to have shoes put on so I didn't tie him up. The next thing I knew, I was rolling ass over teakettle about 15 feet away."

"Well did you get the job done?" Roy asked.

"Oh, yeah. Well, I was madder than I was hurt so we threw him down with a W hitch and he was a pretty good mule."

"You never know about mules," Roy sympathized.

"Well, you know, there's an old saying about mules. They say a horse is liable to kick anytime, but a mule will work for a man all his life just for a chance to kick him once."

Shorty was built small and tough and he held up well through the rigors of his occupation. Besides being kicked several times, he caught a bad cold from working in the rain. He had such tough skin that Thyrza Pelling bent her hypodermic needle trying to give him a penicillin shot.

Having pavements instead of prairies to travel over, our horse shoeing posed special problems. In order to make the shoes last longer we had a special hardening agent, borium, welded onto the bottoms of the metal shoes. Since the horses were in danger of injuring their legs from walking too much on hard pavement, we bought special rubber pads to fit between the shoe and the hoof. The mules, being less inclined to prance, put their feet down easier so they didn't need the padding. The length of our trek forced us to try to preserve as much hoof as possible at each shoeing. Due to the slow growth of the hoof, we often used the same nail holes each time they were reshod. Shorty's job was a little harder because of our methods, but the animals were free of hoof trouble for the entire 2,200-mile journey.

We had a surplus of historians in camp suggesting we go here or there and telling us about the old days. We were also a center of attraction for artists and photographers. The famous artist Thomas Hart Benton came frequently and honored us by using our wagons as models for a mural he was doing in the Truman Library. Several art teachers at local schools brought their classes to camp every day to make sketches of the animals and wagons. Photographers included everyone from those with small Kodaks to those from national magazines and television networks.

Besides buying and begging supplies, supplying information to newsmen and arranging a press party, one of my big worries was to work with the Independence Jaycees to arrange a parade on the morning of the 18th and kick-off ceremonies on the 19th. Part of the arrangements consisted of getting former President Harry S. Truman, a native of Independence, to give the command for the wagons to start their trek.

The starting point was an important consideration because we wanted to have ceremonies at the same historic spot from which wagon trains had started in pioneer days. After several consultations, we decided to have the ceremonies near the old jail at the northeast corner of the city square. The jail's antiquity and role in early Independence history influenced our decision. Also, some of the historians we spoke to maintained that the wagon trains had formed near the northeast edge of town, a few blocks out from the jail.

We changed the plan after I talked with Mr. Truman. It was getting close to Saturday, the 18th, the day of his appearance at our event. I had corresponded with him and talked to him on the phone before and so far he had been eager to please. I called him again to give him more exact details.

"We'd like you to be on the reviewing stand about 10:00 Saturday morning and say a few words, then the next day we'd like for you to give the starting signal right from the street."

"Are they building the reviewing stand yet?" he asked.

"Yes, the Jaycees were getting it started today."

"Which corner of the city square are you starting from?"

"We thought we'd be over by the old jail; sort of on the northeast corner," I told him.

His tone of voice then seemed to go beyond presidential and become pontifical. "Why don't you start from the southwest corner like everyone else did?"

I tried to hide my confusion and told him with a false note of confidence that I would see about getting things changed.

I relayed this to Roger Bessmer and his Jaycee friends. It rocked them around on their heels a bit, but finally, on the day before the parade, they changed the starting point to the southwest corner to keep peace with Mr. Truman.

On Saturday morning the reviewing stand was packed with dignitaries. Tom Vaughn of the Oregon Historical Society was there along with Tony Brandenthaler of the Oregon Centennial Commission. Howell Appling, Oregon's Secretary of State, and Elmo Smith, Oregon's former governor, represented our state government. Dick Smith, president of On to Oregon Cavalcade, Inc., and my boss, Bill Dawkins, were also included. Mr. Truman welcomed them all to Missouri and bid the wagon train bon voyage in a friendly and cheerful speech.

The parade following the speeches was successful up to a point; then it started raining. The wagon train was in the latter part of the parade. By the time they got to the reviewing stand between the Oregon Trail and Santa Fe Trail monuments, all they could see of the dignitaries was damp arms waving from the courthouse windows behind the stand. When the parade was over, we spent the rest of the day staying out of the rain.

It was still raining Sunday morning when we began our trek. The main part of the starting procedure involved loading Ben Griffith's lead wagon with four sacks of philatelic mail that we were taking to Oregon. This having been done, the Rev. Donald McKay stood on the tall gate of the mail wagon and gave a benediction for our wellbeing. Harry Truman arrived to give the starting command and everything seemed to be going fine. The mules, however, were not impressed with their roles.

Mr. Truman raised his arms among the popping flash cameras and said, "Wagons—WAGONS! … roll 'em!"

The flashing camera bulbs were like sheet lightning and the crowd noise was like thunder. It was too much for Ben's lead mules, and Mr.

Truman's waving arm was the final fright. They promptly turned around in their traces and became tangled up with the wheel team. In a few minutes Ben had the animals untangled; a path was cleared through the crowd and the seven covered wagons went clattering down the street.

Tex Serpa and Gail Carnine rode horseback out in front of Ben's mail wagon. Since Ben had a bigger load, his wagon was the only one pulled by two teams. Rudy Roudebaugh came behind Ben in the wagon sponsored by Drain, Oregon. Lowell Blair was third in the Lane County wagon and Pop Clark drove two black mules pulling Hillsboro's wagon fourth in line. The fifth wagon, sponsored by Douglas County, was driven by Shorty Hilliard. George McUne drove his two white mules in the Rogue Valley wagon next and Roy Brabham brought up the rear in the Pendleton wagon. Dave Gastman, looking like Buffalo Bill on a pinto pony, came along behind as a buffer against the cars that always seemed to follow us. The caravan was a fairly authentic replica of an original wagon train. The main difference was the presence of such small items as wrist watches, cameras and transistor radios. There were also chemical toilets in several of the wagons, but these were invisible to the public.

The wagons' route for the first day was along Santa Fe Road, down Crysler Street, along Blue Ridge Boulevard and Blue Ridge Boulevard Extension, then eventually to Red Bridge on the Blue River. We had been told that this route closely paralleled the original Santa Fe Trail. The Oregon Trail started in what is now Gardner, Kansas, three days out on the Santa Fe Trail. This was the route during the early years of the covered wagons. In the later years, from the 1850s on, the settlers went northwest from Independence and through St. Joseph instead of southeast like we went.

Crowds of onlookers sometimes became more bothersome than flattering. When the wagons left Independence, Robbie Roberts, Bob Fineout and I stayed behind to clean up the campground before going on to Red Bridge. While loading hay and surplus equipment from the back of the water truck onto the semi, we were interrupted every few seconds by people in cars asking which route the wagons took. The recitation of streets and boulevards took so long that I let Robbie and Bob do the work while I stood on the back of the truck giving directions. I found that by shouting I could talk to people in about three cars at a time. Along the route taken, cars and spectators made a moving traffic jam. City, county and state police expressed relief as the wagons passed beyond their respective areas of jurisdiction.

That day I started a routine that was to be repeated almost every day for the next four months. As the wagons rolled on to their destination for the day, I drove ahead to explore the route and find a campsite for the next day. Our plans for Monday called for me to find a campsite near Olathe, Kansas. I drove to Red Bridge, which to my surprise really had a red bridge, then followed the route the wagon train would take from there to Olathe. At Olathe, the Chamber of Commerce secretary-manager met me and we drove out to choose a campground below the dam which forms Olathe Lake a few miles east of the town.

The wagon train people had camped and had a meeting before I returned to them. A traffic jam of spectators slowed me down in trying to park near the wagons. When I finally arrived, I found that my group had met and made up a duty schedule. The women formed teams of two each to be on cook shift one day and have two days free. The men had drawn numbers for guard duty and left me with number 13, the last man on the schedule. We were to have three guards on duty each night to watch the livestock and prevent pilferage and vandalism. The first shift was from 8:00 to 11:00, the second was from 11:00 until 2:00 a.m., and the third guard was on duty until he woke up the cooks at 5:00.

Our first day on the trail was over. A sprinkling rain had fallen most of the day and more rain was threatening. Around the campfire that evening we tried to ignore the rain and mud, and expressed our relief that we were finally underway.

I mused that my misgivings about being with these people had been allayed. I missed San Francisco and Medford, but I felt as if my new associates showed promise of becoming friends. Everyone seemed willing to gather firewood, carry hay, cook, stand guard and do all the chores that needed to be done for the good of the community. They were also being helpful to one another personally. Thyrza Pelling fixed a loose seam in my buckskin coat; George McUne helped me set up my tent and Ben Griffith shared his bourbon with me. Perhaps my dream of camaraderie was coming true.

Janell Roudebaugh watches as the famous artist Thomas Hart Benton sketches our wagons. Later Benton copied from the sketches to do murals in the Truman Library.

Former President Harry S. Truman prepares to give a speech at the wagon train's starting ceremonies. He is being introduced by William Dawkins, publicity agent for the Wagon Train.

The wagon train leaves Independence, Missouri, escorted by Jackson County Mounted Sheriff's Posse, April 19, 1959.

III. Pottawatomi Territory

An Indian raid woke us up at dawn. This was the first of many such attacks we were to suffer on the 120-day trip. A local riding club, mostly high school students, decided that for the sake of authenticity they should dress up like Indians and attack our wagon train. They stormed whooping and shrieking into camp and we fired a few blank cartridges at them to add to the realism of it all. The heat of battle was soon cooled by the misty morning temperature, and the "Indians" responded affirmatively to our invitation to share morning coffee.

After breakfast, the burlap-clad, shivering visitors went home and we broke camp. That being our first morning on the trail we were slow in getting started. It took us a week or two to develop a routine of getting up and on the road every morning with a degree of smoothness and efficiency.

For the first time on the trip I realized what a splendid sight it was when the wagons unwound from their circle and started out single file down the road. There was something about the circular movement of the wagons which stirred my emotions. An aura of pride linked our people, animals and wagons together like a chain. The feeling was especially strong from the center of the circle where I stood and measured everyone's mood as they started a new day of travel.

Far from the traditional drawn-out shout of "wagons ho," Tex would usually ride his bay gelding, Reno, up alongside the lead wagon and give Ben Griffith a nod, mumbling something like, "Well, it looks like we can go now."

Ben Griffith was usually so impatient to leave that a laconic mumble or nod from Tex was all the orders he needed. Ben yelled at his four mules, shook the reins, and every draft animal in the wagon train started pulling. Ben first learned to command mules when he was a boy. His parents had moved from a family farm in Nebraska to one in Oregon in

1907 when Ben was five. In 1959 he left a profitable real estate selling job to travel the Oregon Trail with us. He had the distinction of looking like Ward Bond, an actor who was then starring in a TV series about a wagon train. Many sightseers along the way mistook Ben for the actor. He naturally became self-conscious when people stared at him. I suspect that he sometimes yelled at his mules, "Hey, Buck!" or "Hey, Blue!" just to ease his tension.

Besides the seven drivers, three other men regularly rode horseback with the wagon train. Gail Carnine rode a palomino named Chief in front or beside the wagons and Dave Gastman brought up the rear on a pinto.

Our two pintos were named Comanche and Geronimo, and we also had two sorrel mares, Buttons and Bow. Geronimo was nicknamed "Burbles" because of a faulty posterior which was either infuriating, embarrassing or humorous, depending on where you were standing in relation to the animal when he broke wind. The sorrel mares were not ridden regularly by anyone since they served as a relief team for any wagon which might need them.

Blond-haired Val Johnson, 24, often rode one of the sorrel mares. Jeanne Marshall, 22, another single girl, sometimes rode horseback, but usually she either walked or rode in a wagon.

Thyrza Pelling was our champion walker. She could cover the day's 20-mile journey on foot and still have energy left for camp chores. Thyrza had a more cosmopolitan background than the other Oregonians. She had spent her childhood in England, Italy, and on a yacht in the Mediterranean. Her two sons, Rodney, 17, born in Egypt, and Trevor, 13, born in England, were going to join us in Wyoming when they were out of school for the summer. Thyrza was 39 then and had changed from a pretty girl into a handsome woman. She had a rather solicitous, mother-hen attitude towards others. This, coupled with her British accent, often caused the highly independent, provincial Oregonians to resent rather than welcome her acts of kindness. Thyrza's affection for Tex also caused her to be disliked. The more reserved Oregonians thought it was poor taste for her to have Tex as her favorite topic of conversation and to speak so candidly of her regard for him.

I suspect that this ill feeling was the basic reason for our first big argument in camp. We were camped near Lake Olathe in a cold wind. Thyrza saw that Edna Blair was looking cold and tired so she offered to take over her duties on cook shift. Thyrza was so insistent on being helpful that she forgot to be tactful. Edna got the idea that she was being forcibly expelled from the kitchen trailer. The gang around the campfire heard it all and sided against Thyrza.

I was irked at the way everyone got so upset over such a well-intentioned thing. I didn't want to say anything and add to the angry atmosphere, so I retreated to my tent. I wondered if this was how easily people were going to get angry on the entire trip.

In a few minutes Pam Carnine brought Edna over and asked if Edna could sit inside out of the wind. Her nose was blue from cold and her face was red from anger.

She sat down on a camp stool and pouted. I felt that it might help her to talk about it. "What happened, Edna?"

"That woman kicked me out of the kitchen."

"But wasn't Thyrza just trying to be helpful?"

"No one kicks me out of the kitchen!"

"What did she say that made you so mad?"

"Oh, that woman, she just makes me sick. She's so ga-ga over Tex that it's awful."

"Weren't you cold out there in that wind?"

"No one kicks me out of the kitchen!"

I gave up and went back out to the campfire. The incident gave Edna and others something to talk about at every opportunity. Several times after that Tex and I received allusions to the idea that Thyrza was a source of trouble and should be sent home. We shrugged off the idea because we felt the trouble did not come from Thyrza but from the people who resented her.

Schools were dismissed for us in Olathe the next morning. Along with the school children, workers from the Hyer Boot Company and thousands of other spectators watched the wagon train pass through town. The mayor and city fathers officially greeted the caravan while autograph hunters besieged it.

Our route through this area was parallel to the pioneer route which went southwesterly along the Santa Fe Trail out to a point near the present Gardner, Kansas. Local legend has it that in Gardner there was a sign saying "Oregon thisaway." Those who knew how to read turned off to Oregon and the rest went to California. Sign or not, there the Oregon settlers turned northwest while the Santa Fe Trail continued southwest. The Oregon Trail crossed the Wakarusa River then came to the Kansas River near where Topeka is now located. Crossing the Kansas River took from one to five days depending on how heavy the spring rains had been and how big the wagon train was. Once across the river they continued west through St. Mary's where a Roman Catholic mission was established in 1847.

Fenced-off, cultivated fields in 1959 kept us from following exactly the same route. Rather than being able to go straight to our destination, we were forced into a zigzag pattern north, then west, then north, then west. The farmers would have been rather upset had we cut through their fences and across their fields to follow the original route. The zigzag pattern forced us to travel extra miles but it kept us close to what was the original trail.

On our third night out, Tuesday, we camped on the farm of Mr. Herbert Knabe a few miles northwest of Gardner. Wednesday we camped on a patch of virgin prairie belonging to Mrs. W.P. Elkin along the highway between Lawrence and Topeka. A crowd of 30,000 people had watched us come through Lawrence. On Thursday we arrived in Topeka. Because of heavy traffic on other routes, the route I chose for coming into the Topeka Fairgrounds was about ten miles south and west of the original trail.

I went into Topeka Thursday morning, picked up our mail, bought some supplies, had lunch and made it out to the fairgrounds just as the wagons arrived. George Docking, governor of Kansas, and John Landreth, president of the Kansas Centennial Commission, came to greet us. Governor Docking shook hands with all of us, posed for the photographers and gave us some mementos of Kansas to take to Governor Mark Hatfield in Oregon.

By this time we were famous. Newspapers across the United States and even in Europe were carrying daily news stories of our progress. People from as much as a hundred miles away drove to see us. Some of our visitors would come to see us every evening for nearly a week until we passed beyond their part of the state. Wagon train members were signing hundreds of autographs and posing for countless photos each day. At meal times we developed the trick of setting up a section of snow fence between ourselves and the spectators so we would not be harassed by autograph hunters and well-wishers while we were eating. Fame was a new thing to all of us. At first it was somewhat exhilarating, but it wasn't long before we all felt irritated at the lack of privacy.

A steady stream of people came to see us in Topeka. The women on cook shift had set up a long table inside one of the fairground sheds that had cooking facilities. The wagons were circled up outside and the animals were in the next shed. Our visitors seemed to make a circle: first to the wagons, then to watch us eat, then to look at the livestock. All three things seemed to be of equal interest.

Fame almost brought trouble to a couple of our men that evening in downtown Topeka. Dave Gastman and George McUne had wandered off together to see something of Topeka besides the cattle sheds at the fairgrounds. George was wearing his frontiersman costume consisting of a wide-brim slouch hat, neckerchief, Levi's jacket and trousers, and high leather boots. Dave was wearing his mustache, goatee and clothes in the style of Buffalo Bill. Dressed like that, they were easily recognized as wagon train members. As they were walking along a sidewalk, a young man in cowboy costume, complete with "six-guns," pulled his car over to the curb in front of them. He got out, stepped in front of George and Dave and said, "Draw!"

"Who are you?" Dave asked, declining the challenge.

"The Kansas Kid, fastest gun in Kansas."

"Get back in your car," Dave told him. "We're lovers, not fighters, and we intend to get all the way back to Oregon."

"Well, I've come here intending to have a shootout with you guys."

"Get back in your car or we're going to the police."

The Kansas Kid got back in his car, but he only drove a block farther and pulled up in front of them again. Once more he got out and stood in front of them with his hand hovering by his holstered revolver.

Dave said, "You touch that gun and I'll break your arm!"

The Kansas Kid got back in his car and drove off for good.

Dave probably could have broken his arm. He was one of the friendliest members of the wagon train, but he had boxed professionally and worked as a boxing instructor when he was younger.

The incident reminded us of how in the days of the Wild West a gunman's fame would spread. This caused aspiring young gun fighters from all over the world to come and challenge him. However, in our time the Kansas Kid might have just wanted to be an anachronism like ourselves.

When the wagon train left Topeka the next morning, it went due north across the Kansas River, then turned west towards Rossville on an old road south of the freeway. Along here we followed what had been known as the "Overland Trail," as well as the Oregon Trail. The Overland Trail was established in 1852 as a military road between Ft. Leavenworth and Ft. Riley.

My work in planning our route and arranging for campsites was anything but humdrum, yet it lacked the romance and atmosphere of traveling with the wagon train itself. I had to do all sorts of things our pioneer forefathers never found necessary. I kept police alerted as to our position and enlisted their help with the traffic problems we created; I contacted mayors and chamber of commerce secretary-managers for help in locating campsites, and I found people with detailed maps who could tell me the course of the original pioneer trail. I also had to correspond with our home offices in Oregon and with the towns we would pass through later in the trek. Sometimes I borrowed office space in the towns we came to. Of all the people who helped us in this area, I especially remember Bus Zook, Chamber of Commerce secretary-manager of Lawrence, Dale McCoy of the Kansas Centennial Commission in Topeka, and Henry W. Beseau of St. Mary's, Kansas.

While checking on our campsite in Rossville, I heard of an impending Pottawatomi Indian raid at Silver Lake. I decided to drive back and meet the wagons to see if I could get in on the fun. As I drove through Silver Lake, I saw about ten Indians mounted on horses and donkeys coming down the main street. They looked as if they meant business with their costumes, war paint and lances.

The Pottawatomis had been moved here from Michigan after Congress passed its relocation act of 1830. Before that, this had been the territory of the Kanza, or Kaw, Indians. At that same time the Shawnees and Delawares were moved into this area from the East. These tribes were induced to move with the promise that this new land would always be theirs. As it turned out, the white man's "always" didn't last long.

I met the wagon train as it stopped for lunch at the home of Mr. E.A. Moore. Mr. Moore lived in what was reputed to be the oldest house in Kansas. The stone structure had been built in 1826 and served as a station house for many years. Mr. Moore pointed out John C. Fremont's initials carved near the ground in a cornerstone of the building. Somehow I couldn't imagine anyone of Mr. Fremont's stature stooping to carve his initials like that.

Fremont passed this way in June, 1843, on his second expedition west. He too had been bound for Oregon. Near here some Osage Indians ran off a few of his horses. After an exciting chase, Fremont caught up with the Indians and recovered his animals.

Now, 116 years later, the Indians were attacking another band of whites. There, however, the parallel ends. No one in 1959 expected to shed any blood. I wanted to join the fun so I climbed into the Rogue Valley wagon to ride with George McUne. The sun was shining and this put everyone in a good mood. Everyone grinned a bit nervously in anticipation of the Indian foray.

We drove onto the school baseball diamond at Silver Lake and were greeted by the applause of hundreds of students gathered in the stands. That seemed peaceful enough. Suddenly a column of yelling, painted Pottawatomis came galloping from behind a building at a corner of the field. We put our animals into a run and started forming the traditional defensive circle. Everyone was yelling and shooting. I leaned out the rear end of the wagon and fired some blanks at a half-naked, bow-and-arrow-toting Indian riding a galloping donkey. My Colt .45 made a terrific blast. We spent an exciting few minutes going at full speed clockwise while the Indians galloped around us going counterclockwise. As if by plan, both we and the Indians decided to stop before we had any runaways or someone got hurt. The school children applauded mightily. While letting our animals stand and calm down, we shook hands with the Indians and complimented them on their regalia and horsemanship. They thanked us for helping put on the show. In a few minutes we resumed our journey and left the Indians behind in peace.

The next day we had only a seven-mile run from Rossville to St. Mary's. We knew that such a short traveling day would have to be compensated for later to keep our 20-mile-daily averages, but the offer of bountiful hospitality from St. Mary's convinced us to take the short day. We paid for it during the following week on a long, hot day into Marysville. Looking back over the years I feel the pleasure of St. Mary's compensated for the pain of Marysville, but I would have rather not been forced into the trade-off.

Another factor which influenced our decision to stay in St. Mary's was that our animals were showing symptoms of distemper. We felt that almost a full weekend of rest would improve their health and would also give Shorty Hilliard a chance to catch up on his horseshoeing. Tex's concern for the animals at this point was uppermost in his mind. Had it not been for his consideration of them, we might have passed through St. Mary's without stopping.

From a historical viewpoint, St. Mary's was an interesting town in which to spend a weekend. It was founded in 1847 on a Roman Catholic mission to the Pottawatomi Indians and was the site of the first cathedral between Missouri and California. The mission has since become a Jesuit seminary. Regardless of the town's Catholic heritage, the majority of the townspeople seemed to be Protestant.

The St. Mary's hospitality was magnificent. The townspeople provided us with showers and laundry facilities. They brought us a potluck dinner Saturday evening and we followed that with a songfest around the bonfire. On Sunday morning they sent us a minister for services in camp and later took us all to dinner at the Methodist church. On Sunday afternoon we were given a tour of the St. Mary's seminary campus. They also loaned us machine shop facilities to use in applying borium to the bottoms of our horse and mule shoes. St. Mary's set a standard of hospitality that we hoped for on the rest of the trek.

The services on Sunday morning were rustic and colorful. The Rev. Paul Capp of the First Methodist Church was our minister. We put down bales of hay in rows for pews and stacked one bale on top of another in front for a pulpit. We stood flags on each side of the pulpit: the Oregon state flag on the left and the United States flag on the right. On the pulpit we fashioned a crude cross out of branches. The sermon was a touching one about the miraculous qualities of water and the glory of trees. The grey, water-laden clouds overhead made the sermon especially meaningful. We were pleased at the opportunity for peace and contemplation, and gave thanks to God and Mr. Capp.

That night at 2:00 a.m. Bob Fineout, number 12 man on guard, woke me up for my turn at guard duty. I came over to the campfire and reveled in the peacefulness of our world. In the distance coyotes howled at one another. Nearby I could hear the noises made by our horses and mules: the munching of hay, the scuffing of hooves, and now and then a grunt or squeal when one nipped another. I wrote letters by lantern light, kept the fire going, heated coffee in a tin can, made a couple rounds of the camp and generally enjoyed the solitude. At 5:00 a.m. it all ended when I woke up the cooks to begin a new week of coping with crowds, being busy and moving on.

The wagon train "forts up" in a mock battle with Pottawatomi Indians at Silver Lake, Kansas. Hundreds of schoolchildren watched the "battle" from the football field grandstand.

IV. Raiders and Other Ruckuses

We started to be worried about the animals when we were in Topeka. Most had not yet been toughened to their work and a veterinarian there found that some had distemper. We were giving the sick ones millions of units of penicillin each day but it still seemed that some of them might have to be disposed of. Tex was especially concerned because of his ambition to get to Oregon with the same livestock and the same people as those who left Missouri.

The veterinarian in Topeka told us to keep on giving the penicillin even though it may not have been helping. He also told us to try to keep the disease from spreading by watering the animals out of separate buckets. Two horses which were the worst off were Rudy Roudebaugh's black gelding and mare, Dan and Daze. Rudy did his best to care for them but still they were eating very little, had runny noses and were generally dispirited. The veterinarian's prognosis was a pessimistic "they might not make it."

Our route for this second week took us past several historic sites such as the Louis Vieux cemetery, Alcove Springs and the Mormon Trail – Oregon Trail junction. Louis Vieux had been of mixed French and Potawatomi ancestry and had made a small fortune ferrying wagon trains across Vermillion Creek at $1.00 per wagon. Now he is buried on a knoll near the creek with his three wives, most of his children and many members of his children's families. On Monday our wagon train stopped there among the tombstones and oak trees where the Vermillion Home Demonstration unit gave us a picnic lunch. They had cut brush, picked up dead wood and graded out a smooth area for the wagons to park.

We would pass Alcove Springs and the Mormon Trail – Oregon Trail junction on Thursday. On the road near Alcove Springs is a grave marker dedicated to Grandma Kaye who was bitten by a snake and died there in 1846. She was a member of the ill-fated Donner party which passed Alcove Springs on the way to starvation and cannibalism in the High Sierras. Another member of the Donner party, Mr. Edwin Bryant, is said to have given the springs their name. Just north of Alcove Springs, about five miles south of Marysville, the Oregon Trail coming north from Independence joined the Mormon Trail coming west from St. Joseph. The trails joined at Independence Crossing, a ford across the Big Blue River. At this point our 1959 wagon train left the original route and went on to Marysville where there was a nice bridge across the Big Blue.

After lunch at the cemetery, the wagons left for Louisville and I drove to Manhattan, Kansas, to buy supplies. I met the wagons back at Louisville just in time to help unload baled hay from the semi-truck. It was cold and cloudy. After we finished our work, we huddled around the campfire until suppertime. Then the women of Louisville served us a delicious meal in the grade school gymnasium.

We had a cheerful campfire that night. Some local musicians came with fiddles and guitars. The wind died down and it became warmer than it had been during the day. The Louisville people organized a square dance on the grass of the school playfield where we were camped.

At bedtime I sneaked into a small room off the main auditorium of the gym and set up my cot. It was so quiet there that I slept through a great deal of excitement. Some local pranksters thought it would be funny to let our animals loose. One switched off the lights on the field while others came to untie the horses and mules. Dave Gastman caught one young man about a block away from the camp leading one of the mules. Roy Brabham almost overexerted himself chasing the boy who turned out the lights. The boy got away but at least he never came back. Eventually the excitement died down and everyone managed to get some sleep.

Westmoreland was only about 12 miles from our previous camp as Louisville, giving us another short travel day. We agreed to camp there, however, since we had not yet learned to refuse all the hospitality proffered us by the small towns. To keep up with our itinerary we would have to have an extra-long travel day later. As it worked out, that long day could have ended our wagon train.

Westmoreland had been a campsite for the pioneers. One local resident remembered his father telling about the early wagon trains. He had seen wagons camped helter-skelter, filling a field one-half mile square just south of town. We camped at the north end of that same field.

What I think of as a "camp catalog of personal hurts" had another page added to it that afternoon. Tex had given the word that each animal should have its own water bucket, but there weren't enough buckets provided to make the rule practicable. Instead the drivers were watering out of an old tin wash tub as before. I think they intended to water the horses a team at a time and rinse out the tub between each team. This plan was hard to carry out because the drivers had to hold their thirsty animals away from the water while the "sanitation" procedures were followed. Tex noticed what was happening just when Rudy's sick horses, Dan and Daze, were drinking. He looked into the tub and saw floating there a huge gob of phlegm which had come out of one of the horses noses. Without saying a word Tex picked up the tub and dumped the water on the ground under the noses of the startled horses. Not much was said, but it was obvious that Rudy was furious and so was Tex. I think Rudy was more upset at Tex's peremptory handling of the situation than at what he had done. He also felt bad, of course, that his thirsty horses hadn't had their fill of water. Tex was upset at himself for not having provided the buckets necessary for watering the animals properly. Anyway, Tex and I hopped into the Ford and drove to Wamego on a bucket-buying expedition.

At this stage of our trek the drivers were starting to grumble about quite a few of Tex's ideas on caring for the livestock. Each driver had something to say about something: the quality of the feed, the horseshoeing, the harnessing, the medical treatment and anything else they could think of. Looking back at it, I think the basic problem was that the drivers were beginning to get fond of their animals and consequently they each became highly opinionated about what was best for their "babies." It became another problem we lived with for the rest of the 2,000 miles.

That night in Westmoreland we put on a program in the school gymnasium. Tex got up and entertained the audience with a poem about how "Life Gets Tejous," while I provided background music with my guitar. Pop Clark was persuaded to give a talk on our trip. He told why we were making the trek, how far we had come, and how far we had still to go. He also gave a good explanation as to why we had to have our water truck and hay van with us. He pointed out that people now have all the good water holes and pastures fenced off. Our trucks were portable substitutes for those things.

I went outside for some fresh air while the townspeople cleared the floor for square dancing. Over by our wagons some men were unloading a feisty young thoroughbred from a truck. Ben Griffith explained that a man who had taken him to dinner at his ranch the night before was giving him the horse as a gift. Along with the horse, the man donated ten bales of hay and ten sacks of grain. It sounded suspicious that someone would give away such a beautiful animal, but we didn't ask many questions because of the old saying about looking a gift horse in the mouth. Later on in our trek there was a terrific quarrel over the animal and we wished we had investigated the story further. The details were partially filled in at the end of our trek, but they weren't explained to my satisfaction for another 17 years.

The pile of hay and oats served as a dry place for me to sleep that night. After warding off an over-friendly boxer dog, I found a form-fitting depression among the sacks and got a good night's sleep.

From our Wednesday campsite west of Frankfort, the wagon train would go through Blue Rapids, then up the east bank of the Big Blue River to Marysville on Thursday. In an attempt to shorten the day's journey from Frankfort to Marysville, I drove out south of town with John Bernard, secretary-manager of the Marysville Chamber of Commerce. We looked for a place to camp in case the wagon master decided not to push the animals the entire distance into town. However, since the land from Alcove Springs on into town was all fenced off in plowed fields, brush patches and thick oak forests, we didn't find a good alternate campsite. There wasn't even a farm with a roomy, level barnyard. I knew that if the weather turned either too hot or too cold, our livestock would have a hard time. I gambled that the wagon train people would understand the circumstances and not be too upset if the weather betrayed us. I learned later that even the clearest understanding of circumstances is no assurance against being upset.

On Thursday I worked ahead up to Fairbury, Nebraska. When I came back to meet the wagons in Marysville, it was almost four in the afternoon. The day had become unseasonably warm and the wagons still hadn't reached town. Thousands of people lined the shady streets. Incoming motorists kept the spectators informed about the wagon train's progress.

I was heartsick. The day's run was over 26 miles, and never before had the animals gone so far in such hot weather. Had the weather remained cool as on the previous day, it wouldn't have been so bad, but today it was well up in the 90s. I decided there was nothing I could do but wait, so I went on up to the armory. The wagons circled up outside while I was taking a shower.

The wagon train people didn't seem too tired, but the horses and mules looked bushed. I was dismayed when I looked at them. Some were snot-nosed and runny-eyed with distemper. All of them were soaked with sweat and seemed to hold their heads lower than usual. A bystander told me that when the wagons stopped downtown to receive the key to the city, one of Ben Griffith's mules laid down in the traces. Ben popped at him with a BB pistol and got the mule back on his feet. The man who told me that thought it was funny, but it made me want to crawl into a small hole.

No one had much to say to me but I could sense the ill feeling. Normally friendly drivers put on a grim expression and looked the other way when we passed each other.

After tending the animals, the people took showers and sat down to dinner at some picnic tables outside. Marysville Mayor Dick Wieger, my friend John Bernard and other men from town cooked huge steaks for us on some charcoal broilers they had set up. While we ate I was the target of some vituperous remarks from several of the men, especially Ben Griffith. I was judged guilty for not being able to predict the hot weather and for not having found a campsite south of Marysville. Tex and some of the other men realized that our strict itinerary and the lack of a good campsite south of town had necessitated the long day's run. They accepted the situation saying, "It might have been worse." One driver went around urging others to quit and go home with him. He didn't find anyone else who would leave so he stayed too.

From that day on to the end of the trip there were hints and subtle threats of a "big blow up" which would leave our wagon train driverless. For those of us dedicated to finishing the job, this constant foreboding put a cloud over what might otherwise have been a pleasant adventure.

I was reminded of a book I had read in preparation for our journey, First Three Wagon Trains, by Bidwell, Bancroft and Longmire. One of the episodes in the book was about the Elijah White party of 1842. Mr. White, the elected wagon master, suggested that all 22 dogs with the group should be killed. Otherwise, he believed, they would go mad from thirst on the plains. A two-thirds majority of the wagon train members agreed and the dogs were all shot. However, the ill feeling caused by this lasted throughout their journey to Oregon, and for some, lasted even after the people reached Oregon and grew old on the homesteads and in the cities they built there. Just as in the Elijah White party, animosities developed with us in Kansas and lasted to the end of our journey. The incident with Thyrza Pelling at Olathe, with Rudy Roudebaugh in Westmoreland, and then with me and the hot weather in Marysville all added up to lots of discontent. Fortunately the feelings waxed and waned in intensity so life was bearable.

Everyone seemed to feel better after eating their steaks. Gail and Pam Carnine and I drove out to find a new campsite for the next day. I had previously chosen a site at an old abandoned schoolhouse about halfway to Fairbury. In view of the hot weather, we decided to find something closer to Marysville and cut down the length of the next day's traveling. We found a good open area on the Kriensieck farm, about six miles beyond the old Hollenberg Pony Express Station.

Back at camp we received an invitation to a nearby dance hall where Jan Garber's orchestra was playing. As a special honor to us, for one dance the floor was cleared of everyone except wagon train members and we were introduced. I hoped that the socializing would take my mind off the day's troubles, but instead the day's troubles took the fun out of the socializing.

That night I set up my cot alone in the main gymnasium part of the armory. The hugeness of the room compared to the little space I occupied coincided with my feelings of smallness and isolation. I felt that I had been a good soldier for following the supreme command, the order of the itinerary. I had kept a promise to the Marysville city fathers by arriving on the day specified. In doing this, however, I was disloyal to the people and animals of the wagon train. I caused them hardship and discomfort that the steaks and showers of Marysville didn't compensate for.

While I lay there brooding, Tex came in and sat down on the edge of my bunk in the darkness.

"You really got some people riled up at you today." Tex's low voice was amplified by the tomb-like emptiness of the armory.

"Yeah. I can't say that I blame them. But I wish I'd known it was going to be one of the hottest April thirtieths on record."

"Well, besides that it was the most traveling we've ever done in a day and some of our animals aren't in shape for it."

"Gee, the people can understand," I said, "but I wish I could go up to every horse and mule we have and apologize to them."

"The people aren't all that understanding either." Tex contradicted me. "Some of them called Roseburg tonight and demanded that you be fired."

"I figured they would. Do you think anything will come of it?"

"I don't think so. I talked to Dick Smith and explained about sticking to the itinerary and the unusually hot weather. He seemed to understand."

"Another thing that messed us up was the short traveling day from Rossville to St. Mary's, then again from Louisville to Westmoreland. The short mileage of those two days had to be made up."

Tex agreed. "Well, we'll be better off if we learn to say no to people when they demand we get to their town on time or offer us all kinds of hospitality to stay in their towns. The itinerary is important, but not so important that we cause ourselves a lot of suffering."

We talked some more about supplies and the condition of the livestock, then Tex left. As I was going to sleep it came to me that I was just beginning to learn my job, to understand the care and operation of a 20th Century wagon train.

Dave Gastman, (L) and the author lead a nightly songfest.

V. Fairbury or Bust

The next morning we had boiled snake for breakfast. Of course if it had been printed on a menu, most of us would have chosen alternate fare, but the way it was we didn't have the opportunity to decline. There was a small kitchen just inside the armory near where the wagons were circled. The women on cook shift used that and handed the food outside to us where we had our usual stand-around breakfast. The wagon train pulled out at 8:00. Robbie Roberts, Bob Fineout and I stayed behind to clean up the camp area while the women on cook shift cleaned the kitchen. I decided to have a last cup of coffee before leaving on my scouting and foraging duties. I poured the last cupful from our huge pot, drank it, then chewed up the grounds in the bottom of the cup. As soon as I put my cup back in the kitchen and turned away, I heard a scream from Jeanne Marshall.

"Look! Look what was in the coffee!"

Jeanne came outside holding an 18-inch garter snake draped over a wooden spoon. The poor thing had been boiled to a monotone of brownish-white.

"You mean that was in the coffee pot?" I asked.

"Yes! When I went to dump the grounds, this snake came pouring out with them."

"You mean we all drank coffee with that thing boiled in there?"

"Well, we filled the pot last night, then this morning we just turned it on without taking the lid off and looking at it inside."

"How did it get in there?" Robbie and I asked at once.

Jeanne stood there holding the snake draped over the spoon and looked at it thoughtfully. "Maybe it crawled in by itself," she mused.

"I don't think it's likely that it would crawl into the kitchen, up onto the stove, then under the lid by itself."

We speculated on who would do a thing like that, then Jeanne threw it out into some tall weeds. Leaving the mystery unsolved, we concluded that snakes boiled in coffee harm neither the flavor of the coffee nor the health of the coffee drinker, but it doesn't do so much for the health of the snake. I drove off speculating on what extra vitamins we might have gotten that morning. On a different level, I wondered if maybe that is what Adam and Eve should have done with their serpent.

My travels for the day exposed me to the Pony Express. The wagon train was scheduled to stop at the Hollenberg Pony Express Station a few miles north of Hanover, Kansas. This is now the only Pony Express Station in America still intact and restored at its original location. Other stations have been restored, but they have been moved to city parks and museum grounds where they can be better cared for and more easily visited.

The Hollenberg station was built in 1857, three years before the inauguration of the Pony Express. I couldn't find out whether it had been a "way" station or a "home" station. The way stations were set up every 10 miles and home stations were every 50 miles. At the 10-mile intervals the riders changed horses, and at the 50-mile intervals both riders and horses were usually changed. Looking at the low-ceilinged interior of the station, I was reminded that the riders were small men. They must have walked around comfortably inside where, when I wore my Stetson, I had to keep my 6'1½" frame bent slightly. The Pony Express riders were lightweight for speed, and tough and wiry for endurance. The record run for these "swift couriers" was made in 1861 when President Lincoln's inaugural address was carried from St. Louis to San Francisco in 7 days and 17 hours. The establishment of the transcontinental telegraph in 1862 ended the need for the Pony Express and put a lot of colorful young men out of work. The stations were then abandoned, used as farmhouses, or turned into stations for the Overland Trail stage coaches.

G.H. Hollenberg, a native of Germany, built the Hollenberg station. The long, weather-beaten, wood-frame building stands just a few hundred yards from Cottonwood Creek, where the Oregon and Overland Trails met and crossed. Mr. Hollenberg first used the building as a general store, post office and hostelry. In the 1860s it was called "Cottonwood Station." Now it had been preserved as a museum by the Washington County Oregon Trail Association. Mr. Hollenberg came west for his health after an adventurous life seeking gold in California, Australia and Peru. He built the station, married there, and then eventually died from lung hemorrhaging while en route to Germany, where he was planning to recruit German settlers to come to Kansas.

His recruiting efforts must have been carried on by someone, because I noticed while in this area that almost everyone had a German family name. I particularly remember the Reach, Kriensieck and Wieger families. Some of the town names are also German: Hannover, Bremen and Frankfort, to name a few. At our songfest around the campfire at the Kriensiecks', the local people even sang some songs in German.

The wagon train crossed the Big Blue River at Marysville, then about ten miles farther west the caravan came to the Little Blue. We would be generally following the course of the Little Blue up through southeastern Nebraska for the balance of our second week of traveling and all of our third week.

When I left Marysville, I made a side trip to Hanover, and then met the wagons at the Hollenberg station. Hundreds of youngsters who had come by school bus were also there to meet the wagons. The Oregonians were kept busy posing for pictures, signing autographs and fending off kids who were writing their names in axle grease, crayons and lipstick on the wagon canvas. George McUne's white mules were also autographed but they didn't seem to mind. In general, the wonder and enthusiasm of the students was a good reward for all our effort. We seemed to forget the troubles of the day before as we basked together in the warmth of admiration.

I waited until the wagons were rolling north again, then I drove into Fairbury. Because of the distance between the Kriensieck farm and Fairbury, I had to tell my contacts there that we might not make it into town for the weekend on schedule. My announcement caused no end of commotion. The newspaper and Chamber of Commerce people pleaded, cajoled and argued. They wanted me to promise that the wagon train would get to town as we had promised by mail weeks before. However, I was not going to risk another long travel day in hot weather as in Marysville, so I stood firm in my wishy-washiness. I said that it depended on Saturday's weather, the conditions of our animals and the mood of the wagon train people. One newspaper man threatened us with bad publicity if we didn't make it into town. A man from the Chamber of Commerce said they might have to withdraw their offer of dinner and showers. I got miffed and suggested that the wagon train would be closer to the original trail if we passed Fairbury several miles to the east. Leaving it at that, I drove back to meet the wagon train at Kriensiecks', our last campsite in Kansas.

All the wagoneers were in a good mood. Perhaps some sort of serpent had been exorcised. I distributed mail, ate supper and talked to Tex about the Fairbury problem. As I talked, Tex's jaw tightened and his eyes narrowed. When I finished my report, he and Lyle Fenner, our newsman, drove into town. They met the "welcoming committee" in a meeting and told them we were not going to mistreat our livestock just so we could get into Fairbury and gain the town some nationwide publicity. Tex made it clear that if we could not make it into Fairbury the next day, then public sentiment would more than likely be on our side. The committee saw that we were united in our thinking and decided, we thought, to accept whatever happened.

The next morning I received word to call our Oregon headquarters. The committee in Fairbury had not accepted Tex's statements as the last word. Instead they called Roseburg asking that we be "ordered" to make it into town that day. I explained the situation to Dick Smith, and instead of being ordered to do anything, we received backing on our decisions. The run to Marysville had been almost 27 miles. Fairbury was about 25 miles from Kriensiecks'. After the Marysville experience, we had elected to stay with the 20 miles per day that our itinerary required. It seemed hard for the Fairbury people to understand that we were not a company of paid employees. Most of our members were volunteers, and like the pioneers of old, they could not be ordered to do anything.

That morning I saw that attitudes were changing in Fairbury. The manager of the May-Etta hotel told me that no matter where we camped, cars would bring us in to the hotel for showers and a banquet. The Chamber of Commerce manager was still a little put out, but he promised to help in any way he could. While driving up that morning I found an alternate campsite several miles south of town. Everyone hoped we wouldn't need it. The day became rainy. I drove out to meet the wagons to see what the weekend plan was going to be.

I met the wagon train seven miles south of town, rolling north on wet pavement. I suddenly remembered that the highway shoulders were muddy as I pulled off to talk to Tex. My front wheel left the pavement and I lost control of the car. I let go of the steering wheel and applied a slow pressure on the brakes. Mud showered up ten feet in the air as I skidded to a stop out in the borrow pit. I knew I was badly stuck, but I said to myself, "To hell with it. I'll worry about getting out when I've seen how things are on the wagon train."

Everything was fine. The animals were stepping out briskly in the cool weather. The drivers were smiling. Tex said they would make it on in to Fairbury. I stood and yelled, "Only seven miles to go" at each wagon as it rolled past. They all had a remark to make about the spectacular way I had stopped the station wagon.

Getting out of the mud was easier than expected. No sooner had the wagons gone by when a truck stopped, hooked a chain onto my front bumper and pulled me out.

In Fairbury the news that the wagons were coming on in was well received. All of yesterday's friction seemed petty and was forgotten. After passing the good word, I drove out to the city park to be there when the wagons arrived. After a triumphal parade through town, the wagon train formed a loose semicircle among the trees. We worked in sunshine unharnessing and tethering the stock.

A fierce thunderstorm broke later that evening. Fearing that our animals might try to run away from the crackling lightning and booming thunder, we rushed back to camp from a banquet we were attending. The livestock must have been used to such storms in Missouri because they were all taking it calmly. The rain was falling in torrents. In the flashes of lightning we could see our horses and mules standing morose and still with their tails to the wind and their heads bowed.

The wagons stood in four inches of water when the storm ended. Later Rudy Roudebaugh sounded off to one of the local city officials about how terrible they were in having us camp in the middle of a mud puddle. Ben Griffith was with Rudy at the time. Unfortunately for him, the men remembered Ben's name instead of Rudy's. Tex then had to handle a counter-complaint about what a mean-mouthed ingrate Ben was. Tempers died down in direct relation to the rate that the ground around the wagons absorbed the water. Fifteen years later Rudy was still chuckling over the way Ben had been blamed for what he had done.

The banquet we had rushed back from was held at the May-Etta hotel. Besides us, about 20 local descendents of pioneer families were there. Among these were members of the McCanles family. This family has often been referred to as "the notorious McCanles gang" which was supposedly outfought by the "famous Wild Bill Hickok!" The McCanles at the banquet caused me to change my opinion. It seems that Hickok actually was positioned behind a hanging blanket, and was shooting the men down in ambush as they stepped into the room. The McCanles family at the time was made up of honest millers and tradesmen. Journalists such as Ned Buntline, looking for outlaws and heroes in the West, created a legend which maligned them terribly and which still taints the descendants.

We learned more about Wild Bill Hickok the next day. That afternoon there was an official welcoming ceremony on behalf of the city. Afterwards, a number of the wagon train members were taken a few miles northeast of Fairbury to participate in the dedication of the reconstructed Rock Creek Post Office. Rock Creek Station, like Hollenberg's Cottonwood Station, was built in 1857. S.C. Glenn built it there because it was an ideal location for Oregon Trail travelers to ford Rock Creek. In 1859 David McCanles bought the station from Mr. Glenn and built a toll bridge across the creek. He also built an "East Station" on the opposite bank from the original location. Later he sold the East Station to a stage coach company which named Horace Wellman as its agent. Wellman, so the story goes, stole some equipment from David McCanles. McCanles came to try and recover what was his when Hickok, a friend and employee of the Wellmans, shot him down. This is the basic story which Ned Buntline distorted when he decided to glamorize the life of Wild Bill Hickok. Ironically, the idea for Hickok's sobriquet came from McCanles himself. McCanles had started it by calling James Hickok "Duck Bill" because of his long nose. Buntline changed Duck Bill to Wild Bill and a legend was born.

Back in camp that Sunday evening there was a church service which the public attended. It was followed by community singing around the bonfire. We had been having troubles with vandals, so I and several other men stayed back in the shadows to guard the wagons. We caught one boy holding a cigarette lighter up to a wagon and setting the canvas on fire. We yelled at him and he snuffed it out with his baseball cap. Later he had the audacity to sneak back and write by the hole, "I put the fire out." Besides that trick, we had to chase boys out from inside the wagons several times. It all reminded me that our pioneer predecessors had had similar troubles with "friendly" Indians.

The crowd finally went home and we went to bed. We were no sooner comfortable in our sleeping bags on the ground when a policeman drove up and told us that he had just received a tornado warning. It was expected to hit Fairbury around 2:00 a.m. We argued about what to do with the animals. There was a large, open-walled, dome-roofed amphitheatre there which might offer some protection. Even the local people were hard put to give advice. If we put the animals inside, the roof might fall on them. If we left them outside, they might get hit by flying debris. The "insiders" won out, so we set up a tethering line by the amphitheatre stage and moved all the animals inside. Then we debated about what to do with the wagons. Because of the seats in the amphitheatre, we couldn't put them inside. We finally decided to leave them out in the open and hope for the best.

The air was still and warm. We sat around the campfire and waited. Two o'clock came and nothing happened so we went back to bed. I put my bedroll between two rows of seats in the amphitheatre. My last thought before dropping off was to wonder if there would be a roof over my head in the morning. There was.

Fairbury, from our first impressions, had seemed like it wouldn't be good to us. For that reason we felt thankful to God and everybody when we were able to leave town intact that morning. People hadn't stoned us, our animals didn't stampede, and as if we were blessed by the blood of the lamb, the tornado had passed over us.

Photo: Ezra Meeker, American Oregon Trail pioneer and writer (1830-1928) pictured here dedicating the first of many Oregon Trail markers in 1906, Tenino, Washington. The marker, still exists along Sussex Avenue in Tenino. Source: Creative Commons

VI. THE LITTLE BLUE

That Monday morning the wagons were headed for a stop at Hebron, Nebraska, in the watershed of the Little Blue River. I drove ahead to Hebron where I met Vic McLure, a personable and helpful man with whom I had been corresponding. He showed me our campsite in a park near the southern edge of town. There we conferred with the head of the local riders' club about guiding the wagons into the park. Vic and I then drove west to make plans for Tuesday.

We crossed the Little Blue River and followed its course to the little town of Oak. Part of our route was exactly on the Oregon Trail. About a mile and a half east of Oak is the site of a famous Indian attack. The Indians killed several whites so the action is called a "massacre." At first I thought the local people were kidding when they pronounced the word to rhyme with "see" instead of "sir," but I heard the former several times without a flicker of a grin or a glimmer of a wink, so I decided the speakers were serious.

At Oak we met Mr. Harry Follmer who talked with us about the area's history. The Indian raid near there had taken place in August, 1864, and had resulted in the deaths of the stage station keeper, Mr. Joseph Eubanks, and several other settlers. Mrs. Eubanks and her two children were held captive by the Indians for over three years. The hostiles had been Cheyennes under Black Kettle and Arapahoes under Left Hand. Their raiding began in Colorado in June and didn't slow down until they sought shelter for the winter. They didn't completely stop their raiding, however, since it was a fairly mild winter and Indian attacks along the Oregon Trail continued into 1865.

Back in the 1840s, when men like Col. Stephen W. Kearney and Francis Parkman were in this area, the Pawnees were the most obstreperous. Then in the 1860s, the Cheyenne, Arapahoe and Sioux fought the whites in south-central Nebraska. Sporadic fighting on a small scale, especially with the Sioux, continued on into the 1870s.

Besides talking about the history of Oak, Mr. Follmer made some suggestions for campsites in the area. The plans I made were tentative because I had noticed that the road into Oak was dirt instead of asphalt or gravel. This meant that if it rained any more, the road would become too muddy for us. In order to set up a plan in case of rain, I took Vic McLure back to Hebron and set out by myself on Route 3, which goes south of Oak, to find an alternate campsite.

Several miles west of Deshler I located a campsite on some high ground that was fairly solid. Mr. Charley Anderson owned the farm. Across the highway a barn belonging to Mr. John Jensen would serve as an emergency shelter for some of the people, and the barnyard was a solid place for the semi to park.

Because of a driving wind, the wagons in Hebron were parked in a line rather than a circle to form a better windbreak for the animals. It started to rain and Vic McLure got permission for us to use a building at the east end of the park as a shelter for ourselves. It had been a house at one time, but it was moved there to be used as a Girl Scouts' headquarters and general meeting hall. The building soon became muddy, messy, crowded and noisy, but we accepted all that gladly because it was better than the rain, wind and mud outside.

The house became more crowded as the evening progressed. It stormed hard all night and even people who normally slept in the wagons ended up in the house on the floor before morning. The wagon canvas was water repellant, but in a hard rain a mist formed inside that eventually soaked through blankets and sleeping bags.

Some disheartening news reached us while we waded around in the mud eating breakfast. Word came that Lyle Fenner had been called back to Portland by the officials of the radio station he worked for. We hated to see him leave because he was well-liked by everyone. We were also aggravated because he had been doing a great job in keeping the world informed of our progress. Newspapers all over the world were running daily stories about us. Among these were <u>The Manchester Guardian</u> in England and another newspaper we heard of in Bombay, India. But Lyle left and the wagon train moved off into the rain.

We moved off late because Roy Brabham had trouble greasing the wagon wheels. The ground was soft from rain so the jack just sank into the ground instead of lifting the wagons. The rain also caused us to change our plan of going through Oak. We'd had about 1.5 inches during the night. The wagon train had to backtrack a mile south to travel on the pavement on Route 3.

My scouting duties took me to Nelson, then north to Fairfield, west to Holstein, then on up to Minden. In Nelson I sat in on a meeting of a congenial wagon train welcoming committee, and then in Fairfield I searched through a hardware store attic for some badly needed harness snaps and buckles. Between Nelson and Fairfield I chose a campsite on the Boyd Jones farm for Wednesday. For Thursday I got permission to camp on the Heye Buhr farm west of Fairfield on the Clay and Adams county line. Farther west, south of Holstein, I found a campsite on a farm belonging to Mr. Jay Goble. Then I arranged for us to go on into the fairgrounds at Minden on Saturday. In all of this traveling we would be crossing and re-crossing the Little Blue at least once a day until we left its courses near Minden.

Back at the Anderson farm camp it was raining and cold as usual. Wagon train members and spectators were huddled around a campfire in the center of the circle. Everyone cheered when Mr. Anderson drove in with a trailer load of firewood. An impending storm held off until after supper.

Darkness fell at about the same time the storm began. Tex, Shorty and Tres Hilliard, I and several others went across the highway to the Jensens' barn. For over an hour the rain came down in gusty torrents. Dave Gastman was out there on the ground with a tarp rolled around his sleeping bag. He said later that only a trickle of water was running in on him. Had he tried to run for cover, or even move, he would have gotten thoroughly soaked, so he had to lie there wrapped up like a giant cocoon.

In the flashes of lighting I could see the wagons rocking in the wind and the animals hunched up with their tails to the storm. I watched out the barn window and daydreamed. It seemed that in the silver blackness the wagon train ceased to exist. Flashes of lightning brought it back into being, but brought it back out of history instead of out of now. It wasn't mine. Those weren't my friends out there. Something that happened years before was being sporadically recreated by the electronic turbulence of nature. The future as well as the past was more real than the present. Everything that had been was represented by the wagon train while I, a vessel of dreams, represented all that would be. The present was so fantastic that I doubted its existence.

Headlights appeared and brought me back to 1959. Pop Clark had been suffering from stomach trouble that day. His grandson, Bob Fineout, was returning from taking Pop to a hotel in Nelson.

Watching Tres and Shorty get ready for bed was another show. They were probably the biggest fussbudgets in the world. There were many decisions to be made in getting settled, and each decision was momentous. They had to select the exact placement of their sleeping bags, their lantern, their clothes and themselves. Through the entire process they kept up a continual chatter weighing the pros and cons of placing things "here," or "just a little ways over there."

The next morning a welcome, warming sun caused steam to rise from everything. Some confusion in breaking camp started steam rising in other ways and added another item to our camp catalog of personal hurts.

The kitchen truck had to leave the field first. They were sure to get stuck if they didn't get onto the highway before the wagons pulled out and made a quagmire of the gateway. The truck got stuck anyway. Gail Carnine galloped out on his palomino to see if he could help.

Ben Griffith and the men on the three wagons behind him had been ready and waiting for the signal to pull out. When Ben saw Gail leave, he thought Tex had given the signal for the wagons to leave too. He and the ready wagons behind him started towards the gate. Meantime, Bob Fineout and I were still harnessing Pop Clark's wagon, so it and the wagons behind it never moved. Tex got perturbed, so he rode out and asked Ben if he was starting a wagon train of his own. Ben stopped, but not without furrowing his brow, sticking out his jaw and turning red.

In a few minutes some men pushed the kitchen truck out of the mud, we got Jack and Brigham harnessed and hitched, and the wagon train started out as one. George McUne drove Pop's mules and Jeanne Marshall drove George's two white mules, Fibber and Molly.

Pop Clark, feeling better, met the wagon train as it came through Nelson. A high school band and hundreds of spectators also greeted the caravan there. The day's fair weather allowed spectators to be with us constantly that day. They flocked around camp at the Jones', and at least 100 of them were on hand at 7:00 a.m. to see the wagons leave. The Jones children rode proudly on the wagons while Mr. Jones saddled up his beautiful, copper-colored riding horse and escorted the cavalcade to Fairfield. The wagon train passed an Oregon Trail marker about 100 yards north of the Jones farm. There was another Oregon Trail marker about a mile south of the campsite for that night at the Heye Buhr farm.

Late that afternoon I set up my bunk in an empty granary, then Tex and I drove to Holstein to make a couple phone calls to Oregon. While driving along we talked about the personality difficulties among our members. Tex and I both had been involved from time to time, but often we found ourselves trying to act as middle men in arguments we weren't personally involved in. It was hard to keep peace with everyone when complaints often meant asking one of our people to change the way he did things. George McUne, for example, complained once that Ben Griffith was setting too fast a pace. Tex then had to say something about it to Ben which made Ben angry. Had he not said anything to Ben, then George would have been angry. None of us were such King Solomons that we could deal with all those things justly.

Brooding about the incident of the premature start at Charley Anderson's, some of the men that next morning just stood by the fire and weren't going to hitch up until Tex told them to. I had heard what was on their minds and I knew it wasn't very serious. Some of the drivers were going along with it as a joke, and those who started it didn't have that "big blow up" earnestness about them. I just watched to see how Tex would handle the situation. Without looking at anyone, Tex finally remarked offhandedly, "Well, it looks like we better get moving." The men took that as a command and the wagons rolled on towards the Jay Goble farm.

At Jay Goble's we would be between five and ten miles south of the original trail, but on a road with little traffic which was still passable in wet weather. Near here the original trail turned away from the Little Blue River and headed northwest to Ft. Kearney, about two days away across the prairie. This area is now grain fields and pastures, where the roads follow the grid pattern of agrarian societies rather than the natural diagonal and curved pattern of hunter and nomadic tribes.

I worked ahead to Kearney that day then arrived back at the Goble farm just in time to miss an "Indian" raid. Members of the Hastings Saddle clubs had trucked their horses down, put on war paint and costumes and swept into camp as the wagon trainers were finishing supper. They tried to take some mules, but failing that, took Thyrza instead. When the rain changed from a drizzle to a downpour, they decided to let Thyrza go and leave. The "Indians" and spectators all went to their warm, dry homes and left the wagoneers standing around in the rain with several nervous mules and an excited Thyrza Pelling on their hands. Conditions were poor for philosophizing but I did wonder about the extremes people would go to in the name of fun.

I began a stint at guard duty at 11:00 that evening. It was the first time my number had come up since St. Mary's, Kansas. The camp and the prairie at night hadn't changed much since then, nor had it changed since 1846 when Francis Parkman had to stand guard in this same area, a few days' travel from the Platte. There was the same "dank grass bending under the icy dew drops," the same blackness beyond the light of the campfire, the same noises from the livestock, and the same "barks, howls, yelps and whines" of coyotes off in the distance.

These latter noises, plus the "fierce and stern howl, close at hand" that Parkman heard seems to have been made by a wolf, rather than by a coyote as I heard. With the disappearance of the buffalo, the wolves were replaced by coyotes. The wolves used to eat the old and lame buffalo, where the coyotes lived on mice and prairie dogs. Had the white man been able to exterminate the latter animals, then the coyotes would have disappeared too. Of course, when it comes to sport, it's easier to shoot a buffalo than a mouse because the buffalo presents a larger target. It seems that those feats requiring the greatest skill should gain us the greatest honor, yet who ever heard of a famous mouse hunter? Just imagine having a "Mouse Bill Cody" instead of Buffalo Bill Cody. That matches the ridiculousness that Ned Buntline had to change in "Duck Bill Hickok."

With these midnight musings I sat in the rain by the campfire. I enveloped myself in my G.I. surplus poncho and poked wood into the hissing fire until 2:00 a.m. when it was time to wake up my relief and bed down in the Gobles' barn.

Swallows and pigeons in the rafters woke me up with their calling to one another. Someone had thoughtfully let me sleep late. The wagons had just pulled out for Minden by the time I got to the cook shack for breakfast.

Our first big problem for the day was to again get the cook shack out to the road without getting it stuck. I volunteered to drive it out because neither of the women on cook duty wanted to take the chance. Fortunately, I made it.

The next problem was getting the semi onto the road. Robbie had parked it next to the barn we had slept in and the driveway had turned into a rushing stream. After a nervous few seconds when the rig almost came to a standstill in a soft spot, Robbie's expert driving brought the huge machine out onto the solid road.

Rob Fineout was not so lucky. He had to drive the water truck out through the ruts left by the kitchen truck. He did fine for about 20 yards, and then the back wheels started sinking. When he came to a stop, the wheels had sunk in so far that even the axle was mired in the mud. Robbie, however, was able to hook on with his truck and a long cable. Soon we were all on the road.

The grassy spot I had picked for the wagons at the fairgrounds in Minden was under almost four inches of water. Following their instructions, the drivers circled up there anyway and unhitched. Later we borrowed a tractor and took the wagons out of the pond. We put them on a graveled area in the center of the exhibit buildings.

That afternoon we helped Robbie clean out the van, and then all of us went to downtown Minden to visit the "Pioneer Village," probably one of the largest museums of early Americana in the world. The museum covers nearly ten acres and has a model pioneer village in its center. The buildings are either replicas of old stores, churches and shops, or they are genuine antique buildings which have been moved there. We visited there for several hours and then started back to camp.

Getting home was a problem. A traffic jam started a half mile from camp and we were stopped by it. It was ironic that the people were coming out to see us and we wouldn't be there because they were in the way. It took us almost an hour to go the half mile.

At dusk Dave Gastman and I gathered firewood and built our evening bonfire. The singing started as usual with Dave leading, Shorty playing the mandolin, and me playing my guitar. A couple local members of the gathering had had so much to drink that they couldn't carry a tune, and the noise they made discouraged everyone else. We quit trying and finally everyone left. Then Shorty and I picked up our instruments again and stood alone by the fire remembering old songs for almost an hour. An old Bing Crosby song, "The One Rose," was one of our favorites.

The sun was shining intermittently that next morning. We formed an outdoor church out of bales of hay and a Rev. Slagg conducted services. The sermon was one to be remembered. The minister spoke about trees—how each one was an individual, and yet how they all blended together to form a forest. He drew a parallel between the trees and our society, requesting that we respect each other's individuality while regarding ourselves as a member of a whole group. In view of the friction among us, the sermon said what needed to be said. The twenty-one of us were by no means a forest, but we were a pretty tight clump of trees. Some of us would be cut down, but in the meantime we had to live together.

One of the buildings there was being used as a storehouse for antique cars and horse-drawn carriages. The fairgrounds' board chairman gave me a key to the building and several of us set up our camp cots inside. I slept beside a 1924 Hudson. As we settled gratefully into our dry beds, I heard a distant, melancholy mewing of a kitten somewhere in the dark, nether regions of the storage shed. The tiny animal in the huge building reminded me of myself in the armory at Marysville. I recalled the feeling of desolation and felt glad that time and distance separated me from it.

Thyrza Pelling sells souvenirs. In her lap is the extensive journal she kept which was lost near the trail's end in Oregon.

VII. THE PLATTE

Three hundred and seventeen miles out from Independence the pioneers came to Ft. Kearney. The fort was established in 1847 and served until 1871 as an immigrant supply station and military base. When we passed in there in 1959, the fort consisted only of a monument and a grove of giant cottonwood trees. Now a stockade and other buildings have been rebuilt there to represent the fort as it was over a century ago.

Our plan to arrive at the Platte River at 11:00 a.m. to meet the Kearney welcoming committee meant that we wouldn't have time to stop at the site of the fort. As we learned later, a local historical society had planned a welcome speech there. A lady from the group stood by the road smiling as the wagons approached. Tex nodded hello and the wagons kept on rolling. The train passed by and the lady realized it wasn't going to stop. Her indignation was high caliber. Dave Gastman, faithfully bringing up the rear, caught the full force of her wrath.

I had to find a campsite for the next day, so while the wagons were parading through Kearney, I was driving west on Route 30. I wanted to find a route to travel besides the main highway because the traffic there was murderous. Route 30 followed the river, however, and to get away from it would mean going back to the zigzag, north-then-west pattern that was half-again longer.

We were the center of some controversy at this point about which side of the Platte we should travel on. The people living on the south side believed they were "on the trail," and the people living on the north side were convinced that they were "on the trail."

Actually, the trail went on each side of the river depending on the weather, how easy the river was to cross and the availability of food and forage. Ezra Meeker, one of our heroes whose explorations gave us a path to follow, was an advocate of the north side. Francis Parkman went up the south side, but he was accustomed to being off the trail anyway. Since the river has changed its bed in the past century, the original trail is in the middle of the river in some places. In other places what was the south side is now the north side. Someone told me that the buffalo used to eat sapling trees and keep them from growing on the river banks. Now that the buffalo are gone, trees have grown up which help keep the river in a permanent course. The majority of the Mormons travelled along the north side of the river and a large percentage of the Oregon and California settlers did too. After all these deliberations, and after some planning sessions with the Kearney greeters, we chose to cross over to the north side of the river at Kearney.

I did my work up in the Overton-Lexington area and met the wagons at our campgrounds. I had arranged it to be at a commercial camp near Kearney called "Tent City." There were no tents there, but there were restrooms, showers, and fences to which we could tether the animals.

That evening we had an Indian raid that wasn't as ho-hum as the one back at Holstein. A group of about 40 boys in their late teens had rented horses, dressed up like Indians and put on the appropriate war paint. While we were eating supper they charged around us whooping and kicking up dust. Some of us drew our pistols and fired a few blanks just to be courteous, but we were really more interested in our food.

When the dust billowed up towards us, we began to think the boys were being obnoxious. Gail Carnine grabbed a garden hose, and when they circled around again he gave the horses and boys a good dousing. The horses were baffled and refused to run through the stream of water. The boys didn't know what to do either, until one got off his horse and tried to take the hose away from Gail. The rest of us sat there laughing until a couple more boys got off their horses to help their buddy. Without hesitation, all male members of the wagon train jumped up and into the fray. Except for a few horse-holders, the rest of the boys joined in. There were a few minutes of hard wrestling in which everyone got a little wet, but we managed to keep control of the hose. The boys got back on their horses and rode away. We cheered them as they left and they yelled back complimenting us on being good sports about it all.

That evening we all seemed to be closer together than before. It occurred to me that we should have a little Indian raid every day so we could unite in fighting something outside rather than among ourselves. We sat around the campfire singing a few songs, but mostly we talked about home, the wagon train and the weather.

I'm afraid our feelings of mutual solidarity were not shared by the men on the home front. Three different factions in Oregon were battling over the glory, blame and credit for everything that had transpired on the wagon train. These factions included my own firm, William Dawkins & Associates in Medford, On to Oregon Cavalcade, Inc., in Roseburg, and the Oregon Centennial Commission in Portland. Each faction was afraid they were not getting enough credit when things were going well, and each was blaming the others about things which were going badly.

Our feeling on the wagon train was that none of the three was in charge of us. We were slightly contemptuous of them all because it seemed they wanted to get in on the glory without having to wade around in the mud. We had financial ties to all three groups, but for a while souvenir sales had been going so well that we were largely self-supporting. We also felt independent because there was no way anyone could be an absentee manager of a wagon train. The hundreds of day-to-day and sometimes minute-to-minute decisions that had to be made could not wait for the chiefs in Oregon to have a conference.

My employer, Bill Dawkins, decided that he had had enough of the controversy so he resigned from the account. I could have gracefully left the wagon train at that time, but it never occurred to me to do so. I had developed a loyalty to our purpose and to the people on the train so I chose to stay. I resigned from William Dawkins & Associates and was made welcome by my new employers, the Oregon Centennial Commission and On to Oregon Cavalcade, Inc.

I was surprised to hear from Ben Griffith that he and a couple others had phoned Oregon asking that I be allowed to stay with the group. This surprised me because Ben had been one of my biggest detractors at Marysville only two weeks before. However, this "spirit of Kearney" didn't last long. The discomforts and hazards of Route 30 brought me under fire again.

Gail Carnine was one of my loudest critics but he tended to keep his remarks indirect. He complained about my idea of staying on Route 30 rather than about me personally. He was vociferous about wanting to get us off the main highway. In my mind the ongoing problem was that we had an itinerary to follow. Going on side roads would have meant traveling 30 miles to get 20 miles farther west. Not only would this have taken longer, but it would have meant more horseshoeing needed to be done. Shorty Hilliard was hard-pressed to keep the animals shod as it was. The condition of their hooves and the short supply of borium-tipped shoes was a constant worry.

I sympathized with Gail's viewpoint, but except for short excursions to go past schools or to turn off to camp, we were forced to stay on the main highway. The traffic was a constant strain on everyone's nerves and the shoulders of the highway were too soft for wagons to give way. A police escort in front of and behind the train enabled us to move and kept traffic moving around us.

At noon that Tuesday I drove back from my advance work to meet the wagons, distribute mail and have lunch. I stopped on a side road just as the wagons pulled off and down into the borrow pit where the cook shack was waiting. An icy wind had given everyone a blue nose. Gail Carnine glared at me as he guided Chief over to the fence. He swung down from the saddle, tied Chief to the fence and walked towards me.

The wind turned up the brim of his Stetson and his eyes looked watery from the cold. His angular jaw was clenched as if tight muscles would help keep him warm. It looked as if he couldn't straighten his legs because his buckskins were permanently set in the riding position. He also walked funny because his legs were stiff from having ridden horseback for four hours without dismounting.

"Good God, Dick! Can't you get us off this damned highway?"

"I could if you wanted to take half again as long to get to Oregon."

"This traffic is driving me nuts. The animals are all spooky and anything could happen. Some of the people stopping to gawk at us have no sense at all. They stop where they block traffic both ways."

"You'll just have to yell at them."

"Yell, hell! I've yelled myself blue in the face now."

"I can ask for a larger police escort if you want."

"No, the only thing that will help is getting us off Route 30."

I tried to change his line of thought. "You know it's just as cold no matter what route we follow."

Tres Hilliard extricated me from the conversation by yelling over from the cook shack. "That's right, Gail. Now come and eat and you'll feel better."

While we were eating our hot bean soup, a Union Pacific train came by on the tracks paralleling the highway. The engineer thought he would be friendly and whistle a greeting. Our animals were terrified. Those which weren't tied close up on the reins reared up on their hind legs. All of them kicked and screamed. They calmed down some when the whistle ended but they were agitated all the while that the long freight train roared past. They weren't used to trains screaming by less than 50 feet away at 80 miles an hour. The diversion served to take the people's minds off the cold and the traffic. It gave them something else to complain about.

I drove to Overton, found a phone and called Union Pacific. The management got word to the engineers and we were not subjected to freight train whistles anymore. Later that week, when the offending engineer was off duty, he stopped by camp and apologized. We saw him occasionally for the next thousand or so miles whenever the railroad followed the same route as the Oregon Trail. Eventually the animals became accustomed to train noise. They also became accustomed to the noise made by diesel trucks as they passed the wagon train. Sometimes the drivers would have their engines revved up to shift gears as they came by. Both our people and the animals had some frightened moments until the animals seemed to learn that there was no harm in the noise.

Along this part of the Platte we were in Rudy Roudebaugh's home territory. People recognized him easily because he had the same black beard as he had when he was a high school football star in Lexington. After serving in the navy in World War II, he married and settled in Oregon where he became a logger. His mother and other close relatives still lived around Lexington, and every day he had some old friend or relative riding on his wagon with him. Newspapers and radio stations mentioned Rudy often and this brought even more people to come and see him.

I envied Rudy his old friends. My worries about traffic, campsites, the weather, publicity, town welcoming committees and intra-wagon-train squabbling made me long to see some old friends too. Perhaps it was an established pecking order, or perhaps it was a modus vivendi, but it seemed that my old gang in San Francisco could complain to one another in a way that didn't jeopardize long-term relationships. Complaints on the wagon train were often punctuated by threats of the "big blow up" which would destroy our organization and our purpose.

The complaints about who didn't like whom spilled out of camp and back to Oregon in the form of phone calls. The specific complaints were too petty for me to remember now, but in general the Blairs' dislike for Thyrza Pelling and Gail Carnine's dislike of everything seemed to be at the heart of the controversy. The Oregon Centennial Commission decided to send one of the commissioners out to try and smooth things over—not so much for our good, but for the good of the State of Oregon. Our trek was so successful that our dissolution would be a real loss to them.

They sent an Oregon farmer named Jack Lively. He was a slim, soft-spoken man in a light-blue suit. He had the demeanor and reputation of a sage and I think his visit did some good. He listened to stories ranging from the petty to the ridiculous. He heard all the details about Olathe from Edna Blair; he heard about how upset Tex had become in Minden when Bob Fineout drove the wrong car to town to take a shower; he heard about the time that Tex leaned on the cook shack counter to eat instead of leaving the entire eight feet for access by the hungry horde, all 22 of us. Mr. Lively had a good lesson in how some people can be small even when on a grandiose mission. He stayed with us two days and studied the problems.

When we camped at Darr, Mr. Lively had a long talk with Thyrza to try and iron out some of the camp's difficulties. I felt sorry for Thyrza because I knew she wanted to be friends with everyone. She had the knack, however, of making one faux pas after another that kept the camp in turmoil. Edna Blair told Tex either Thyrza went home or she would. Tex didn't honor that. He simply told Thyrza what had been said and that she could make up her own mind. Thyrza and Edna both stayed a while longer.

The morning that Jack Lively left was sunny and there was dew sparkling on the green stubble. He asked us to gather around the ashes of our campfire so he could talk to us before he left. He impressed upon us that what we were doing was the greatest part of the Centennial celebrations, and that all Oregon was watching us and counting on us to get through. With that in mind we should forego any personal differences which might endanger our mission. No one said much before we went our separate ways, but I found out later that his words did make an impression on some of the dissidents.

The wagon trainers that day were given the red carpet treatment in Cozad and Gothenburg. At Cozad they had coffee and donuts at the Willow Springs Pony Express Station. The station had been moved into the city park from its original location south of the Platte. Later in Gothenburg everyone was presented with gifts. Riders' clubs and police cars escorted the caravan nearly all the way.

That night when we were camped on the Lincoln-Dawson county line, we thought we were being vandalized again. Our animals were tethered in some trees about 50 yards from the wagons. Dave Gastman came to the campfire and went unobtrusively among us, alerting about six of us that someone was out by the tethering line. He didn't want to make a stir and tip off the would-be marauders that we were after them. We slipped out into the darkness and ran quietly over to see what was happening. I saw three figures douse cigarettes and start running as we came close to them. I yelled at them to stop at the same time that Dave, who had sneaked around behind them, yelled at them from the other direction. They had no choice but to stop. We went up to them and demanded to know what they were doing. Instead of finding anyone vicious, we found three frightened teenage boys who had sneaked away from their parents at the campfire to come out and smoke cigarettes. The boys had seen us coming and thought we were their fathers. They were relieved to find out that we weren't and we were relieved that they were only smoking.

The weather had become drier the past few days and I stopped bothering to put up my tent and camp cot. Instead I unrolled my bedroll wherever I was away from the noises of camp. I had improvised a bedroll which could be adapted to any weather. It consisted of a 7' x 9' tarp, an army comforter and a cheap sleeping bag. If it looked like rain, the tarp folded both under and over me. In clear weather it simply served as a ground tarp. The comforter was under me as a mattress on warm evenings and it folded completely around me on chilly evenings. Instead of using an air mattress, I usually found tall grass to cushion me. If that failed, I sprinkled some hay on the ground. At camp that night west of Gothenburg I invented another essential item for my bed. The prairie was smooth enough for sightseers to drive around camp on all sides, which they usually did. My bedroll was hard to see because it was the same color as the grass. As a precaution against getting run over, I hung my Stetson on a six-foot stake and stuck it in the ground beside me. I slept peacefully and woke up warm. The sun was shining, and sparkling white frost covered my bed and my world.

Our next campsite was on the Marvin Lehman ranch near Maxwell. The wagons circled up on some pasture beside a grove of large oak trees. The trees gave us something to tie the animals to, and the pasture was large and solid enough so our motor vehicles could drive up to where they were convenient. There was no rain and everyone agreed that it was the best campsite we'd had so far on the trip.

A few years after we stayed there, a historical marker was set up only a quarter mile east of where we camped. The marker notes the presence from 1863 to 1880 of Ft. McPherson just a few miles south. The fort was a base for the 1869 campaign which rid the area of marauding Cheyenne Indians. In 1871 Prince Alexis of Russia used the fort as a base of operations for his famous buffalo hunt. Buffalo Bill Cody was his guide on that excursion. Rudy Roudebaugh, Pop Clark and several others from our group went and visited the site of the old fort. The commissary building was all that was left of the original buildings.

Keith Blackledge from the <u>Telegraph Bulletin</u> in North Platte visited our camp that evening. He wanted to camp out and ride along with us to get the feel of the wagon train before writing about it. I set up my tent for protection from a predicted rain shower and we had our usual campfire sing. At bedtime as Keith was walking past my tent towards his bedroll I called to him, "Hey, Keith, you want a nightcap?"

"Sure, I'll have one with you."

I reached back into my tent and came out with a bottle of bourbon. I took off the lid and handed it to him. "There, that will take the chill off the evening."

He looked at me, perplexed. "You mean straight?"

"Well, you came out here to rough it didn't you?"

He agreed and went ahead on it. His reaction to the plain opened bottle made me realize how unimportant such amenities as glasses, chasers and mixers had become.

Other amenities we had become unaccustomed to were bathrooms, sinks, running water and privacy. The next morning I saw a large group of sightseers coming towards us and said to Gail Carnine, "Those people are just in time to watch me brush my teeth."

Gail had a sarcasm of his own, "Yeah, I was going to relieve myself a little while ago, but there wasn't anyone to watch so I decided to wait."

A drizzling rain started about the time the wagons left the next morning. Keith Blackledge stood in the middle of the circle with me and took pictures of the wagons as they uncircled and pulled out of camp. He underestimated the speed of the wagons, almost five miles an hour, and had quite a run to catch them when he finished taking pictures. He climbed aboard George McUne's wagon and rode along with him.

Later he wrote in his newspaper about an interesting, and to me gratifying, part of his conversation with George. He quoted George as saying, "I wouldn't any more go back home without finishing this trip than anything. If anything happened to the caravan, I guess I would just keep on going by myself. There are a lot of others that feel the same way."

I was delighted to see in print that George felt that way. It made me feel that finally some of our people had developed a certain loyalty to the group and dedication to its purpose. It made me think that Jack Lively's visit and campfire oration at Darr helped considerably. However, every time I heard a wagon trainer complain about the presence or actions of another, I felt the whole thing was being jeopardized. As Jack Lively reported in Oregon, we were "suffering from too much togetherness."

Just before getting into North Platte, the wagon train came to where the North and South Platte Rivers join. A long, narrow bridge across the north fork was closed to all traffic while the wagon train crossed. From North Platte to Ogallala, a distance of 52 miles, the train would be following the north bank of the South Platte. Mormon immigrants and some others had followed the North Platte instead of crossing as we did. Another branch of the trail followed the south side of the South Platte, parallel to the route we took. This was the trail followed by the pioneers who didn't cross the Platte near Kearney as we did. They went along the South Platte until they found a place where the river could be forded; then they went to the north side, and eventually, to the north side of the north fork. This route changed from year to year depending on how swollen the river was from the rain and snow runoff.

Our wagon train was greeted in North Platte with another "key to the city" to add to our collection. After a brief stop, the caravan rolled on to the Steel Ranch about seven miles west of town. We made our weekend stop there.

Our livestock by this time was pretty well toughened up to traveling. We still had some distemper in our remuda, however, and a veterinarian came that evening to break a fever boil and otherwise take care of one of Rudy Roudebaugh's horses. It was an interesting but gory operation to watch. The vet hit a certain spot with his probe and puss squirted out five feet into the air. He said the horse would be all right but it would take longer to get well if we worked it too hard.

It began to rain, but the townspeople didn't let the storm interfere with their sightseeing. They stayed in their cars and circled camp just as the Indians used to do when they were attacking. As the rain continued, soon there was a wide, muddy strip where the cars drove around us. Finally one car bogged down and that ended the tourist attack.

A new member of our expedition arrived that day: nine-year-old Robbie Roberts II. He was definitely of the same mold as his dad, not only physically, but with the same good nature. I first called him "Robbie Junior," but he protested that he wasn't a junior; he was "the second." As time went by we called father and son "Robbie One" and "Robbie Two," thinking also of "Robbie too." Except for Robbie One's red beard and advanced years, they were very much alike. Robbie Two had the same wiry build, humpy nose and friendly grin his father must have had twenty years before.

On Monday Tex left Gail Carnine in charge of the wagon train and went ahead with me to scout the trail and meet with the Ogallala welcoming committee. We returned to our camp near Paxton and found that another new member had joined us. Ivan Hoyer, a member of the Board of Directors of On to Oregon Cavalcade, Inc., had come to be our publicity man. All 300 pounds of him had been flown to Kansas City where Lyle Fenner had left his station wagon. Ivan got the car out of storage and drove out from there. Several of the wagon train members had known Ivan in Roseburg. Everyone liked him and we were thankful that someone had come to do a job which badly needed done. My own duties of keeping the wagon train moving had involved so much time that I couldn't be a publicity man too.

The glory of the Ogallala arrival was dulled by an accident near town. An elderly couple had slowed down to see the wagons while they were pulled off into the borrow pit for lunch. A car coming up behind the couple failed to slow down fast enough and hit their car. The car was knocked about 50 feet, barely missing one of our wagons. By the time some of our people got there, the lady was dying and the man was in critical condition.

Traffic on Route 30 being as heavy as it was, we had expected an accident of some kind in the 150 miles we were on it. With the less-traveled and safer Route 26 within a few miles, the accident had a touch of irony to it.

Most of the early-day pioneers had gone farther west from present-day Ogallala before turning north to go up to the North Platte. On that route they had a 1½-mile slog up what they called California Hill. As soon as possible we chose to turn up to Highway 26, which follows the North Platte. This responded to those who wanted to get off Highway 30 and it also allowed us to avoid the climb up California Hill.

In Ogallala we made camp at the fairgrounds, took care of the stock, had some hullabaloo with "Indians," and went to a school for showers. While climbing into a red convertible en route, I had the door slammed on my fingers. I lost some skin off my ring finger and my little finger turned a deep purple color.

Back at camp later, I found that the accident on Route 30 had caused another fight of sorts. Gail Carnine maintained that the accident was our fault because we shouldn't have been traveling on that highway.

Our arguments didn't mollify him and he said he was going home. He seemed to calm down that evening, changed his mind and didn't go home after all.

That day we noted the anniversary of our first month "on the trail," or more appropriately, "on the trail of the trail." We tried to forget our troubles at a banquet in a restaurant. The steaks were delicious and Tex bought a huge cake decorated for the occasion. Afterwards some of us went to a dance at the Legion Hall, then to the Elks club for more festivities. It was pouring rain so we weren't worried about a dearth of spectators and vandals at camp.

We called the van of the semi-truck "Robbie's Hotel." That night it was a sanctuary from the storm for all of us not sleeping in the wagons. The bales of hay made a perfect platform for our sleeping bags. At times the thunder actually shook the van. Besides being kept awake by the violence of the storm, the pain in my purple little finger didn't let me sleep. I had a good think about the "big blow up," everybody's bickering and our route to Ash Hollow from Ogallala.

Roy Brabham putting clean canvas over the new bows of Arkansas oak. During the trek Roy could be seen every evening putting axle grease on each of the 28 wheels of the caravan.

VIII. The North Platte

It was raining hard when we took Route 26 out of Ogallala. Tex and I had scouted the trail previously and we hoped to take what is called the Canyon Road. This would have had far less traffic and it would have been closer to the original trail. However, the previous night's deluge made Canyon Road impassable.

The change in plans meant that I had to pick a new campsite. The wind was blowing cold across the tableland from the west. I found a swale on the Floyd Grape ranch, about five miles east of Ash Hollow, where the wagons would be sheltered from the wind. As luck would have it, by the time the wagons arrived the wind had shifted to the north and the swale became a wind tunnel instead of a shelter. Everyone let me know about "Carter's wind tunnel" when I came back to camp that afternoon.

While the wagons were on their way to the Grape ranch, I drove ahead to arrange for our camp in Oshkosh the next day. That town was a milestone for the wagon train because its newspaper had printed an article saying we wouldn't come there. The article also said we were not interested in history and knew nothing about the original trail. It gave us a certain acrid pleasure to come to Oshkosh.

I contacted Doc Jenkins in Oshkosh. He was a cousin of Paul Jenkins who had been of help to us in the Gothenburg area. He helped me find a place where our people could take showers, then went with me to look at our future campsite on the riding club grounds at the east edge of town.

I met Tex at Lewellen while on my way back to camp. He had come in to call home about the state of our finances and about the latest controversy going on in camp. Little of it was new. Some people were still upset about the accident at Ogallala, others were still unable to get along with Thyrza and others were worried about the condition of the animals.

At camp the wind blowing up the swale was causing some bitter complaining. As many as were interested gathered in the lee of the water truck and took part in a gripe session. I explained the wind shift and Tex listened to the other complaints. Being able to talk things over helped tremendously. Although little was accomplished at the meeting, we each left with a feeling which approached union and solidarity. Gail Carnine still had an unmollified attitude, but all he did was talk about going home instead of doing it.

That night those of us not sleeping in the wagons were fortunate to have a concrete block barn in which to sleep. We stretched our bedrolls out on the clean hay and listened comfortably to the cold wind howling outside.

Rudy Roudebaugh's mare, Daze, was lame the next morning. She was so bad that we knew we would have to replace the team. We theorized that another horse had kicked her during the night. The bruise was compounded by the horse's sickness. These things plus suffering from the cold wind that had blown all night added up to the end of the horse's wagon train days.

Buttons and Bow, the two sorrel mares we had been riding, were hooked up to Rudy's wagon. It was a steep climb out of the swale and the animals didn't want to push on the cold collars. Pop Clark led the way out by circling around the sides of the depression and doubling back to the top. The other wagons followed; Rudy's rather hesitantly because the horses hadn't worked in a harness for some time. It was one of the more impressive mornings for me to watch the wagons leave camp.

Rudy's horses, Dan and Daze, were almost frantic to see the wagons leave without them. Old lame Daze hobbled to the top of the hill with Dan to watch the wagons leave. The anxious expressions on their faces almost brought tears to my eyes. They whinnied and shook their heads so pathetically that I couldn't bear to watch them. I was amazed at how attached they had become to the wagon train in only a month's time. We all felt as if we were deserting two old friends.

I was having some blank cartridges made back in Ogallala. After picking them up and leaving town, I met Tex and Floyd Grape in the Grapes' stock truck heading east. They were taking Dan and Daze back to the auction sale at North Platte. Some of our people had expressed a fear that the horses would be sold for dog food, but Tex reported later that they had no trouble keeping them from the "killers," because they were even too poor-looking for that. However, we've never been convinced that they didn't end up as dog food.

Farther west on Route 26 I passed the wagon train, then stopped at Ash Hollow. Besides being the site of several Indian battles, Ash Hollow had been a stopping place for pioneers. They had been on barren, high tableland since crossing the South Platte and coming up California Hill. At Ash Hollow they found green grass, firewood and fresh water for the first time in a couple days. They were forced to pause at the top of the hollow and lower the wagons down Windlass Hill to the level of the North Platte. A stump stood like a large post at the top of the hill. To get the wagons down, the pioneers tied a rope to the rear axle, rough-locked the wheels, and wrapped the rope around the post to use it as a windlass.

I climbed to the top of the hill and looked at the stone monument which now stands where the windlass post was. In my imagination I could see the pioneers playing out the rope to lower all their possessions down the precipitous incline. What at one time were trail ruts down the slope have now been eroded into deep gullies.

In Oshkosh that day we had two newcomers. Tex had bought a fine-looking pair of brown mules to replace Rudy's horses. Jan, the biggest, weighed about 1,300 pounds and her half-brother, Doc, was about 150 pounds lighter. Janell Roudebaugh gave them their names. The mules had good sense and definite personalities. As time went by, their antics provided us with many laughs and chuckles.

Breakfast in Oshkosh was memorable. Mud was two inches deep around the whole camp. There was no place to get out of the rain, so we all stood out in the deluge eating breakfast. Every time I bent my head over to take a bite, the rain would run off my hat brim and pour into my plate of hotcakes and eggs. Being hungry and tired from having had the two to five a.m. stint at guard duty, I was beyond caring about a little water in my food.

The next evening our camp was by the river on the Rush Creek Ranch near Lisco. Our host, ranch foreman Ruby Ellis, took several of us on a tour of that section of the 6,000-acre ranch where they raised horses. The rain kept to a sprinkle and the breeze was mild so the campsite was rated excellent.

Our weekend camp was at the Bridgeport fairgrounds. The last seven or eight miles of the trip from Lisco had been in sight of Courthouse and Jail Rocks, landmarks which had been guides for the pioneers. Our caravan's route along the highway took them within a hundred yards of Amanda Lamon's grave. She died during the great exodus and now a monument has been erected there. Besides the usual details, it points out the location of the original trail several hundred feet to the north. The river, now a half-mile north, had once run almost where the grave is.

One visitor in Bridgeport was a locally-owned covered wagon drawn by four Scottish Highland oxen. Because of their long red hair and short, heavy stature, they didn't look at all like the oxen used to settle the West. However, their lumbering, slow gait impressed on us the difference between being drawn by oxen rather than by horses and mules. The oxen's top speed was about two miles an hour, whereas we averaged at least four an hour. The oxen's slow speed meant that they had to travel all day to traverse the 20 miles that we covered in just over six hours.

While we were in Bridgeport, Tex and several others of us were invited to Paul Henderson's house for a briefing on the Oregon Trail through Wyoming. Paul was, in many people's minds, America's authority on the Oregon Trail. A railroad engineer by profession, he spent nearly every moment of his leisure time studying the trail. He took treks, made maps, and collected historical data. He had one file cabinet drawer filled with nothing but diaries written by people who made the original crossings. His help to us was invaluable.

The main thing Paul talked about was the trail through Wyoming. He showed us slides of the desolate rangeland we would be going through and told us about the history of the trail through places like South Pass, the Sweetwater, Rocky Ridge, and Green River. He set up his projector and showed us slides of what was left of the original trail. He told us that if we made a circle on a map using the old mining town of Atlantic City as the center, then 50 miles out from there in all directions we would find more artifacts and places of historical significance than anywhere else in the United States. The way he told it and listed his reasons for saying that, it didn't sound like an exaggeration. When we came to that area, we saw what he meant.

The antique car club of Bridgeport provided us with an excursion the next day to Courthouse and Jail Rocks. It took us all back about 25 years to see the old cars chugging up the hillside. To make things even more anachronistic, some of us had to get out and push the last several yards up the hill to the parking area. Some people were intent on climbing to the top of Courthouse Rock; others were satisfied with exploring around the sides. After I tried to find a path to the top and failed, I settled for the exploring jaunt with Thyrza Pelling, Tres Hilliard, Val Johnson and George McUne. We had been warned about rattlesnakes so I walked ahead tossing clods and sticks, hoping to stir up any snakes with my missiles rather than with my feet. We had almost followed the narrow trail completely around the side of the mesa when suddenly there was an ominous rattling in a bush by my shoulder. It was only 12 inches from me. I'm sure if the snake had been impolite enough to strike without warning, he could have had me in the neck. We all backed off and threw clods at the three-foot-long rattlesnake until it fell into the trail in front of us. Then we were stymied. It was too far to go back and we couldn't go forward either. The clods of dirt were too soft to hurt the snake and there were no rocks or sticks that we could find. Finally we walked back on the trail until we did find some rocks to throw. We then managed to knock our badly-damaged adversary down into a deep gully off the trail. I decided after that to carry a round or two of live ammunition in my gun belt with my blanks.

That afternoon Tex and I drove ahead to Chimney Rock to inspect the site for our battle with the Sioux the next day. Scotty Hamilton, the Chamber of Commerce representative from Bayard, toured the area with us and told us that the Indians had come out and rehearsed the day before. We worked out an order of battle and the script for the action, then left with the feeling of boys anticipating a football game.

Two new members and a visitor joined us in Bridgeport. The first of these was a relief driver and some much-needed help for Shorty Hilliard with his horseshoeing. Dick Melton was a slow-talking, backwoods-type man from Azalea, Oregon. His craggy jaw and squint eyes gave him a disdainful expression that had no connection with what he might be thinking, and he was usually thinking rather than talking. Besides being a good worker he turned out to be a good fiddle player.

The other new member was Dave Gastman's wife, Lillian. School was out in Oregon so she was able to leave her teaching job and come "keep an eye on Dave." She and Dave joked that that was why she joined us, but I wondered where joking ended and the facts began. Lillian, a slim woman in her early 40s, was made welcome by promptly being put on the women's cooking duty roster.

Tex's wife, Ludy, was our visitor. Tex and I picked her up at the airport when she flew in from Oregon. As a girl, Ludy had come from east-coast society. She had a degree from a famous women's college, and had even been a debutante. But as Tex described her, her background didn't keep her from reaching up into a cow having trouble giving birth and pulling the calf out with her bare hands. I found her to be friendly, matter-of-fact and beautiful. She had a firm smile, dark-brown hair and a good stride. Of the six or seven wives Tex had had, she was his favorite. Ludy and Tex were glad to see each other. We had a drink at the airport, then a grand time driving back to camp through a spectacular sunset.

Beautiful weather helped our good mood last through the next morning and early afternoon. I did some business in Scottsbluff and Bayard, then met the wagon train in a field near Chimney Rock. Everyone was waiting for the starting time of our Indian war games. Robbie Roberts, Bob Fineout, the women on cook duty, and I all parked our separate vehicles at a service station so we could get on board wagons and participate in the fun.

Riding clubs from Bayard and Sydney had come to meet us. While we waited we enjoyed visiting with them. They got their eyes full of wagon train while we admired their horses. Some of us borrowed the riders' horses and took rides to pass the time before leaving for the "massacre." I got onto a trim sorrel gelding and started galloping across the pasture. No sooner had the horse got into a good run when it suddenly felt like he was falling. He sank straight down into the ground so both my feet almost touched the ground at the same time. I looked down and saw that we had run into a mud bog which had crusted over and looked solid. The people watching from the wagon train saw me lose altitude so fast that they thought I had fallen. The horse seemed smarter than me about mud bogs, so I gave him his head and he had us back on solid ground in a minute. The horse's owner was perturbed when I brought back his finely-groomed animal coated in mud almost up to his belly. For the next 15 minutes I dipped clear water out of a pond with a paper cup and washed the horse's legs.

At zero hour minus one half, Robbie Roberts and I climbed onto Shorty Hilliard's wagon. A traffic jam of spectators made the wagon train slow in getting to the battle ground.

"Look at the chief up there on the ridge," I said to Robbie as we pulled onto the field.

"Whoo boy! He sure looks real," Robbie said.

Then I saw where the spectators were gathered. "My God, look at those damned tourists. They've filled up the place where we're supposed to have the fight."

"Hey, Tex!" I yelled out of the back of the wagon. "There's people all over the place we picked."

In reply he yelled to Ben Griffith in the lead wagon, "We'll have to circle up right in front of those people, Ben."

"But I see ditches and boulders there," Ben yelled back.

"We'll have to trust to luck," Tex told him.

Meanwhile the chief was still riding along the ridge parallel to us about 75 yards away. He waved his lance and shouted at us in Sioux. Tex raised his pistol and fired, signaling for the action to begin.

"Holy cow, Robbie! Look at those Indians come over that ridge. There's oodles of them."

"Don't fire until you see the whites of their eyes." Robbie's cliché seemed apropos somehow.

"Hey, look! The ones on horseback are getting here too quick. They're outrunning those on foot and getting to us before we have time to circle up."

"Hang on!" Shorty shouted, "We're going over a ditch."

We hung on while each wagon wheel in turn dropped into the 12-inch deep ditch and came up out of it. Crossing at a 45-degree angle caused the wagon to careen left and right for each of the four wheels. It was breathtaking to try and hang on while being screamed at by Indians.

"There goes Rudy," Robbie said and pointed up a nearby hill. Rudy's mules had decided that in case of Indian attack, the best thing to do was to leave immediately. Rudy finally got Doc and Jan under control and convinced them to rejoin the group.

While we finished our circle, the Indians rode and ran in another circle around us. Tex, riding Reno, decided to cut in front of Roy Brabham's wagon to chase one of the marauders. Roy's frightened horses were going faster than Tex judged, so Roy's wagon tongue got caught under Reno's stomach. Tex and Reno rode the tongue about 20 feet before they got loose.

"Those Indians look like they're not used to riding bareback," Robbie said. "Look at those two coming there."

Robbie and I both fired at them when they were only a few feet from us. The shots made the horses jump sideways and both Indians fell off. "Well, we got them," Robbie and I both said at once.

We staved off the initial attack and the braves pulled back to the ridge. All this was in keeping with the battle's libretto. During the lull we organized our defenses. We formed a tighter circle, let Rudy back into place and unharnessed the animals. The second attack was delayed while we chased sightseers out of camp.

In ten minutes the second attack began. Our fight this time didn't last long because we ran out of ammunition. All of us, except for some women hiding in the wagons, were captured and herded into a circle on the side of the ridge. The women in hiding soon got lonesome and joined us.

One Indian in a bright blue costume had actually been wounded. He went around proudly showing off his bleeding shoulder. A small piece of brass had come off a shell casing and had almost the same effect as a bullet.

We held a short powwow and smoked the peace pipe with Chief Man-Afraid-of-His-Horse, the one who had challenged us from the ridge earlier. During the ceremony, five Indians took Dave Gastman down with the intention of cutting off his hair. They desisted after some pictures were taken.

After the powwow we formed a 60-foot circle and the Indians put on a show for us in the middle. Crow Dog, one of the chiefs, demonstrated the full peace pipe ceremony while another chief narrated the proceedings over a loudspeaker. The ceremony was followed by colorful and impressive Indian dancing. The squaws wore their best decorated buckskin dresses ranging in colors of white, grey and various shades of brown. The men all had on war paint and feathers. Bells tied around their legs made a constant rhythmic jangle as they danced. After some dance demonstrations, they invited us to dance with them. We learned the steps soon and enjoyed ourselves immensely.

After the dancing we are beef and beans from paper plates using a car hood for a table. Things were quieter then. Most of the Indians left and I got out my guitar, sat on the tailgate of my station wagon and started playing. Ludy and a flock of children started singing. Ludy's beautiful soprano voice blended in with the children's voices and made a fine combination. Not wanting to stop, we stayed there for nearly an hour entertaining ourselves. Then we went over to the campfire and sang with the other people until bedtime.

As I lay in my sleeping bag I thought again of how amiable everyone was when they had an Indian attack. The entire day was spent without grumbling or gossip. The Indians gave us something outside ourselves to fight so we had a great time. When I first signed on to take the trek, I imagined it would be like this all the time. I remembered how the Russian novelist Sholokhov brought out in his books that some men at war feel a sense of belonging that borders on contentment for the only time in their lives. When we band together to fight a third party, we forego bedeviling one another and fight some other devil. Having an outside menace deemphasizes the group pecking order, and the people function as a group rather than as a collection of individuals jostling for better positions. This isn't always good, however, because continually needing an outside element to fight can lead to xenophobia and racial prejudice. Anyhow, it's a natural human trait that I observed that day and I welcomed its respite from our daily squabbling, complaining, and general discontent.

The wagons rolled on to Scott's Bluff National Monument the next morning. In talking to the National Monument ranger about the trail in that area, I learned that the Monument buildings are right at Mitchell Pass, a division in the bluffs where the trail went through. South of the bluff there had been a blacksmith shop and trading post operated by a man named Robideaux, one of the original Oregon Trail pioneers. Some settlers detoured the bluffs and went south to the trading post, but since it wasn't in existence during the entire period that the trail was, the bulk of the settlers either went through Mitchell Pass or followed the Oregon-Mormon Trail on the north side of the bluffs, across the North Platte River.

The traffic jam getting into camp that evening was worse than the one we'd had at Minden. Several rangers were directing the parking, and a couple more were on the highway directing traffic. One of those on the highway was also counting our visitors. At 9:00 p.m. he stopped counting when he reached 10,000. At least 2,000 more people came after that, making 12,000 for the day, our biggest crowd ever.

It was so crowded that our people found it impossible to do any of the necessary chores. The visitors always wanted to talk to us or take pictures, so it took us at least a half hour to do a five-minute job. I spent 20 minutes bringing a bucket of water from the water truck to a horse at the picket line.

Our animals were taking the constant harassment of people in two ways: some became meaner and some became gentler. It was meaner for most of them and we had to be watchful to keep people from being bit or kicked. I watched a boy giving one of our sorrel mares a handful of grass. The trouble was that he was teasing her rather than giving it to her outright. The mare soon tired of that so she reached out with her mouth, grabbed the boy's baseball cap by the bill and threw it onto the ground. The boy got a horrified expression on his face, then turned and ran crying to his mother who was nearby. The mother and I both had been watching the boy and I was afraid she would be angry. The boy cried into her bosom while she comforted him. Between sobs I heard him say, "I'm going to kill that god damned horse." I looked at her inquisitively. She smiled and nodded at me in a way that I knew she knew the boy got what he deserved. I retrieved the boy's hat for him and the mother took him home, thoroughly chastised by the horse.

Ludy Serpa left the next morning for Oregon, the wagons pulled out through Mitchell Pass and I drove ahead to find a campsite for the evening. From Scott's Bluff National Monument the wagon train took its familiar zigzag course following the roads past a terrible-smelling fertilizer factory and past the South Morrill railroad station. From South Morrill the best roads for our purposes went north across the river through Morrill, then west again on Route 26. The route we took allowed us to avoid California Hill, a 1.5-mile-long slog up and over a hill to get to the North Fork of the Platte.

Cultivated fields occupied both sides of the highway where our daily quota of 20 miles ran out. I took a side road 100 yards north and found a likely camping spot on the farm of an elderly couple, Mr. and Mrs. Vern Luth. They said we could camp there, and then Mrs. Luth invited me in for coffee.

Mrs. Luth was like a character out of Gogol's novel, <u>Dead Souls</u>. Although her name implied she was of German heritage, she seemed to be of the same unsophisticated and earthy peasant stock that Gogol found on the steppes of Russia. She chattered away and bustled around her kitchen like Nadara Korobochka who invited Chichikov for a bite and gave him a banquet. I had been thinking of how the Nebraska prairies compared with the Russian steppes, so I sort of expected to meet someone like Mrs. Luth. Mr. Luth meanwhile sat outside under some trees in the back seat of an old junked car. Mrs. Luth explained that he liked to do that because of his "gas problem."

My pistol was dirty from the black-powder blanks I had fired the day before so I borrowed some hot soapy water and cleaned it. All the time I dismantled, washed and reassembled my six shooter, Mrs. Luth fixed coffee, cake and cookies and entertained me with the story of her trip to the Chicago World's Fair in 1933. I gathered that the wagon train's arrival was to be the biggest event in her life since then.

That evening the Luths had a wonderful time visiting with our people. After supper a violent rainstorm came up and we all had to find shelter. Most of us sat it out in the back of the semi. When the storm abated, Thyrza, Val, Tex, Dave and I went into Morrill. The only place open was a private club called the "Stock Feeders." They said we qualified as stock feeders and let us in. While there we fortified ourselves with huge steaks in anticipation of entering Wyoming the next day.

An early-morning picture of the wagon train at Scott's Bluff, Nebraska.

Near Chimney Rock, Sioux Chief Crow Dog goes through the peace-pipe ceremony with wagon master, Tex Serpa.

IX. Ft. Laramie Relived

In Wyoming we relived history best of all. We were often in the wilderness by ourselves because of the state's scarce population. Also, civilization had not obliterated vestiges of the original trail. For miles we traveled along wagon wheel ruts left from the last century. There were fewer towns to greet and entertain us so I didn't have the constant task of coordinating welcoming events as I had in Kansas and Nebraska. This gave me some time to leave my Ford and ride with the wagon train itself, usually on horseback.

In Wyoming frequent visible reminders of pioneer days made the lapse of a century seem inconsequential. In the first part of the state we went past the sites of three U.S. Army posts which had been used during the Indian wars: Ft. Laramie, Ft. Fetterman and Ft. Caspar. Forts Laramie and Caspar, both partially restored, gave us a feeling of traveling forward through space but backward through time. A colorful, fun-loving and helpful para-military group of men known as the Fifth Wyoming Volunteer Cavalry contributed to the aura of timelessness. In the latter part of the state, the ghost towns and barren lands allowed us to live and travel in a way similar to people a century before us.

Also like our pioneer forefathers, our quarreling sometimes turned into physical violence and sometimes led to people quitting the wagon train. I've often wondered how much of the territory between Missouri and the West Coast was first populated by people who, being unable to get along with their traveling companions, left their wagon trains and settled where they were. The old diaries and journals I've read tell of several such instances.

Our plans for the wagon train to stop at Ft. Laramie meant that it would be impossible for us to stop in Torrington, the first town in Wyoming. The distance between Torrington and Ft. Laramie was too great for one day's travel and too short for two days. Remembering the incident at

Marysville, I didn't want us to have a short travel day that would have to be compensated for later. For that reason I went six miles west of Torrington and found a good campsite in a basin-shaped area off the highway. The owner, a Mr. Stephenson who sold cars in nearby Lingle, Wyoming, gave us permission to use the property.

The newspaper editor and several Torrington businessmen were indignant that I chose to camp there rather than in town. The editor wanted Torrington boosted by the nationwide publicity and the businessmen wanted people to shop in their stores when they came to see the wagon train. After the news of the campsite selection reached town, Ivan Hoyer was the first of us to find out how angry some of the townspeople were. He met me on the road and told me how the Chamber of Commerce secretary had "read him out." Then I went to town and talked to the secretary too. After telling him about the miles we traveled per day and of our desire to stop at Ft. Laramie, he understood why we had to camp beyond Torrington. However, this was another instance when someone understood the logic of the situation but was miffed anyway.

I was in Torrington talking with a three-man welcoming committee from Casper, Wyoming, when the wagon train passed through town. A strong thunder shower hit them on the west edge of Torrington. In a few moments the rain turned to hail. I suggested to my companions that perhaps by the time the hail stopped, we wouldn't have a wagon train to reach Casper.

We had feared and expected a storm like this somewhere on the trip, and here it was. The hailstones were up to an inch in diameter. We hoped that our animals would simply hunch up and suffer through the storm, but we were afraid the stinging hail would make them stampede.

As luck would have it, there was a huge auction sale barn near the wagons when the storm struck. The doors were open, so the two lead wagons drove right inside, almost filling the barn. The other men had to quickly unhitch and drive their animals in, leaving the wagons outside. They had several exciting moments, but everyone got inside safely and they weathered the storm without mishap.

That day the Torrington newspaper printed an uncomplimentary editorial in my honor. The editor had not known that we were stopping at Ft. Laramie when he wrote it. Consequently, he belabored us and me in particular, for being so neglectful of history. I was gratified that the wagon train people backed up my position. They commented that our purpose was to get to Oregon, not to stop in every town to be entertained and attract thousands of people to the downtown stores. Over 1,000 people visited us in camp that evening. Their friendliness indicated that the newspaper was not the opinion leader in Torrington, and it didn't matter to most people where we camped.

While we were there another new member joined us. Kiwanda Roudebaugh, Rudy's wife, arrived from Oregon. She had not been with us from the start because their oldest daughter, Judy, had to be seen through her last year of high school. Ki's friendliness soon won over everyone in camp and she was a willing helper with the camp chores. Her ancestry was one-eighth Indian, but in appearance she was more like three-fourths. She had a dark complexion with brown eyes, black hair and a square-shaped face characteristic of some northwest Indian tribes. She was refreshingly free of the psychological defense and attack complexes that afflicted most wagon train members in their interactions. She was fun to talk to because she could think objectively about the group's conflicts and even laugh about them.

We were not destined to get much sleep on our first night in Wyoming. I went to bed at ten and was barely asleep when Bob Fineout brought me a copy of the Torrington newspaper and read me the abovementioned editorial. It took me a while to mentally straighten out the editor before I got to sleep again. At 1:00 a.m. the noise of yelling woke me up. Some teenagers on a knoll 40 yards away were yelling at Dave Gastman who was on guard duty, "Come on and get us, Buffalo Bill, come up and fight!"

"Hey you guys, get up! I might need some help," Dave shouted at us and started running up the hill.

I shouted after him as I grabbed for my boots and pants, "Wait Dave, don't go by yourself!" But he had disappeared into the darkness by the time I got started.

I ran over the crest of the knoll and down into what seemed like a black abyss on the other side. I couldn't see anything. "Dave!" I stopped and yelled. There was no answer; I was alone. I listened, expecting at least to hear the sounds of running or of struggling. There was only darkness and silence. I ran another 30 steps, stopped and yelled again. Again there was no answer.

By starlight I made out two figures coming towards me from the left. "Who's that?" I asked. They didn't answer. "Who the hell are you? Speak up." I was getting ready for a fight.

"Cavalry!" one of the figures answered.

By then they were close enough that I could see what looked like striped pants legs and light-colored neckerchiefs. "What do you mean, cavalry?"

"Fifth Wyoming Cavalry from Cheyenne. We've come up for the weekend to escort you into Ft. Laramie."

"You're kidding."

"Oh, no. We've got this club organized to do these things."

"Well, you're just in time," I said, "One of our guys is out here somewhere chasing some high school kids. They ran back this way—away from camp."

"Let's go!"

The three of us started running in the direction where our quarry might have gone. The hills we ran over seemed like they would never end. Coming down a hill we would slow down in anticipation of the terrain taking a sharp upturn. But sometimes after we slowed down, it would be another 100 steps before the ground did go up. Going uphill, the problem was reversed in anticipation of the terrain turning down.

I lost track of the cavalry about when I came to the first upslope. I ran blindly up and down two more hills, then 100 yards ahead of me I saw someone turn on their car headlights and drive away to the west.

I yelled again for Dave and this time he answered. The cavalrymen joined us and we discussed what to do next. Figuring that our challengers might circle around and go back to camp, we ran back through the darkness toward the wagons.

It was quiet back in camp. The teenagers didn't come back. Several of the wagon train people were up getting acquainted with the cavalrymen. There were 14 of them in all. I talked to the group's organizer and commander, Col. Robert S. Lee who described himself as a "shirt-tail descendent" of the famous Civil War commander. Col. Lee was light, slim and wiry; the kind of man that Jeb Stuart, one of my Civil War heroes, said made the best cavalryman. Col. Lee's men obeyed him out of feelings of fun and friendship. He and several others in the group were employees of the Convair Aircraft plant in Cheyenne, Wyoming.

Col. Lee and I discussed plans for the cavalry escort into Ft. Laramie the next day. The men's horses were to be at the fort. They were driving over to get them in the morning, and then they would ride out to meet the wagons near Ft. Laramie village.

The wagon train made an unprecedented six miles an hour the next morning. Their route was along the north side of the North Platte, across the river from where in 1854 Lieutenant Grattan and 29 of his soldiers were killed by Indians. Lt. Grattan had tried to forcibly arrest a

Lakota Sioux Indian for killing a stray cow. When Bear Chief, the Sioux leader, refused to hand the Indian over to the army, Lt. Grattan ordered his men to fire at the Indians. Bear Chief and his brother were wounded in the first volley. There was never a second volley because the soldiers were immediately wiped out by the thousand or more Indians that surrounded them. This incident was the closest Ft. Laramie ever came to being under siege.

Our wagon train crossed to the south side of the river about five miles north of the site of the Grattan Massacre. Their speed put them at the rendezvous point a half hour before they were supposed to meet the cavalry. Col. Lee and his men galloped out from the fort and formed up in town in front of the wagon train. Tex nodded and mumbled to Ben Griffith for the wagon train to start and Col. Lee shouted a precise "Forward, Ho!" for the cavalry. They rolled on towards the fort in the grey morning past green pastures and empty prairie. They passed an Oregon Trail monument and went along the entrance road parallel to eroded wheel ruts of the old Oregon and Overland Trails.

I drove ahead to the fort to watch the arrival. There were flags: the United States, Wyoming and Oregon flags, plus the guidon of the Fifth Cavalry. The wagon train, the handsome horses, the uniformed men and the flags flying blended together into a glorious sight. The pageantry of the procession and the romance of parading into a real fort made my eyes water. The scene was undoubtedly one of the most colorful episodes of our trip. Unfortunately there were few spectators on hand to see it. The impending rain, following the rain we had earlier that morning, kept most sightseers at home. Also, the scarcity of population in that area meant that there were not many potential visitors anyway.

A chain of events occurred in the midst of that rustic pomp to remind us that we couldn't escape from the petty animosities among ourselves. First, one of the cavalrymen was so badly hung over from drinking that he fell off his horse. Thyrza Pelling was walking, so Col. Lee urged her to ride the trooper's horse. She tried to decline but the Colonel assured her it would be all right and she agreed. Then they needed someone to carry the American flag. Since Thyrza was near the head of the column, that was urged upon her too. The women who had come ahead with the kitchen truck and were watching the parade with me thought it was awful. Edna Blair, Thyrza's most vehement critic, said, "Oh, if she only knew how out of place she looks." Several of the other women agreed and told Thyrza about it as soon as she got off the horse. Thyrza was hurt to the point that her efforts to defend herself were feeble. I had considered Thyrza's flag carrying a slight thing, but I was reminded again how even little things are subject to strong group condemnation, especially when the group is suffering from "too much togetherness."

That afternoon we took tours of the fort. In the early evening the cavalry stood retreat. It was cold and windy, but the troopers weathered it fine and looked impressive against Old Bedlam and the other old buildings of the fort.

Ft. Laramie was first built in 1835 and was called Ft. William. In 1841 the American Fur Company built adobe walls around it and renamed it "Fort John on the Laramie." This was soon shortened to Ft. Laramie and it was purchased by the U.S. government in 1849. The military abandoned it in 1890, then the government purchased it again in 1937 to be preserved as a National Monument.

We wanted to camp there to be as historically authentic as possible and also to make up for not stopping at Ft. Kearney. On the other hand, we would have still been authentic had we not stopped at the fort but stayed on the north side of the North Platte instead. In the 1850s and 60s the Oregon Trail did not come through the fort, which is on the south side of the river. Many westbound travelers simply sent someone on horseback down to the fort for mail and supplies while the wagons waited on the trail about four miles north.

Ray Ringenbach, the ranger in charge of Ft. Laramie National Monument, showed me around the restored and ruined buildings of the fort, then drove west with me over the route the wagons would take out of there. Directly north of the west edge of the fort, Mr. Ringenbach showed me a deep gully which was once the main trail west. Pioneers had called it either the Oregon Trail or the Overland Trail, depending on where they were going. We secured permission in Ft. Laramie village from the property owner to go alongside the gully, then we plotted a course over the tableland and down to the river edge at Register Cliff, a traditional campsite for pioneers on their first night out of Ft. Laramie. The cliff is now also a National Monument where thousands of names carved in the soft stone are enshrined. I saw several names dating as far back as 1843. The cliffs were teeming with swallows when we stopped and got permission to camp there.

Mr. Frederick, who owned the property near Register Cliff, pointed out to Mr. Ringenbach and me the approximate location of Mexican Hill, the place where the old trail came down off the tableland to the level of the river. He said the swallows in the cliff came every year on May 23, stayed a week or so, and then left until May 23 of the next year.

In this part of the country we were coming into actual hills for the first time since leaving Kansas. The green grass, clear water, and juniper and pine trees in the area were a pleasant change from the plains of Nebraska. We were all used to the mountains and hills of Oregon, so we felt much more at home in this terrain.

That night I went to bed in Ft. Laramie's old powder magazine which has been restored. The walls are two feet thick and there is only one window in the building. The thick walls deadened all outside noises and made the building both weather and sound proof. This afforded me my best night's sleep since our stay at the Lehman Ranch in Maxwell, Nebraska.

We had a flag-raising ceremony with the cavalry after breakfast. It was Memorial Day and we commemorated it in an appropriate manner. We lined up in two groups: the men from the wagon train on the right and the dismounted cavalry on the left. A bugler and color guard from the cavalry marched to the flagpole in front of us. The bugler blew "First call," then the men from the wagon train fired a three-gun salute with their pistols. After the salute, the bugler blew "Call to Colors," and the flag was raised to full then lowered again to half mast in honor of the dead. Gail Carnine gave the commands for the wagon train men and Col. Lee led the troopers.

That being Saturday, we planned to spend the weekend at Register Cliff. Tex wanted to scout the trail ahead with me later, so I took the opportunity to ride on one of the covered wagons. Ivan Hoyer in his car followed behind me in mine to Register Cliff, then took me back to meet the wagon train. I climbed up and rode with George McUne on the Rogue Valley wagon.

As the wagon train rumbled out of Ft. Laramie, the cavalry troop stood in formation by the road and presented arms with their sabers. As on the day before, I lamented that there were so few of us to admire the color and pageantry.

X. The Upper North Platte

We left Ft. Laramie on May 30, the day that summer came. But first we endured a cold morning. A strong wind blew rain horizontally into our faces. The hilly and rough road added to the discomfort of traveling by covered wagon. The scene, however, was fascinating. We stayed within a few yards of the original trail on a ridge overlooking the North Platte. I took turns with George driving the white mules, and the wagons trundled through the uncultivated land like grey ghosts. Off to one side Val Johnson looked like an Arabian princess riding along on a sorrel mare with her poncho flowing in the wind. In the distance antelope ran along looking at us wide-eyed with curiosity.

Some 14 miles from Ft. Laramie we left the graveled road and followed a gully down off the tableland. It was a precipitous slope and we applied the brakes all the way. We came down into one of Mr. Frederick's pastures about 200 yards east of our campsite. As we went by Register Cliff, I noticed that all the swallows had disappeared.

We circled the wagons by the river next to our semi and kitchen trucks. I remember being cold and wanting badly to build a fire and have a hot cup of coffee. Then the clouds overhead seemed to disappear. In the space of a few minutes the wind stopped and a warm sun came out. It was the first warm day since Marysville, Kansas. We had lunch and celebrated summer. Some of our people carved initials in the cliff, others went fishing and all of us did some lounging around camp.

Some of us were talking near the tethering line when Rudy Roudebaugh speculated as to whether or not Doc, his small mule, could be ridden. Someone in Oshkosh had told him that Doc was broke to ride. The discussion led to Rudy daring me to try. He offered to hold the mule while I got on. We stood Doc under a tree then I climbed up and lowered myself down from a limb. The mule went into a frenzy as soon as he felt my weight. The first buck put me back on the limb. Doc moved out with his hind feet flying in all directions. Rudy held onto the halter rope and got a better ride than I'd had on Doc's back. Doc jerked him around like the boy on the end of the line in a game of crack the whip. Finally Doc calmed down; I climbed out of the tree; we had a good laugh, and the rodeo was over.

That day someone gave Roy Brabham a baby raccoon. Val Johnson fixed a bottle for it to drink from. With all of us wanting to pet it, it had more parents than it knew what to do with. It soon developed a fondness for Korn Puffs and would refuse any other kind of "newfangled breakfast cereal." We named him "Racket." He would ride along on Roy's shoulder alternately burrowing his nose into Roy's white beard and looking for mischief with his bright black eyes.

Most of us went into Guernsey that evening to celebrate summer and take part in the town's Saturday nightlife. We enjoyed ourselves immensely and came back to camp in a jovial mood. I went right to bed, but I heard next morning that Pop Clark had "raised old Ned" with some of the people who had chosen to linger by the campfire. They were having a few laughs over the day's events and at the antics of Gail Carnine. Gail turned his hat brim down, puffed out his cheeks and pretended to be a sheepherder. That lasted until Pop broke up the party.

Pop Clark was a vehement prohibitionist when it came to drinking. He complained loudly any time he saw someone taking a drink. Sometimes he complained when he only saw evidence of someone drinking. I remember seeing him in Minden, Nebraska, standing on the tailgate of his wagon, telling all the local visitors what a doomed bunch of sinners he was traveling with. In one way he was a sobering influence, but in other ways his complaining caused more ill feeling than was caused by the drinking. Pop had his mind made up that all drinking was immoderate, and the people accustomed to moderate drinking felt infringed upon by his intolerance. His outburst at Register Cliff marred what had otherwise been a day of good fellowship, the kind of day that I imagined they would all be like when I signed on for the trip.

The next morning a couple local men took Tex in a jeep through Guernsey and up the course of the North Platte to Glendo. The original trail went that route and Tex reported seeing several old graves alongside the road. Highway 26 goes west out of Guernsey then turns north to Glendo instead of following the northwesterly course of the river as the trail did. We decided to take the wagon train over the original route even though the roads were too primitive for our motorized division to follow.

In preparation for this back-country journey the cooks took the stove, ice chest and food supplies out of the cook shack and loaded them onto a wagon. We also had to fill water casks in anticipation of the wagons being away from water that Monday evening.

Ivan Hoyer and I had work to do ahead of the wagon train, so we agreed to camp at Glendo Reservoir where the wagons would be on Tuesday. Robbie One and Two and Bob Fineout, who had trucks to drive, came ahead and camped with us.

The Oregonians enjoyed their day in the wilderness. The trail was rocky and steep sometimes but there was no traffic to worry them. A few determined visitors in trucks managed to find their camp on the George Bob ranch. Mr. Bob was made welcome and so was a fiddle player, probably the best one they met on the entire trek from Missouri. Another welcome visitor was Dean Winegar from Cozad, Nebraska. He had helped us through the Cozad area and made friends with us there. Later he drove out to Wyoming to visit for three days. He repaid our hospitality by giving us prints of the many photographs he took.

Two visitors, however, were not made welcome. While Ivan and I were in Glendo making phone calls to various news outlets, two miffed reporters from the Denver Post found us and complained that they hadn't been well received at the wagon train. They surmised that our people must have been getting a bad time at the hands of the public in order for them to be so lacking in cordiality. I told them they were partially right, and then explained that they had hoped to not be bothered by reporters or the public back there away from civilization, and it was no wonder that the reporters were not greeted cordially. I also explained to the reporters that our people were not chosen simply for their public relations abilities. They were ordinary people and not a group of press agents on a joyride. My line of talk salved the feelings of the men and convinced them that we were real people doing a real thing. They left in a more pleasant frame of mind and said they would see us the next day.

We camped at Glendo Reservoir by a combination restaurant and service station belonging to Mr. and Mrs. Bob Cozar. The weather, the fishing, and the Cozars' hospitality were all outstanding. I think that just as the wagon trainers benefited by being away from an inquisitive public for a day, I benefited by being away from the tension and friction. Besides the usual, ongoing problems, I learned at Glendo that Lowell Blair had created a new situation by going around making remarks against Shorty Hilliard. Lowell's dissatisfaction with Shorty's horseshoeing caused them to come to blows later, but in the meantime it was another worry to live with.

Meanwhile, I was meeting people in Douglas and enjoying their help and hospitality. For three days in a row I was invited to give talks at service club luncheons in Douglas. Tuesday I spoke to the Kiwanis Club, Wednesday was Lion's Club day and Thursday it was the Rotary Club. Every day after lunch, men who were up on the history of the trail and the old forts and stage stations in the area went out with me to find campsites.

Rex Haddon, the Chamber of Commerce man in Douglas, on Tuesday introduced me to Mr. Henry Bollin, who offered to show me the best route from Glendo to Douglas. I wanted the wagons to avoid as much traffic as possible, and also avoid the long hill southeast of Douglas on Route 26. To accomplish this we chose to travel over a graveled road along the northeast bank of the North Platte out of Orin, a small town about halfway between Glendo and Douglas.

I found a place to camp in a dry reservoir on the ranch of Mr. Ben Kohrs. Mr. Kohrs gave us his permission to camp and told us how a mile northwest of the campsite was an old Oregon Trail river crossing. Some years the pioneers came up the north bank and crossed to the south, and other years it was the other way around. The Oregon Trail, for example, went on the south side of the river in 1850 and on the north side in 1851. Our campsite also was to be across the river and three miles away from the site of the old La Bonte Stage Station. The station was maintained by the government and used as a supply depot and horse-changing station on the Oregon and Overland Trails from 1863 to 1869.

The next day Lyle Hildebrandt, an employee of the state fairgrounds in Douglas, met me after the Lion's Club lunch to help find the best route from the Ben Kohr ranch through Douglas and west to Glenrock. We drove west and chose a campsite at the Natural Bridge Junction. Lyle pointed out that the junction is two miles south of the site of Ft. Fetterman and one-half mile north of an Oregon Trail marker.

Ft. Fetterman was built in 1867 and was named after Lt. W.J. Fetterman, who along with 80 other cavalrymen, had been wiped out by Indians near Ft. Phil Kearney in northern Wyoming in 1866. The fort was built for the protection of travelers westbound on the Oregon Trail and northbound to Montana on the Bozeman Trail. After it was abandoned by the army in 1878, the civilians living there stayed on until 1886. Then they moved about ten miles east to establish the town of Douglas.

After the Rotary Club lunch in Douglas, I drove to Glenrock and met my guides there: Mr. Nile Plummer and Mr. William L. Brown. We met for a cup of coffee at a downtown Glenrock restaurant, then walked a block south to a vacant lot which was the site of Deer Creek Station—burned the day it was abandoned by the army in 1866. The army said the Indians burned it, but the local people suspect that the army itself burned the station so there would be a reason for getting more money and troops from the East.

From the site of Deer Creek Station we drove west towards Casper and stopped to visit Ada Magill's grave. Ada Magill died of cholera during the great migration and was buried beside the trail. The trail is now a busy highway at that point. Near there we found a campsite for the following Friday in the heart of an oil field.

The first wagons into this area came in 1830 in connection with the fur trade. On April 10 of that year William Sublette left St. Louis with ten wagons and two carriages, bound for a trappers' rendezvous on the Wind River. His expedition followed roughly what was later to become the Oregon Trail up to what is now Casper, Wyoming. There he turned north and went to the rendezvous which was held at the head of the Wind River that year.

My advance work seemed to take me back and forth between the 19th and 20th Centuries. I located the route of the old trail and picked up information on its landmarks, which in this area were mostly army forts and stations. Having done that, I shifted my thinking back to the 20th Century to determine where we could travel and still remain close to the original trail. Besides keeping that in mind, our 20th Century route was also dependent on such things as existing roads, traffic volume, steepness of hills and the location of campsites. While I carried on my explorations between centuries, the wagon train moved west at its own anachronistic pace.

That evening at Glendo Reservoir we did well at fishing, then after dark we sang songs around the campfire. The reporters from the <u>Denver Post</u> took pictures with their flash cameras. They were in a good mood and our people were cooperating with the posing and patience demanded of professional models.

In a way the picture taking was not a good idea. Some of the wagon trainers complained that they didn't get their pictures in the papers as much as Tex did. I mentally filed that among the other ongoing complaints such as, "That's no way to take care of livestock," and "Why don't you do something about that Thyrza?" Each person had his favorite gripe and we couldn't respond to one without creating a new dissatisfaction somewhere else. All we could do was hope the conflicts wouldn't become violent.

Our hopes, however, were in vain because there was a fight the next morning. Dawn came up red and beautiful over Glendo Reservoir. The men cared for their livestock while the women cooked trout for breakfast. Lowell Blair didn't want to eat. Instead he went around from driver to driver complaining about how Shorty Hilliard shod, or didn't shoe, his horses. I noticed what he was doing and mentioned it to Tex. Tex told me that Lowell had been working himself up like that for a couple of days and was trying to get the other drivers worked up too. While we stood by the cook shack eating, Lowell walked over to Shorty and started the fight. "Come on, Shorty. It's time we had it out."

"Well if that's the way you want it, OK," Shorty said and set his plate on the cook shack counter.

He walked back to Lowell who promptly took a couple swings at him. Shorty ducked them both then moved in and clinched Lowell with his hands around the back of Lowell's neck. Shorty said, "Now I don't want to hurt you, Lowell. I used to fight professionally and I could hurt you if I wanted."

Both men were in the bantam-weight class, so it was not a battle of titans. Lowell was shaking with rage and frustration. He tried to move back to get a swing at Shorty but he couldn't break out of the clinch.

One of the women yelled from the kitchen truck, "Why don't you stop them, somebody?" We all just went on eating our trout and scrambled eggs. The consensus was that it would be good for Lowell to have the fight as an emotional outlet.

They wrestled and glared at each other for several minutes then Shorty told Lowell he would let him go if he promised to quit. Lowell agreed and that took care of the morning fight. Everyone except the Hilliards and the Blairs was sort of chuckling as they hitched up and moved out towards the Ben Kohr ranch.

After the wagons left, I went up to the cafe and offered Bob Cozar some trout we had left over. He accepted and reciprocated by giving us almost 30 pounds of venison, antelope, pheasant and rabbit from his deep freeze. Besides being the best trade I ever made, it was another example of the generosity we found so often among the people we met during our journey.

I gave the meat to the cooks, passed the wagons on the road and drove up to Casper. There I picked up the mail, dropped off our laundry and met Ivan Hoyer at the Chamber of Commerce office. Ed Billie, who was helping to publicize the wagon train's arrival in Casper, took us to lunch. Afterwards, Ivan went back to Douglas and Mr. Billie and I met with two other members of the Casper welcoming committee: Norm Roberts and Jim McNair. We drove out to Ft. Caspar where the wagon train was to camp.

The confusion over the spelling of Casper came about in 1867 when someone at army headquarters in Washington, D.C., mistakenly named it with an 'e.' Efforts to memorialize it as Ft. Caspar have been somewhat successful, but the nearby city has kept the "e."

The men from Casper showed me the fort's headquarters buildings and barracks which have been restored where they were in the 1860s. We also looked at the abutments of the bridge which from 1863 to 1867 went across the river in front of the fort.

I caused trouble when I mentioned that the Fifth Cavalry from Cheyenne was coming up to spend the weekend with us. The Casper men told me that there was a rivalry between Caspar and Cheyenne that was almost feudal. To have men from Cheyenne participate in something in Casper would be to invite trouble. Being an outsider, I considered the argument juvenile— something high school kids might concern themselves with, but not adults. I was candid but untactful in relating this opinion to the Casper men. The argument intensified. I was told that if we invited the Fifth Cavalry, we would be given publicity that would hurt our relations with people the rest of the way through Wyoming. I reciprocated with the idea that we could, if necessary, roll right through Casper and past Ft. Caspar without stopping. We finally agreed that the Fifth Cavalry could come if we didn't publicize that they were from Cheyenne, and the argument ended.

We ate venison that night at the Ben Kohr ranch. After supper Kyle Hildebrandt took a group of us to the museum in Douglas, one of the best museums I visited on the trip. The building was new and well-lighted. It was not like many museums where you have to strain your eyes to see the artifacts and where the museum building belongs in a building museum.

A strange fascination kept pulling me back to look at one artifact. I've never been strong on extrasensory perception or clairvoyance, but a bugle found at the site of the Custer massacre made an unusual impression on me. I seemed to feel an aura of passion emanating from that twist of faded green and crumpled brass. The emotion made me picture General George A. Custer yelling at the bugler to blow the call rallying his scattered troops to him on that hillock by the Little Big

Horn. I felt the terror of the bugler as he blew frantically even while arrows were piercing his body. I felt the passion of a Sioux warrior grabbing the instrument and smashing it against white bodies, then throwing it aside where frantic horses trampled it into the bloody earth.

There are, of course, countless other ways the story could have happened. The bugler might have thrown away the instrument as he tried to run back to Major Reno's command. Then the discarded bugle was smashed by galloping horses. Somehow, however, no story but the former, my first imaginings upon seeing it, could explain the terror and fascination I felt when I looked at it.

That night we camped at the Natural Bridge junction; the next night we were west of Glenrock amid the oil pumps—huge, black, perpetual-motion monsters of the 20th Century. It was ironic that the pioneers in search of fortunes in the West passed over a fortune in oil beneath their feet. We were warned in that area to watch out for rattlesnakes, but with the wagons in a circle and our livestock tied to the wagon wheels outside the circle, I had no compunction about sleeping on the ground in the center. It was unlikely that a snake would crawl past the animals and wagons and come near the fire.

It worked out, however, that I had little opportunity to sleep. I was to go on guard duty at 11:00 so I sat by the fire until it was time to take my shift. Thyrza sat up with me and we talked about Mahatma Gandhi, Leo Tolstoy and the importance of humility. I reflected that I hadn't been very humble with the men from Casper. Several times on the trek I was accused of arrogance, and I'm afraid the accusations had some substance. That gave me something to think about when I was alone feeding the fire and taking an occasional turn around the outer perimeter.

At 2:00 a.m. three cars drove up to our camp and stopped. I suspected it was teenagers like our visitors in Torrington. I woke up Dave Gastman and told him to expect trouble. We were relieved to see that it was our cavalry friends from Cheyenne who had come to escort us into Ft. Caspar. They were thirsty for coffee so I put on the pot. Several Oregonians got up to visit with them. I unrolled my bedroll and slept solidly on the ground until 5:00 a.m.

Publicity man Ivan Hoyer types up a news release using the tail gate of a wagon as a desk.

Rudy Roudebaugh, Robbie Roberts, and Dick Melton hold down a reluctant mule while Shorty Hilliard puts on a new shoe.

XI. Antelope Country

Members of the Fifth Wyoming Volunteer Cavalry salute as the wagons leave camp bound for Casper, Wyoming.

The Casper welcoming committee set up a reviewing stand and organized a parade. Riding clubs, drill teams and dignitaries in convertibles participated. The Fifth Wyoming Cavalry rode horseback behind a drum and bugle corps of youngsters in more frontier army costumes. I rode behind the wagon train with Robbie One in our brightly colored semi-truck. The parade stopped while a senator from Wyoming gave a speech. Rudy's mules, Doc and Jan, broke into a chorus of braying from their position in front of the podium. The lady senator sputtered a bit and cut her speech short. I heard later that she thought the mules had been trained to do that.

The parade was long and hot. Many spectators stood behind plate-glass windows in air-conditioned bars and waved their cold beer at us. When we reached Ft. Caspar, the welcoming committee met us each with a can of cold beer and eased our discomfort.

The U.S. Army gave Ft. Caspar its name after the location had had two other names and after a series of tragic events in 1865. The site was originally called "Mormon Ferry" because the Latter Day Saints operated a crude ferry across the North Platte there between 1847 and

1858. In 1858 a man named Louis Guinard built a $60,000 bridge across the river and some U.S. Army troops were stationed there. The troops called it "Platte Bridge Station." In July of 1865 the Oglala Sioux, Cheyenne and Arapaho Indians joined forces to stop traffic on the Oregon Trail. While the Indians were moving south, a young army lieutenant, Caspar W. Collins, stopped at Platte Bridge while traveling from his permanent post at Sweetwater Station, about 50 miles to the west. Lt. Collins stayed at Platte Bridge Station overnight, then word came that an army wagon train was being attacked near Willow Springs, 17 miles west of there.

The three wagons and 23 men were under the command of Sgt. Amos J. Custard, who was also from Sweetwater Station. Lt. Collins was put in charge of a contingent of 25 cavalrymen to go to the rescue of Sgt. Custard and his men. Unlike the movies where the cavalry arrives in time to save the beleaguered wagon train, it was wiped out and so was Lt. Collins. Only a few of his men made it back to Platte Bridge Station alive. The 50 cavalrymen, including Sgt. Custard and Lt. Collins, were fighting a force of some 5,000 Indians, so it was no wonder that they were overwhelmed. From 1865 on, the post at Platte Bridge was named Ft. Caspar, except for the confusion over the spelling.

The Roundup Club has its clubhouse adjacent to the reconstructed fort buildings. I was sitting in there Sunday afternoon reading about fighting Indians when Tex came in and told me we had a fight of our own to worry about. I tried to call a meeting to find out who was fighting whom and what about, but the main adversaries were busy telephoning our Roseburg headquarters.

We met the next morning before leaving Ft. Caspar. Jeanne Marshall didn't come because she was busy frying eggs in the cook shack and crying. The Carnines didn't come because they were busy packing to go home. The Blairs came, but they were threatening to leave. Edna Blair complained that her cooking partner, Jeanne, couldn't fry an egg, and she demanded someone new to work with. The Carnines were reportedly going home simply because they were tired of all the squabbling. Pop Clark complained about someone drinking a can of beer and said a prayer asking that we all be reconciled.

I knew that something deeper was wrong, but it took me several years of retrospection to figure out what it was. Physical problems were at the root of the emotional ones. Two weeks later Gail admitted that he was in pain from hemorrhoids. His offers to trade jobs with me or work ahead with me instead of riding his horse makes me believe that he was hurting at Ft. Caspar. His problem was so personal that it took him two more weeks to get up courage to talk about it. Saying that he was leaving because of the constant quarreling was his way of coping with his problem without telling us what it was.

I suspect that Edna Blair's problem was also physical. She was suffering from age and asthma. Four days later she admitted having asthma and had to leave. Her 57 years also didn't help her endure the hard work, outdoor living, and poor sleeping conditions. At Casper we were at an elevation of 5,123 feet and still going higher before crossing the Continental Divide. The elevation aggravated both her breathing and her disposition. We surmised later that in complaining about Jeanne and demanding a new cooking partner, she was in fact looking for an excuse to leave without admitting that she was having trouble physically.

The trouble had not been a matter of group and personal interests clashing, but instead only separating. The wagon train had its needs and its purpose and Gail and Edna both had personal problems that couldn't be satisfied by helping the wagon train.

Our Monday morning meeting was, as usual, like the opening of a safety valve. After letting off steam pressure, even though the steam didn't come from its basic sources, everyone felt reunited and kindly towards each other. We decided to try to talk the Carnines into staying with us.

We went over in a group to where he and his family were waiting for transportation beside their packed suitcases. Gail refused to stay at first, so we invited him to at least have breakfast with us. The food must have made him feel better because he decided to stay. We were glad he did and felt that we had accomplished great things with our meeting. Morale was fairly high when we left Ft. Caspar. Three things, however, were causing sorrow: Edna Blair was still feeling badly, someone had stolen a new Polaroid camera from Bob Fineout, and Roy Brabham had lost his pet raccoon.

I went to buy supplies and pay bills, then caught up with the wagons on the Iron Creek road near Willow Springs. Acting on an impulse, I offered to trade places with Dave Gastman who was riding along on Buttons in his usual position at the rear of the wagon train. Dave agreed and drove the station wagon on into camp while I rode horseback. It was a real treat for me. I especially enjoyed the surprised, cheerful greetings from each wagon as I rode up alongside them.

After making camp amid the sagebrush, a carload of us drove out the next day's route ending at the Sanford Ranch headquarters. During the drive Gail Carnine invited me to trade places with him the next day and ride his palomino, Chief, while he took care of the station wagon. I readily agreed since there were no towns up ahead which needed help in planning welcoming festivities.

Back in camp I was surprised to see a girl from Oregon who I had known in grade school. Mrs. Gracie Cole, her husband, Warren, and their youngsters had driven the 1,250 miles to see us. The publicity we were receiving, plus the fact that they knew George McUne and me personally, had given them an urge to see for themselves what our wagon train was really like. Several other Oregonians in the vicinity had come to see us too. Looking at the visitors' cars, there were as many license plates from Oregon as from Wyoming.

Two other visitors who had driven a long ways to see us were Mr. and Mrs. Eldon Judd of Independence, Missouri, some 750 miles back. Eldon had been almost a constant visitor at our camp in Independence. We all remembered him by the rope halters he had braided for our livestock. We were all glad to see him and flattered that someone should drive that far to see us again.

After a pleasant evening campfire, everyone went to bed and our visitors went back to their motels. I no sooner fell asleep when Indian war whoops and galloping horses woke me up. Tex, Dave Gastman and I were bedded down outside the perimeter of the wagons, so we were the first to greet the raiders. Dave yelled out to everyone in camp, "Get up, dammit, it's a raid."

Tex rolled over in his sleeping bag and fired a blank from his six-shooter. I yelled about having been awakened and started loading my pistol in the dark. I had to be careful because I had both live and blank ammunition in my gun belt. By the time I was ready for them, the raiders could be heard talking things over out in the darkness beyond camp. Everything was quiet for a few minutes. Then they came whooping in again. We let them have a good volley of blanks that time. They swept past camp, then we heard them having another powwow. In a few minutes they fell silent and never came back. I wondered later if they knew we were firing blanks. Maybe they thought they'd better not take the chance. I went to sleep wondering about the lengths some people would go to for horseplay. We were several miles from the nearest house, so our phantom visitors had come at least that far to have their fun.

The next morning we were up at 4:30 in order to break camp by 6:00. I rode Chief and Gail drove ahead in my station wagon. The Iron Creek road climbed steadily, most of the time within a few yards of, or right on, the old Oregon Trail. The hills and a headwind slowed us down to three miles an hour.

We saw lots of antelope that morning. Sometimes they were grazing with cattle, interspersed into the herds. One especially curious antelope came within 30 yards of us, and Chief and I decided to chase him. As soon as we were into a gallop, my hat blew off so I had to stop and pick it up. We saw more curious antelope and my hat blew off several more times. At one time a herd of seven ran alongside and away from us. Young Robbie Two solved my hat problem by giving me a braided red and green boot lace to use as a chin string. My Stetson wore out years ago, but I still use the string to hang up my guitar. I remember the Wyoming antelope whenever I look at it.

We arrived at the Sanford Ranch headquarters at noon. Instead of making a circle, we pulled the wagons into a double line behind some trees to give us protection from the incessant wind.

The short night's sleep we'd had caused us all to be tired and sleepy after lunch. I unrolled my bedroll on some grass, covered my head with my poncho to keep out the wind and took a short siesta. The sound of the wind made me nervous so I only slept 15 minutes.

Ben Griffith hadn't been able to sleep either, so he and I went and found Stan Sanford, the ranch owner. We interrupted him in the hay mower repairs and got him to show us around the numerous, well-built log ranch buildings. Besides equipment sheds for hay mowers and tractors, there were cattle sheds, grain storage sheds and a barn or two.

When we were between buildings where we could see the horizon, I asked Stan, "How big is your ranch?"

He pointed off to the west. "You see that range of mountains over there?"

I looked and saw some mountains so far away that they were low on the horizon and hazy blue in color.

"Well," he went on, "if you stand up on those mountains you can see the other side of our land."

I could tell that Ben, a real estate salesman in Oregon, was especially impressed because his eyes got bigger. We were both somewhat awestruck to hear that the Sanfords controlled about 500,000 acres. On that land they grazed 5,000 head of cattle. It took our wagon train three days to go from one side of the ranch to the other.

After our tour I helped Roy Brabham put linseed oil on some of the wagon wheels which had dried and shrunk. It was the first time since the trip started that we needed to worry about the wheels shrinking away from the iron rims and leaving them rattling. We would have to worry about it from there on because of the dry wind and heat we were encountering.

Without Roy's diligence, the wagon train could not have made it to Oregon with all its wheels intact. Every evening while the other wagoneers chatted with tourists or rested, Roy could be found removing wagon wheels, applying mica-laced axle grease inside the hubs, then moving on to the next wagon. He did this for the entire trek with no complaining and few thanks. By the time we reached Independence, Oregon, we had all come to appreciate his hard work and jovial attitude.

Later the wind died down, everyone's nerves stopped jangling, and we enjoyed more of the Sanfords' hospitality. Mrs. Sanford brought us punch and ice cream and young Mike Sanford showed us his school. The Sanford children and sometimes children of hired hands attended there when they were in grade school. When they reached high school age, they moved to Casper. Mike showed us a tiny, one-room building containing desks, a globe, blackboards and the alphabet in big letters on the wall. Except for the view of fields and hills out the window, it was like an elementary school classroom anywhere. Mike then showed us a nearby cottage called a "teacherage," where the teacher lived. Sometimes the parents hired a teacher to live there and teach as few as two children. The isolation of the ranch made these facilities necessary. Casper, the nearest town, is 40 miles away. The nearest telephone was 17 miles away at an office of the Pacific Power and Light Company.

The wind was blowing again when we woke up the next morning. It was so cold that our fingers turned numb while we were eating breakfast. The two Robbies and I spent most of the morning waiting for the water truck to fill from the ranch well. Bob Fineout had taken my station wagon back to Casper on a fruitless trip to find his lost camera. When the tank finally filled, we had a race between the semi-truck, the water truck and some antelope to see who could get to Independence Rock the fastest. The antelope would have won but they lost interest and stopped to satisfy their need for food. It somehow reminded me of some wagon train members having other needs to satisfy.

Meanwhile the wagons were taking a route closer to the original trail on their day's journey to Independence Rock. They came to our next river, the Sweetwater, just before arriving at the ocean-liner-sized rock that protrudes out of the sagebrush like a huge, grey turtle. When they came to the river, they were less than a mile upstream from the site of Sweetwater Station, where Lt. Caspar Collins and Sgt. Amos Custard were stationed before they were killed. The station was also a famous spot in the life of Buffalo Bill Cody when he was a pony express rider. As the wagon train approached the rock, a herd of wild horses on the open range raced across their path, then stopped and stared in wonderment at the phenomenon of so many of their kind pulling the grey-topped wagons.

Father Pierre Jean De Smet, the first Jesuit missionary in Wyoming, called Independence Rock "The Great Register of the Desert." When he first came in 1840, passersby had already carved numerous names in the side of the rock. Later the rock was also known as the "Emigrants' Post Office" because early pioneers left mail and messages there.

After the wagons circled up and we had lunch, men from two different film companies arrived to make movies of us. Both Coronet Films from Chicago and the Centron Corporation from Lawrence, Kansas, were going to make films of pioneers and overland crossings using us as models. We felt the publicity would be widespread and long-lasting, so we cooperated as much as we could. Since Ted Stromquist and Herk Harvey of Centron both wanted to see what the terrain was like up ahead, Tex and I took them with us to look at the next day's route and find a campsite.

We drove west along Highway 220 past Devil's Gap and stopped at the Tom Sun ranch. There we talked to Bernard Sun about where the trail had been and if the same route would be passable to us. He told us we could leave the highway just beyond his ranch house and follow the original trail along the river, but we probably couldn't take the two large trucks because of the deep sand and narrow road. We drove on following the route Bernard Sun had pointed out to us. We went across the Sun ranch and the Turkey Track ranch to the deserted Bill Crane ranch near where the Split Rock Pony Express Station had been. We could look up at the rugged mountains north of the river and see the deep cleft in the range that inspired the pioneers to name the station "Split Rock."

While driving there we often went through sandy swales which were originally wagon wheel ruts. The wagons passing through 100 years before killed the sagebrush whose roots had held the sandy soil in place. Subsequent erosion had made gullies 20 and 30 feet wide where the original train had been.

We explored the deserted log buildings of the Bill Crane ranch and decided to camp there the next evening. Before returning to camp at Independence Rock, we scouted the trail farther west to Highway 287 to make sure the route of the original trail was passable.

That evening at camp, people from nearby ranches brought us a potluck supper. After we were all full of fried chicken, potato salad and Boston-baked beans, the people took us to a dance at the Sweetwater Community Hall. Everyone enjoyed themselves immensely; we danced polkas, schottisches, square dances and modern dances. At one point I noticed that the rafters were low enough to swing from, so I did that too. At the height of the festivities, Roy Brabham came in smiling with Racket the raccoon wrapped around his neck. Someone in Casper had found the lost waif and returned him.

I hated to leave, but I had guard duty at 2:00 a.m. I had time for only an hour of sleep before Dick Melton woke me up and I went on duty. Firewood was scarce there. For a campfire we were burning the stoneboat which we had built in Independence, Missouri, to haul hay with and break in our teams. The night was quiet and it would have been lonesome except for some truck drivers who took breaks from their journeys to stop by the campfire and talk. They left an hour before dawn and I was alone. Too tired to think, I sat by the campfire and gazed blankly at the shadow of a covered wagon on the side of Independence Rock.

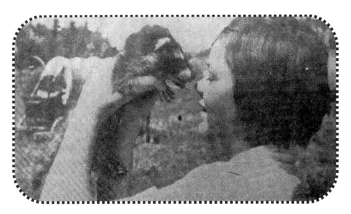

Janell Roudebaugh with "Racket" the raccoon.

XII. The Sweetwater

The trek from Independence Rock to South Pass was the best part of our whole journey. Besides having time for historical and geographical explorations, we had time to sing in the moonlight and enjoy some isolation. There were sudden storms but the weather was generally fair. The closer we came to 7,000 feet in elevation, the more rapidly the weather changed back and forth from bad to good.

The rigors of our journey were nothing in comparison with those of the first white men to go through South Pass, the Robert Stuart group in October, 1812. En route east from the mouth of the Columbia, Stuart's small party faced starvation, hostile Indians and fierce winter weather. While carrying messages east for John Jacob Astor's fur company, they had their horses stolen from them in present-day Idaho, and were overtaken by winter in what is now Wyoming. First they built a hut at Bessemer Bend between Independence Rock and the North Platte, but Indians frightened them away from it. They moved east to a prairie location near present-day Torrington where they built another hut and waited for winter to pass. In coming through South Pass, following the Sweetwater and then crossing over to the North Platte, they pioneered the route that was later to become the Oregon Trail.

Our wagon train's journey going west from Independence Rock to the Bill Crane ranch was roughly the same as the pony express run from Sweetwater Station to Split Rock Station. The caravan moved along the ancient sandy trail over and around low hills along the Sweetwater. Antelope alternately scurried away and ran up to get closer looks. Visiting photographers alternately ran alongside and popped in and out of the wagons to get different camera views. A light dust came up from the sand and marred an otherwise clear, sunny landscape. The wagon train moved along in silence because the sand muffled the sounds of iron wheels and iron horseshoes.

The drivers turned their stock loose in the corral at the Bill Crane ranch. I set up my cot in an empty log cabin and tried to make up for the short night's sleep at Independence Rock. But life was too interesting to sleep long. The youngest wagon train members went swimming, others went fishing and I went rock hounding. My best find was a one-inch diameter Sweetwater agate right outside the cabin door. Besides the heavily-mossed Sweetwater agates, the area was rich in Wyoming jade, quartz and jasper.

The evening was more pleasant than the day. There were not many visitors because we were hard to find, but two young teachers from San Francisco managed to find us and joined us for an evening of songs by the campfire. Maybe the moonlight made us sound better, or our almost two months of practice might have helped, or it could have been the voices of our visitors, but somehow our singing seemed especially good that night. Sometimes our visitors were fond of singing but they weren't singers. The two ladies from San Francisco, however, had excellent voices. Between songs like "Moonlight Bay" and "The One Rose" we talked about our rustic setting and the bright moon while I quietly played flamenco runs and *rasgueados* for background music. One of the visitors, a classic-featured girl with an olive complexion named Betty, spoke with me about places we knew in the Bay Area. We spoke in Spanish about flamenco music and San Francisco nightclubs. The company, the red coals of the campfire and the moonlight gave me a mood of charmed nostalgia. *Todo me encantó mucho.*

Gail Carnine, silently nursing his infirmity, went with me on my trail scouting the next day. We stopped at Keith Walker's store at Home on the Range and enlisted his help in finding a campsite. Our 20-mile daily distance ended at a spot between some snow fences about a mile west of town. The presence of billions of mosquitoes alarmed us, but Mr. Walker said he would have someone spray the area with DDT for us. Back at the store he pointed out a gap in the hills about a mile northeast of town and said it was called Three Crossings because the Oregon, Bozeman and Mormon Trails crossed there. It was also the site of the Three Crossings pony express station.

I noted that Home on the Range and the adjoining Jeffrey City was made up mostly of trailer houses and asked Mr. Walker about it. He said that it was a uranium boom town. The boom had been on for only two years when we were there.

Three miles before the Oregonians came to Home on the Range they were graced with a visitor from above. Senator Gail McGee of Wyoming landed beside them in a helicopter. He walked the length of the wagon train shaking everyone's hand, then offered Tex a ride with him in his flying machine. Gail, I and two women who had come to town to do laundry were waiting in Ed Badger's restaurant. The helicopter landed behind the restaurant and Tex and the Senator came in. Senator McGee finished being introduced personally to each wagon train member, then went back to his helicopter and ascended.

The wagon train passed through town and circled up at the campsite between the board snow fences. The mosquitoes were gone and the weather was fair so everyone gave me their approval on the location.

Two teenage boys joined us that evening. Ivan brought them into camp looking self-conscious in their new buckskins and shy about being among so many strangers. Rodney Pelling had the build and demeanor of someone in his 20s rather than 17. Trevor, 14, immediately got acquainted with the other youngsters and became one of them. We were thankful that both boys were independent and resourceful. Perhaps it was hereditary, or perhaps it was their travels that helped them become adaptable. Rodney was born in Egypt and Trevor in England while their mother, Thyrza, was living out a World War II adventure with their soldier father. The summer before joining us they had backpacked along part of the Oregon Trail in western Wyoming. They had just been released for summer vacation from Shawnigan Boys' School in British Columbia.

When we left that campsite near Home on the Range, we had to decide whether to travel on the north or south side of the Sweetwater. For the past six days of traveling, the traces of the Oregon Trail, Pony Express and Overland Stage routes had been the same. Between Independence Rock and South Pass, the Oregon Trail had meandered back and forth across the river as many as nine times, depending on water level, forage for the livestock, and what everyone else was doing that year. On leaving Home on the Range we would pass historic Ice Slough and then come to where the Oregon Trail separated from what is now Route 287 to follow the river more closely. Our itinerary, our energy and a much-changed river made it impossible for us to attempt the same crossings that the pioneers had used. Instead we had to choose to stay close to the river or to follow other pioneer routes which stayed away from the river on higher ground.

In looking at the terrain, it seemed that the south side had more hills, but the north side had more rocks. The north side was a few miles closer to South Pass, but also on the north side was Rocky Ridge which was notorious for causing many pioneer wagons to fall apart. We wanted to avoid that, but we also wanted to take the shortest route.

The same Paul Henderson who had helped us in Bridgeport, Nebraska, came to help us here in the middle of Wyoming. He was spending his vacation as usual studying the Oregon Trail. He stopped to say hello and we presented him with our problem. He was delighted to be able to put his years of study to practical use. We watched as he spread his maps out on the hood of his station wagon and started expounding on all the "Well ifs" of both routes. After a long talk, it was decided that he would take Tex and Gail to run out the route on the north side while I would ride Chief with the wagon train and be in charge there.

Looking back, I see that here again a decision was made that was related to Gail's secret infirmity. It normally would have been my job to explore ahead but Gail suggested that he do it instead. I readily agreed because I enjoyed the change.

But I didn't simply saddle up Chief and ride on out the next morning. Somehow it became my job to go to Paul's motel, wake him up and wait for him. When he was organized, we drove out to catch up with the wagon train. Tex tied Reno to the rear of a wagon, I got on Chief, and then Paul, Tex and Gail went exploring in my station wagon.

The wagon train passed a long pond bordered by green grass which the pioneers had called Ice Slough. They often found enough ice there to cool their water barrels through the next day. We were close to 7,000 feet in elevation so the ice was available almost all year. We trundled along the asphalt of Route 287, climbed a long hill and pulled off the road for our noon break. While we were there Robbie came by in his semi and gave us instructions to camp at a rodeo corral near the next bridge across the Sweetwater. The corral had stalls attached to it so we would have a secure place to keep the animals, boding well for a comfortable weekend. The camp would be near what the pioneers called "Sixth Crossing."

Hitching up after lunch involved the usual wait for Roy to get ready. He seemed to always be busy smoking his pipe and talking while everyone else was getting ready to leave. We were used to his habit by then and there were usually more jokes than complaints about the delay.

It was three or four miles downhill to where we turned off to camp. Ben Griffith, driving the Independence wagon in the lead position, didn't see me turn off to open the gate into our campground. I thought my actions were obvious or I would have yelled at him. When I got the gate open, I looked up to see Rudy in the second wagon leading the train into camp. Ben was alone halfway across the Sweetwater bridge.

I pointed out to Rudy where the wagons should circle up by the corral, then galloped back to retrieve Ben. He was embarrassed. There was no place to turn around so we went on across the river to a combination service station, bar and grocery store. I offered Ben a beer to smooth over the situation and he accepted. One of my youthful dreams of cowboy life was then realized. I rode up to the tavern door and without dismounting, yelled in for two beers. The proprietor went along with the game and served us outside, me on my horse and Ben in his covered wagon.

The other drivers had saved a place for Ben in the circle of wagons. Several of them made remarks about Ben's being the "independent wagon," rather than the "Independence wagon."

Tex, Gail and Paul came back from their path finding soon after we made camp. They had explored the route on the north side of the river and were pretty sure that we should go that way. There was a good enough graveled road past Rocky Ridge that we wouldn't have to fear that ancient obstacle. Tex decided, however, that the next day, Sunday, June 14, Gail and I would arrange for Keith Walker to show us the route on the south side of the river just to make sure we weren't missing an easier route.

That Saturday a welcoming delegation from Cody, Wyoming, drove 150 miles to see us. Kid Wilson, a 77-year-old former stagecoach driver, led the group. Everyone was dressed up in costumes of famous mountain men and other old-west characters. There was a Calamity Jane and a Buffalo Bill Cody in the group, along with a Jim Bridger or two. They brought lots of venison and watermelons, so that was supper.

The wind blew bad and good the next morning. It kept the mosquitoes away, but it also blew dust into our eyes and food. We had a magnificent breakfast of venison backstrap and hotcakes—with dust for seasoning.

Gail and I went out with Keith Walker in his pickup truck. We drove off Route 287 out of Ice Slough and up the Bison Basin Road to Warm Springs. From there we went on west to Ladyfinger Spring and on to the Yellowstone Ranch. Our trail dead-ended at the Sweetwater where there had been a pioneer crossing. The river seemed to have changed, so a fording for us would have meant risking our wagons on steep banks and in deep water. A bridge which normally crossed the Sweetwater near there was out that year or our plans might have changed. Just across the river we could see Burnt Ranch. In 1859 the ranch was the site of the South Pass Stage Station which was burned twice by Indians.

We drove back past Ladyfinger Spring again and drove on until we got stuck trying to cross a slough at what is called Upper Mormon Springs. All four wheels were mired deep. We jacked up the back of the pickup to put dirt and rocks underneath, then we repeated the jacking operation for the front wheels. That enabled us to move the pickup back a few feet—until the front wheels sank down again where the back ones had been. We jacked up the front again and threw in more dirt and rocks. The mosquitoes were having a feast at our expense while we worked.

When we tried to back up again, the pickup went sideways instead of straight back. It stopped on the grassy bank with its wheels spinning uselessly. We tried putting chains on one rear wheel but that only enabled us to back up a few more feet until the wheels hit a hummock of earth. Then we decided to put chains on the other rear wheel.

At this time the pickup was sitting sideways on a 30-degree slope with a muddy slough downhill, a mound of earth behind and a steep incline ahead. When we tried to move ahead, the truck only slid sideways toward the slough again. Gail and I got the idea to push uphill from the side while Keith tried to drive ahead. Keith gunned the engine, released the clutch and the rear end of the pickup started turning downhill onto us. There was more weight than Gail and I could hold. It seemed for a few seconds that we would either be run over or forced down into the mud. I almost ran over Gail getting out of the situation. The pickup moved forward a bit with its wheels spinning and throwing clods of dirt at us. Gail hit me in the forehead with the back of his arm and knocked me backwards while we dodged the clods. I rolled down to the edge of the slough, the pickup roared up the hill and Gail stood there in the flying mud. I don't know which made me laugh more, the feeling of relief that we were unstuck or the sight of Gail taking a mud shower.

Having failed to get across Upper Mormon Springs, we went to Emigrant Springs where there was a rock-covered pioneer grave and the water tasted like cows. We couldn't get across the slough there either, so we went back past Ladyfinger Spring again and stopped where the water tasted pure.

During the day we had seen hundreds of antelope: some bucks, some does with fawns, some small herds and some herds with as many as 30 in them. The animals were often so curious that they ran towards us or alongside us rather than away from us.

For supper we had buffalo. A group of people from Thermopolis, Wyoming, brought the barbecued meat to camp. It was the first buffalo most of us had eaten and I found the taste similar to beef. However, the flavor can be explained by the fact that the animals were fattened on grain before being killed. Mr. Ivan Million led the group from Thermopolis. We were flattered to think that the groups from Thermopolis and Cody had traveled so far to make us welcome in Wyoming.

Among the group from Thermopolis was an Episcopal minister, Mr. John Tierney, who conducted Sunday services and gave a sermon on remembering God in our daily lives. I missed meeting the minister that day, but we met 15 years later when he was brought to my house-painting party in Seattle by a mutual friend. As we painted my son's bedroom wall, I told him about the book I was writing and we discovered that he was in it.

After supper, Dave Gastman made friends with three college girls from the University of South Carolina: Mimi Johnston, Phyliss Garrett and Carolyn Carter. They were on their way to work for the summer at Yellowstone National Park. The women on cook shift were put out when Dave offered the girls some buffalo meat sandwiches. The anger focused on Dave because he had fairly often brought company home to eat. I don't suppose the fact that the girls were young and pretty helped matters any.

The girls and a half-dozen wagon train members visited the agate and jade museum down by the bridge, had coffee where Ben and I had had beer the day before, then went back to camp for a song fest. I picked up my guitar and we went out into the sagebrush on the leeward side of camp where we wouldn't bother people trying to sleep. We sat on the ground and sang for an hour or more. Pop Clark joined us and even taught us some new words.

At bedtime Pop said a benediction for us. We thanked God for our wellbeing, for our companionship and for the beauty of the night. The scene touched our esthetic natures.

We helped the girls up into the van of Robbie's semi, tossed them some blankets, and then went into the night to unroll our bedrolls onto our respective patches of ground.

The next morning it took real nerve to ask the cooks to feed our three guests. After a serious consultation and much trepidation, Tex finally agreed to do it. It was all right because Tres and Jeanne were fresh on cook duty and were more hospitable than the tired women of the previous day's shift. The wrath of the cooks was something we strove to avoid.

Edna Blair went home that morning. The asthma had been bothering her in direct proportion to our gain in altitude. Her disposition hadn't improved any either. She mentioned to several people that she might rejoin us when we reached lower elevations in Idaho and Oregon. Everyone gave her a sympathetic "sure, Edna," but actually, no one wanted to encourage the presence of someone neither physically nor temperamentally an asset. The look of anger on her face as she was driven to a bus station led me to believe that she was bothered by more than asthma.

The wagons pulled out, the girls from South Carolina went on to Yellowstone, and Robbie One, Bob Fineout and I stayed behind to clean up the campsite. Tres and Jeanne stayed behind to make lunches then I had to drive them to catch up with the covered wagons.

Somewhere I took the wrong fork in the road and drove along the river rather than two or three miles north of it as the wagons had done. We realized our mistake when we noticed that there was no fresh horse manure in the road. However, we did get to see a branch of the Oregon Trail that the other Oregonians didn't see. We were almost to the horseshoe bend in the river where pioneers had made their seventh and eighth crossings before we turned back. We felt some anxiety about being lost until we finally saw a beautiful pile of fresh horse manure on a road leading to the north. We caught up with the wagons as they were rumbling up a hill near Rocky Ridge. Roy Brabham was following his usual distance behind everyone, taking it easy on his "colts" as he called them.

I dropped Tres, Jeanne and the lunch off with Roy, then turned around and drove to Lander, Wyoming. I had lunch with the local wagon train welcoming committee chairman, H.E. "Kit" Carson, Robbie One and Ivan Hoyer. I left Ivan with Kit Carson and took Robbie with me to buy hay and oats. Robbie needed to know where to pick up the supplies in his semi.

Our business taken care of, Ivan, Robbie and I went back south to the ghost town of Atlantic City where we again met Paul Henderson. He was with his old friend and fellow historian, Jim Carpenter, who was a permanent resident of Atlantic City. They were going to show us the best way for the wagons to come through from that night's campsite near Diamond Springs to South Pass on the Continental Divide. Jim Carpenter took us in his pickup truck to go exploring.

We drove west on Route 28, crossed to the south side of the Sweetwater, and turned off the highway towards Pacific Springs. Ivan and Robbie, riding in the back end of the pickup, got soaked in a rain shower.

At Pacific Springs we looked west with the glad feeling that it was downhill to Oregon. From there on we would be traveling downhill more than uphill until we reached our destination. To the north we could see the Wind River Mountains and the Oregon Buttes were to the south. We were at what in the early 1800s had been the western boundary of the Louisiana Purchase and the eastern boundary of Oregon Territory. It was interesting that the pass wasn't a declivity between mountains as I was accustomed to passes being in the Oregon Cascades. Instead it was a broad, sagebrush-covered plain with hills and mountains off in the distance on both sides. The slope up to the pass was so gradual that it didn't even seem like we had reached a high point in elevation.

From Pacific Springs we drove back east, crossing and re-crossing the original trail, until we came to the South Pass marker erected by Ezra Meeker in the early 1900s. The marker pays tribute to Narcissa Whitman and Eliza Spalding, the first white women to travel west through the pass. They were with their missionary husbands, Marcus Whitman and H.H. Spalding in 1836.

The pass looks desolate now, but Paul Henderson guessed that nearly a half-million people came through there by foot, wagon, horseback and handcart during the pioneer immigrations.

Paul talked about history and I thought about the wagon train as we drove back to meet it. We went past the ghost town of South Pass and chose a campsite for the next evening on a hill near the cemetery looking down on the town. Paul told us that the town is famous because it was the first one in America to give women the right to vote. The Territorial Legislature legalized the town's grant of suffrage that same year, 1869, by granting it throughout the territory.

South Pass City only boomed for five years. Gold was discovered there in 1867. The town reached its peak in 1870 when it had a population of 4,000. By 1873 it was deserted again. The miners left behind their log cabins, clapboard shacks, false-fronted business buildings and a land scarred by test holes, abandoned placer mines and gold dredge tailings.

When we were there it was the custom of several hundred old prospectors to come to South Pass every summer. They went gold panning, rock hounding or fishing, or they sat on wooden benches in front of the town café. Some of them whittled, some chewed tobacco, some did both and some just sat. All of them dreamed of a new gold strike and the part they might play in it.

After surveying the town from its hilltop cemetery, we drove southeast along Willow Creek. Then we crossed an antelope-speckled plain to the site of the former town of Lewiston on Strawberry Creek. We forded the creek and stopped to look at the few piles of old boards and rubble which is all that is left of Lewiston. We drove east a few miles farther and came to Rock Creek. There was a monument showing where a Mormon group called the "Willie Handcart Company" got caught in a blizzard in 1856. Fifteen people froze to death and are still buried there. After seeing and hearing about these places, I remembered and appreciated what Paul Henderson had told us in Bridgeport, Nebraska, about the Atlantic City area being so rich in history.

The wagons were supposed to have been at Diamond Springs, several miles northeast of a deserted mine once known as Copperopolis. However, when we arrived at Diamond Springs, we saw that the wagons had decided to travel farther. We drove west along a nearby ridge and found them camped two miles northwest of Copperopolis.

The windy and cold weather should have made everyone uncomfortable, but instead they were laughing about the two incidents of the day. The first of these involved Pam Carnine and Ki Roudebaugh riding on the water truck and misappropriating someone's beer supply stashed there. Pam and Ki had thought it was funny at first, but by the time my group arrived, one of them was sleeping and the other one didn't feel very well. The other incident involved George McUne taking a horseback ride with a lady from the area who offered to show him Copperopolis. He somehow didn't hitch his horse securely while they explored the old mine. The horse caused some concern when it came running into camp with its stirrups flapping. A half hour later the concern changed to laughter when George came in with a red face.

Immediately after our supper of buffalo and elk meat, a terrific storm broke. The high winds drove the rain underneath our shelters and even into the wagons. It penetrated the canvas wagon covers and formed into a mist inside. Several of us slept under a tarp draped over the side of the water truck, but we got wet like everyone else. At that time we were at an elevation of 7,300 feet so that accounted for the ferocity of the weather. There were even patches of snow near camp.

The sun shone the next morning and everyone was amused at the steam rising off the canvas wagon tops, tarps and bedrolls. The boys in the group, Gary, Trevor and Robbie Two, sang songs and the adults chuckled about the previous day's adventures. I ate breakfast, helped break camp and after the wagons left, rode out to Atlantic City with Bob Fineout in the water truck. He hoped to get to Lander and fill the truck with water before the wagons got to the next campsite at South Pass City.

Getting water took longer and the wagons reached their camp sooner than expected. Bob was in trouble with everyone because the stock went thirsty for an hour after reaching camp. Mostly, however, he caught "Old Ned" because the lunch was on the water truck. Everyone had gone down to South Pass City for hamburgers by the time he arrived.

Late that afternoon another storm with high winds and rain hit camp. Everyone was fearful of the wagons blowing over in the strong wind. There was some discussion about Richard Carter's choice of campsites, and more discussion about moving down the hill to a more sheltered area. Then, as happens at that altitude, the storm suddenly stopped. The sky cleared, the wind calmed and we had a beautiful sunset. An elk-stew supper combined with fair weather improved everyone's mood again. The Oregonians began laughing and joking, even with Bob Fineout and me.

In keeping with the mood, a group of us walked down to the town café and had a party. We fit naturally into the old West surroundings with our buckskins, Levi's, beards, and sidearms. The old prospectors looked on us as a sign that the town was coming back for sure. They said "town," but they meant "past."

We sang and danced to "Colonel Jackson on the mighty Mississippi," then woke the town up by firing some blank ammunition. As sometimes happens, there was a moment's lull in the party. Rudy Roudebaugh said, "What'll we do now?"

"Let's take off our clothes and look for ticks," I answered.

"Yeeaa, we'll have a tick-picking party!"

Rudy jumped up, tore off his shirt, and sure enough, there was a lively brown wood tick crawling across his chest and down onto his side. Rudy caught the varmint, then we had to celebrate that we had most likely averted a case of Rocky Mountain spotted fever. Rudy put his shirt back on and the others chose to find more private places to inspect themselves. It was a bad night for ticks.

This high in hilarity took place at the Continental Divide, a high point geographically. During the remainder of the week we were to hit some highs in anger and dissension.

Gail Carnine, lead scout, receives a peace pipe from Shoshone Chief John Treharo near South Pass, Wyoming.

XIII. Green River Rendezvous

We had passed through Sioux country and now we came to the land of the Shoshone and Arapaho. Over 30 chiefs, braves and squaws from those two tribes met the wagon train near Pacific Creek on Highway 89. The Fremont County Sheriff's Posse also met the wagons and rode with them the last mile into camp. The palefaces brought lunch and gifts of jade, and the Indians brought dances and a peace pipe. Chief John Treharo gave us the peace pipe after the ceremony. Kit Carson and his friends from Lander arranged it all.

Tex missed the festivities because he was scouting the trail in my station wagon. Val Johnson and I missed them because we stayed behind in South Pass City to catch up on the wagon train's correspondence with cities in Idaho and Oregon. Everything was over and the guests were gone by the time Tex came and got Val and me and we caught up with the main group. Our people were full of comments about how colorful the Indians had been.

Late that afternoon we had more Indian visitors, but it was an unofficial visit and didn't go well. As a matter of fact, I was embarrassed. Our visitors were a Shoshone Indian woman and her teenage son who the woman said was a great-grandson of Cochise, the Apache. They wanted to eat with us, but our cooks had complained so much about feeding extras that we had to say no. The woman and her son sat cross-legged on the ground about 50 feet from us and watched while we self-consciously ate supper. When we finished, they came back and visited some more. The only ill feelings were their hunger and my embarrassment at being uncharitable.

That night I went to sleep in a foul mood. Pop Clark was haranguing Tex within earshot of where I had set up my cot. He was going on about everyone drinking beer. Pam and Ki's adventure on the water truck had caused him to start delivering temperance lectures, and then he heard about our party the night before and got really upset. Pop told Tex that we were all alcoholics and were "on the downhill road to ruin." It irked me to hear him carry on because I felt that what drinking there was had contributed to a feeling of camaraderie that might not have existed otherwise. Robbie One and I, for example, joked often about a bottle of Jim Beam we kept hidden in a supply barrel in the van. What we used in friendship, Pop used in rancor. No one tried to change Pop's way of life, but he put a strain on the entire group by trying to convert us to his. I fretted and Pop ranted until fatigue won over vexation and I fell asleep.

However, Pop's side of the story was demonstrated the next evening when an excess of beer was partly to blame for a ruckus we had. We were camped several miles out of Farson where Highway 28 joins Highway 187. The area had been especially desolate for the early pioneers and was to be our jump-off point for leaving the pavement to cross the Little Colorado Desert. I reached camp at 6:00 p.m. after a day of trail finding and advance work in Kemmerer. No one had had supper because Tex had read in a local paper that a group from Rock Springs was bringing us a potluck meal. I thought it strange that no one had contacted us personally with the offer, but we felt we could rely on what we saw in print. A mounted group came and put on an exhibition of horseback drills for us, but they didn't finish up saying, "Now we'll bring out the food." We thanked them for coming and they left. It was after 7:00 and everyone was hungry. Rudy Roudebaugh especially needed to eat because he had been drinking beer for several hours. Tex finally told the cooks to warm up last night's stew.

I stood by the kitchen truck and explained the mix-up as our people came to see what was happening as far as supper was concerned. They didn't find my explanation nutritious, but at least they saw that supper was being prepared.

Rudy came up to me scowling. Before I knew what was up, he grabbed the knot in my kerchief and twisted it tightly on my neck with his powerful hands. This was the first of two times on the trek that I felt my life was in danger. It felt like he was trying to squeeze me into a size 15 collar when I wear a 16½. He twisted the kerchief so tightly that even a slight bit more would snap a neck vertebra. I couldn't struggle or fight back for fear of bringing that extra twist onto myself. I could smell the beer he had been drinking as he backed me into the side of the cook shack, shoved his face into mine and told me that it was all my fault. Since I couldn't move, the only way out was to talk and that was hard because of my squeezed throat. I managed to croak out, "What do you expect me to do?" But that didn't help. It occurred to me that he didn't want to talk. He wanted to vent his anger. Roy Brabham told me later that if I had turned a shade purpler he would have hit Rudy with an oaken single tree that was lying at his feet. It must have looked serious for peace-loving Roy to have thoughts of violence. Finally, Rudy eased up on my neck and listened to reason.

I explained that there was no way I could have made any advance supper arrangements because no one had contacted me or even asked me to contact them. Rudy knew that guest dinner arrangements were in my realm of responsibility so that was why he blamed me when something in that area went wrong. The beer he had been drinking didn't help him keep calm about it. On the other hand, had I been drinking with him, he would have seen my side from the start and there wouldn't have been any misunderstanding. He finally understood that I was as much a victim of rumor as he was. We were back on normal speaking terms the next day, but it took me at least a year to figure out that he felt badly over what had happened and I was able to enjoy his company again.

Meantime there was something else going on with the Roudebaughs which gave us something outside ourselves to think about and helped normalize relations. Ki and Rudy's oldest daughter, Judy, was going to meet us in Kemmerer to get married. Judy wanted her folks to be at the wedding but she didn't want to wait two months for them to come home, and they didn't want to make a special trip home. Instead, she and the groom, Tom Hollaman, and the best man, Don Work, were driving out from Oregon to have the wedding when the wagon train reached Kemmerer.

Ivan Hoyer's wife, June, came to help with the wedding arrangements. On her first night in camp she provided some entertainment by sleeping in her pajamas. It wasn't so much the sleeping, but the getting up that was entertaining. Ivan was accustomed to sleeping in the back of his station wagon, so naturally, June crawled in there too. Getting to bed was all right because it was dark, but when she started to get up in the morning, she found herself in bright sunlight in the middle of camp with no blinds on the windows. The antics and contortions she went through trying to take off her pajamas and put on her clothes inside her sleeping bag were a wonder to watch. Some of us tried to be polite and look the other way, but the snickers and grins were hard to hide. Ivan laughed loudest of all.

It reminded me of Phyllis Lauritz, a reporter from the Portland Oregonian, who visited us at Bridgeport, Nebraska. I saw her in the morning flopping around in her sleeping bag like a butterfly trying to break out of its cocoon. She saw me gazing at her in wonderment and laughed, "Have you ever tried to put on a girdle in a sleeping bag?" I laughed and walked politely away, just as with June Hoyer on the desert near Farson.

I had to take care of trail finding, Ivan publicity, and June the wedding, so the three of us went to Kemmerer while the wagon train rolled on to Farson. But first we got lost. We drove through Farson, crossed the Little Colorado Desert and came to the Green River. Once across the river, we turned south when we should have driven west another ten miles to turn south on Highway 189. The road we turned onto played out into a cow path and then disappeared. Seeing a power line, we decided to follow it across the prairie to see where it went. We soon came to a huge mineral refining plant just north of Little America on Route 30.

An armed guard escorted us from the main gate into the air-conditioned office of the plant manager who had read about us in the newspaper and was glad to meet us. We learned that the plant manufactured soda ash, a white substance refined from a mineral called trona which is abundant in that area. Soda ash is mainly used in the manufacture of glass, but the manager told us that there were at least 146 other uses for it, some of them in secret government projects. The classified uses explain why we had to get special permission to pass through the area and why we had guards escort us.

We ate ice cream sundaes at Little America, and then drove on to Kemmerer. Kemmerer is the hometown of James Cash Penney. His home is still standing, and near it is Penney's No. 1, his first department store in the nationwide chain. In the center of town across the street from Penney's No. 1 there is a small park with an Oregon Trail marker in one corner.

We found parking space beside the park. It had been so long since I had seen green grass that I didn't wait to walk onto it. Instead I rolled out of the car and onto the lawn. Its moist freshness soothed my dried and dusty body.

I had been in correspondence with Mr. George Sawaya who operated a shoe and leather goods store there. I looked for him first. While June made wedding arrangements and Ivan contacted the newspaper and radio stations, Mr. Sawaya took me to look at some prospective campsites. We found a good one at Frontier, a small town on the north side of Kemmerer.

June, Ivan and I had lunch, talked to Lyle Fenner in Portland on the phone, visited with some people we met from Oregon and started back to Farson where the wagons would be camped. We went north out of

Kemmerer on Highway 189 and turned east off it to reach what the local people called the C.C. Bridge. I presumed that they called it that because it was a 1930s Civilian Conservation Corp project. Near it was a good place to camp for our weekend at the Green River. Leaving the bridge we took a wrong turn and went several miles north of the shortest route to Farson. Our confusion was a blessing in one way because we got to see a cairn of rocks which had been erected by the original pioneers to mark the Oregon Trail.

That was the evening I had the suppertime mess with Rudy. The next morning I asked him if he approved of the fact that we were arranging a wedding for his daughter. He said, "Well, you know how it is. Once they get it in their heads, it isn't long before they get it somewhere else." I took his joke as a green light for the wedding and for our old friendship too.

That morning marked the end of our second month of traveling. The wagons moved out with one of George's white mules, Molly, limping badly. One of Lowell Blair's chestnut horses had a running festicule on its neck, and Lowell was grumbling that the rough going over South Pass had caused it. Tex said it was caused by Lowell not adjusting his harness correctly. That morning we also discovered that one of Rudy's mules had had distemper without anyone knowing about it. The usual symptoms hadn't appeared, but we found where a fever boil had broken under its jaw. Even with these difficulties with our livestock, the people were all in better moods than they had been in the night before.

I passed the wagons and drove into Kemmerer again. George Sawaya's brother, Bill, loaned me his desk in the mayor's office so I could write letters to the towns up ahead. Ivan and June met me for lunch again at the town's hotel. We met Mr. Howard Mason, the new Episcopal minister in the area, and invited him to conduct Sunday services for us in camp that weekend.

That day I received a telegram from Col. Lee saying that the Fifth Cavalry would arrive late that night.

That evening the wagons made a dry camp in the middle of the 40-mile-wide Little Colorado Desert. It was a pleasant camp in spite of the fact that there was nothing there but sagebrush and sand. I took a carload of people out rock hounding. On one of my trips to town I had found a place where agates, jasper and flint were strewn like gravel on top of the ground. The blowing sand had polished the stones as well as if they had been tumbled in a lapidary shop. I picked up several stones resembling streaked black and brown jasper. Later I learned that the local people call them black agates.

Back at camp several of us sang songs until bedtime, and then Gail Carnine and I rigged up a lantern on a pole above the semi to serve as a beacon for the cavalry.

I set up my cot outside the camp perimeter, but I didn't want to sleep because of the beauty of the desert in the moonlight. I felt that if I closed my eyes it might vanish.

Col. Lee woke me up at 3:00 a.m. by shining a flashlight in my face. I thought at first it was the moon bouncing around in the sky, but then I realized that the moon wouldn't be talking to me too. Also, it had been only a half moon and the flashlight was full. The cavalry, along with some of their wives and children, had arrived from Cheyenne. The beacon light that Gail and I put up had guided them the last ten miles into camp.

During breakfast we traded Stetsons for Civil-war-style forage caps, played with swords and took pictures. I gave everyone instructions on getting to the campsite at the C.C. Bridge, then drove into Kemmerer to check on some wedding arrangements and have my station wagon repaired. The driving over rough roads had jarred the latches loose on the rear door and had ruined one tire.

Our weekend campsite was on a green meadow by the Green River. Here the earliest pioneers had to dismantle their wagons, make crude boats out of the wagon boxes, and float their belongings across the river. In later years the Mormons built a ferry north of the present-day C.C. Bridge, and there was another ferry called the Lombard Ferry to the south. Eventually bridges were built, but by then the Oregon Trail was beginning to be closed by barbed-wire fences and replaced by the railroad.

The Green River first became famous as the site of the annual rendezvous for fur traders and trappers in the 1820s. Two of the most famous of these were the ones on Henry's Fork of the Green River in 1825, and in 1827 125 miles farther north on the bank of the main stream. Perhaps "notorious" would be a better word than "famous" to describe these events, because they were noted for the amount of drinking, fighting, fornicating, gambling and general sinning that went on there. The year 1835 marked the end of that era, however, when the Rev. Samuel Parker preached at the rendezvous. In 1836 Dr. Marcus Whitman and Rev. H.H. Spalding showed up at the rendezvous with their wives, the first white women some of the trappers had seen in years and the first white women to travel to the Oregon Territory. The coming of Christianity and the dwindling supply of beaver heralded the end of one era and the beginning of another.

As far as my group was concerned, I didn't see any general sinning, but we did have drinking, fighting and preaching. Also our rendezvous was with the Fifth Wyoming Volunteer Cavalry rather than with any fur trappers or traders.

That afternoon there was a gripe session with Lowell Blair griping and everyone else listening. No one took his side as he tried to promote the perennial "big blow up," so he decided to go home. I was on my way back to camp from Kemmerer at the time of the big scene. When I was about a mile from camp, I met Ivan on his way into town. Behind him was one of the cavalry cars with Lowell Blair in the back seat. He had his baggage with him and was going home. In camp I learned that Lowell had accused Tex of profiteering on the educational film being made by Coronet. Tod Stromquist, the Coronet film producer, made an emphatic denial of this on Tex's behalf, but that didn't satisfy Lowell. Lowell also claimed that Tex was being cruel to the animals. No one in the group seemed to agree with Lowell and since his continual grumbling had been wearing on everyone's nerves, no one tried to talk him out of leaving.

Dave Roberts, travel editor for <u>The Cincinnati Inquirer</u>, arrived that day. I chatted with him then went over to the cavalry tent where a music fest was going strong. Lee Heath played the mandolin, a trooper nicknamed "Tiny" played one guitar and I played mine. Lee took the lead on more old southern hoedowns than I knew existed.

After supper the music started again, only this time it was by the evening campfire. Shorty Hilliard played the mandolin while Lee Heath called square dances. We were able to organize two squares of people who knew what they were doing. The dust boiled up in clouds but no one wanted to stop. The music lifted everyone into gladness and held them there for hours. Some "medicine" administered by the "dispensary officer" in the cavalry tent helped keep people dancing.

Considerably past our normal bedtime I carried my bedroll a quarter mile down the river where I could sleep undisturbed. I woke up with hot sun in my eyes and ants everywhere else. The "medicine" from the night before made me lightheaded. When I came back to camp, Dave Roberts was happily cooking breakfast for everyone. He wore a dish towel around his portly waist and waved his spatula like a baton to punctuate his conversation. I settled for two raw eggs in some grapefruit juice.

After breakfast Dave and I talked about South Pass, Ezra Meeker and the Oregon Trail in general. Dave loaned me a copy of Meeker's book,

Ox Team Days on the Oregon Trail, which I promptly read. It was the first book I had read all summer—a far cry from my usual two a week. I read while sitting up in the shade of a tree by the river where I could look up and imagine Mr. Meeker working to convert his covered wagon into a boat, then crossing the Green River at almost the very spot where I was sitting.

That Sunday afternoon the cavalry left with the promise to meet us August 15th in Oregon. We were by ourselves again. Our remoteness from any town even kept local sightseers at a minimum.

Dave Roberts insisted on frying chicken for dinner. He was the first visiting reporter who demanded to feed us rather than vice versa. While we were eating, George Kolzow, manager of the Hillsboro, Oregon, Chamber of Commerce, came visiting with five gallons of fresh strawberries from home. Between the chicken and the strawberries, it was the best meal we had on the trip.

The Episcopal minister, Howard Mason, came at five that afternoon and conducted the Sunday service. A small organ mounted on the back of a pickup truck provided accompaniment for the hymns. Mr. Mason had heard of the incident with Lowell Blair the day before so his sermon was on loving our neighbors.

Pop Clark had complained the day before about not feeling well, and that Sunday morning he seemed worse. His grandson, Bob Fineout, took him to Kemmerer to find a doctor. Towards the end of services, Bob returned with Pop. The doctor had diagnosed his illness as Rocky Mountain spotted fever. Pop had caught it from the ticks he'd found on himself several days before. The doctor had begged Pop to stay there in the hospital, but Pop didn't want to be away from his mules, Jack and Brigham. I didn't have the gall to say it, but it occurred to me that if Pop had been at our tick-picking party at South Pass City, he might have averted the fever.

The wagon train camped at Independence Rock, Wyoming.
Some of our wagoneers added their initials to the side of the rock.

Our camp at the Bill Crane Ranch along the Sweetwater River
near Home on the Range, Wyoming.

XIV. Weddings and Graves

The "On to Oregon Cavalcade" crossed the Green River on June 22nd. According to the old diaries and journals I read, we were at least two weeks ahead of the date when the early-day pioneers crossed. Many of them celebrated July 4th at the Green River. Our increased speed was mostly due to the fact that we were driving horses and mules rather than oxen. Our ability to cross rivers on bridges and travel on good roads also set us ahead of our forefathers.

Tex left Gail Carnine in charge of the day's journey and came ahead with me to help determine our route beyond Kemmerer. We had to go over a high mountain range in order to come down into the Bear River Valley on the Idaho border. Route 30 goes directly west out of Kemmerer and it would have been the ideal route except for its heavy traffic. Remembering our sad experience along Route 30 in Nebraska, we wanted to find another trail.

The Oregon Trail through southwestern Wyoming had three major branches, each about 30 miles apart at their most separated points. The southernmost branch went southwest from near what is now Farson, Wyoming, followed the Big Sandy down to the Green, then over to Black's Fork of the Green and up it to Ft. Bridger, some 30 air miles south of present-day Kemmerer. This branch is what the Mormons followed to the Salt Lake area and what some ill-fated Californians such as the Donner Party followed. Oregon-bound pioneers who took this route turned back northwest at Ft. Bridger and came into the lower end of the Bear River Valley. Ft. Bridger was often a disappointment to travelers because Jim Bridger was always more of a roving mountain man than he was a storekeeper. His store and blacksmith shop were often closed while he was off on a trading or trapping venture.

The middle branch of the Oregon Trail, known as the Sublette Cutoff, went from the Big Sandy across the Little Colorado Desert as my expedition had done. It then went into the mountains a few miles north of present-day Kemmerer, crossed Ham's Fork, threaded its way around some steep slopes, followed Rock Creek Canyon, then came down in the Bear River Valley near what is now Cokeville. The brothers Milton and William Sublette both charted trails across the mountains while in the fur-trading business in the 1830s. At times they were partners and used the same route, and at other times they were competitors and crossed by different routes. None of their routes completely avoided the steep slopes.

The third branch of the trail, known as the Lander Road, was some 30 miles north of the Sublette Cutoff. This road, not opened until 1859, was surveyed by Frederick W. Lander and built mostly with Mormon labor. It was a boon to the pioneers because it was the most direct route from South Pass to Ft. Hall. Frederick Lander estimated that he rode over 3,000 miles on horseback to stake and survey the 346-mile stretch of road.

Tex and I had heard that the Sublette Cutoff was steep and rocky. We wanted to avoid Route 30 because of the traffic, and we were several days' travel west of where we might have turned off on the Ft. Bridger or Lander routes. With these things in mind we wanted to find still another route to the Bear River Valley. We thought that perhaps we could go partway on Route 30, then turn off the main highway and go northwest over the mountains and come down at Cokeville. To explore that possibility we drove to the town of Nugget, then turned north on what is called the Sage Stock Road. The sagebrush grew as high as the car and as thick as a briar patch along the road. About six miles southeast of Cokeville, we came down a swale which showed signs of ancient trail ruts, probably those of one of the Sublette Cutoffs. The ruts led us to the highway at the main buildings of the Thompson ranch four miles south of Cokeville.

We talked to the two men by the ranch house. Two days later we were in trouble because we presumed that one of the men was a Thompson. The men were interested in our project and seemed hospitable. They told us that there probably was a better route than the one we had followed, and advised us to get in touch with a man named Ralph Sutton whose ranch adjoined the Thompsons' on the east. We took their advice since we had saved nothing in mileage over the route we had just followed.

Ralph Sutton turned out to be an old friend of Rudy Roudebaugh. While still a teenager Rudy left his home in Nebraska one summer to work "way out west." He went to work for Ralph Sutton's father, Ed, here in Wyoming. Ralph said that he knew of a passable route that was generally along the Sublette Cutoff and offered to show it to us the next morning. Most of the route was across his ranch.

At 5:30 the next morning Tex and I met Ralph Sutton at Frontier, where the wagons would camp that evening. We left my station wagon there so we could go exploring in Ralph's pickup truck. Four miles northwest of Frontier we turned west off the main road and climbed a three-mile-long hill to an elevation of 7,900 feet. The vestiges of the Oregon Trail across the plateau consisted of deep, eroded gullies similar to those along the Sweetwater River. Headstones in this area marked the graves of people who had died of cholera. We figured that for every grave which was marked by a stone, there must have been ten marked by boards which had long since disappeared. It was like driving through a cemetery. We drove past Nancy Hill's grave and made a mental note to visit it later. Four miles farther west we came to a campsite-sized grassy area divided in two by a long cattle watering trough. As usual, the springs there were named Emigrant Springs. We marked that as a campground, then drove on to explore the remainder of our route across the mountains.

Seven miles beyond Emigrant Springs we came to a bench marker which told us that we were at 8,200 feet, the highest elevation we reached in our four-month trek. From there we drove a short ways down a 35-degree slope and came out onto a green pasture called the Rock Creek Canyon which was part of the Thompson ranch. We turned north across the pasture, crossed Sublette Creek and came to a steep drop down a canyon into the Bear River Valley at Cokeville. This was the main branch of the Sublette Cutoff. The road was rocky and narrow. Ralph told us that as far as he knew, we were the first people to come down that gully in a vehicle in a long time. Tex and I figured that if we rough-locked the wagon wheels and removed the canvasses, the wagons could make it through. The canvasses had to be removed to keep them from tearing on the aspens and willows. The mileage saved and the traffic avoided by not following Route 30 made the hardships and risks worthwhile. We also would take pride in traveling one of the original trails. Another Ezra Meeker marker stood waiting for us at Cokeville. It was almost like the old man himself was standing there giving us a word of encouragement.

We had gone exploring at 5:30 a.m. because we wanted to be back in Kemmerer in time for the wedding. Tom and Judy were being married beside another Oregon Trail marker in the city park. Crowds of interested townspeople and tourists filled the park before the ceremony. The groom and best man arrived at the prescribed hour but the minister and bride were late. The minister arrived and the mayor cleared people away from around the trail marker to make room for the ceremony. The wagons arrived and formed a backdrop for the trail marker but the bride was still late. I had a frantic discussion with the Hoyers.

"Well, who was supposed to give her a ride?"

"I thought you were."

"No, I wasn't. I thought you were."

Ivan and June were just leaving to get Judy when she arrived. One of the townspeople brought her from the house where she was putting on her wedding dress.

It was a simple wedding. The crowds, covered wagons and blue sky made it colorful. Everyone was happy as the young bride and groom rode off in a covered wagon. For me, however, the wedding was ruined by an accident.

Someone on the wagon train decided that we should fire a salute with the blanks in our pistols. It was a warm day and a second before we were to fire I had touched my sweaty face with my thumb. The moisture left on the thumb was enough to cause the hammer of my Colt to slip so the pistol fired when it was pointed ahead rather than up. Jeanne Marshall was standing in front of me. I was horrified to see tiny red splotches appear on the back of her arm where she was hit by burning powder and wadding. She looked around with a startled, pained look on her face. In my surprise I could only give a confused and abject apology. Someone took Jeanne away to give her first aid and I was called away on another matter. The superficiality of Jeanne's wound and the merciful passage of time allowed me to get over the shock of what I had done.

Two men from Cokeville wanted to talk about our stop there on our second day out of Kemmerer. I hadn't finished talking to them when two more men from Pocatello, Idaho, wanted to talk about our July 4th stop in their town. Tex came into the restaurant where we were meeting and took over the discussions.

The Carnines had separated themselves from the rest of us and gone back to camp. Suspecting that something had upset them again, I went out to see what it might be. I found Pam packing clothes and Gail lying in the shade under the semi. He cleared up the mystery of his behavior of the past two weeks by admitting that he was suffering from a bad case of the piles. He told me that he and Pam were going to go home until he was better. Horseback riding was especially difficult for him so there was no use trying to dissuade him from going.

That night I slept on a horse-manure mattress. The townspeople feted us at a banquet at the Kemmerer Hotel and I was especially worn out when I got back to camp. There were no lights and I was too tired to be careful so I simply unrolled my sleeping bag on the closest spot of ground where no horse harness or people lay. It was a deep sleep. When I woke up, I noticed the ground felt lumpy. I was rolling up my bedroll when I discovered that I had been sleeping on a huge pile of fresh horse manure. My body weight had flattened it somewhat and my ground tarp had kept it from seeping into my sleeping bag. Still, it took me some time to clean up. I considered it retribution for my sins and shortcomings of the previous day.

My work up ahead was done well enough that I could ride with the wagon train that day. The Carnines were leaving Gary and Cheryl with us and taking the train home. They would leave my station wagon at the train station where I could find it the next day. I saddled up Bow, one of the sorrel mares, and assumed Gail's place at the head of the caravan. Tex sometimes rode up front, but usually he was beside the wagon train where he could watch the condition of the animals and wagons as they moved along.

We left shortly before 6:00 a.m. and followed the same route that Ralph Sutton had shown us the day before. There were no traffic problems to force the wagons to stay together, which allowed the wagons to string out over at least a half mile. Ben Griffith with his four mules was way out in front and Roy Brabham with his two grey "colts" was way behind. It was a steep climb for our horses and mules, but we made it to our campsite at Emigrant Springs by 10:30.

We didn't make the traditional circle for camp. Instead, we pulled helter-skelter up onto the hill behind the cattle-watering trough. Each wagon stopped wherever it found a relatively level area.

I rigged up my tarp for shade and took a nap as soon as lunch was finished. It was siesta time for almost everyone because we were tired from the altitude and from the long day in Kemmerer. That afternoon we went exploring. Some of us contented ourselves with playing in a nearby snow bank rather than taking a hike.

Back in camp two college-age boys were waiting to talk to us about an Indian raid in Cokeville. Lyman Dayton seemed to be the leader and his companion was named George Johnson. We walked some 50 yards from camp and sat cross-legged on the ground to have our powwow.

"Something you guys should know," I explained, "is that our wagon train has already been raided so much that most of our people are tired of playing cowboys and Indians."

This surprised the boys a little but they didn't give up. "Well, how about if we came up with a new idea?" Lyman asked.

"That might work. We've been raided in front of a grandstand full of school kids, we've had water fights, we were once raided and captured by real Indians and we've had any number of small skirmishes at all hours of the day and night. You might be hard put to think up something new."

George Johnson came up with an idea. "How about some hand-to-hand combat?"

I reflected a moment. "You mean like wrestling matches?"

Tex came walking up about then and we explained the idea to him. He seemed intrigued so we worked out a more complete scenario. The more we talked about it, the more fun it seemed. That settled, the boys went home to talk it up among their buddies while Tex and I sold our people on the idea. We got everyone's approval, but it ranged from skeptical to half-hearted.

After supper three men from Kemmerer came to camp with a pickup truck and took some of us to Nancy Hill's grave. Rudy Roudebaugh knew more than the local people about Nancy Hill. While Rudy had worked on the Sutton Ranch he had heard the full story. A man who had been with her wagon train in 1847 had returned years later and told Ed Sutton, who had in turn passed it on to Rudy.

Nancy Hill had been a beautiful girl. The man who told the story to Mr. Sutton had left camp early on that July morning to go hunting. When he left, the girl was happy and laughing. By the time he returned that evening, she had taken sick, died, and was buried. She died of cholera, the disease which was responsible for the majority of deaths on the trail to Oregon. It was an especially virile strain of the disease which has now mutated itself out of existence and was spread by people drinking water from wells and springs which had been contaminated by the previous passers-by.

The date on Nancy Hill's headstone, July 4, 1847, was barely legible when we were there. After taking some pictures, we drove a quarter mile back towards camp and stopped at the graves of a Mr. A. Gorum and two others whose headstones had become illegible. Mr. Gorum died a year to the day after Nancy Hill.

At camp that night we had one of the most cheerful bonfires since the Green River. We had plenty firewood, few visitors, corn to pop and marshmallows to toast. The starry sky, the firelight flickering on people's faces, the laughter and the cool fresh air made it a beautiful night.

While trying to sleep I discovered that I had tethered Bow too long. Twice she worked her nose underneath my bedroll and I woke up to find her rolling me over so she could eat the grass on which I was sleeping.

The wagons moved west towards Cokeville the next morning while Ivan, June and I drove back to Kemmerer. I picked up my station wagon and the laundry then drove to Cokeville via Route 30. There I met Lyman Dayton and George Johnson again and we chose a campsite for that evening. We looked especially for soft, level ground that would be suitable for our fight that afternoon. We found a spot in an alfalfa field by a small stream only a city block away from Ezra Meeker's monument.

The wagons were just coming out of the canyon and onto level ground when I drove out to meet them and tell them where our campsite was located. Our people had experienced firsthand the steep, rough trail that Tex and I had told them about. All had gone well thanks to the use of rough-locks all the way down. Rough-locks are pieces of sheet iron attached by chains to the wagon frames. They reach from the frames to the ground. This keeps the wheel from turning and, in effect, turns the wheels into sled runners. The original pioneers had not all had these devices, so they had to drag trees along behind to slow their descent down some slopes. On the steepest hills they had to lower the wagons with ropes. The descent was a nerve-wracking experience for our people, but it contributed to their pride in themselves as a group.

We made camp, ate lunch, then Tex and I left to plan our route for the next day, our first day's travel in Idaho. We were back in time for supper and the big Indian raid.

I passed out firecrackers to the youngsters and all the men who still had blank cartridges put on their pistols. Then we had to shoo the spectators out of the camp. One lady with two little girls just smiled at me when I told her that pandemonium was going to prevail there in a few minutes. I didn't want to speak harshly so she thought I was kidding.

Whooping and shouting, Lyman Dayton and some 40 other young men with painted faces, riding bareback and dressed like Indians, came galloping and splashing across the stream and into camp. There were shots, shouts, screams, hoof beats and fireworks. I noticed the lady with the two little girls. They were huddling on their knees under the water truck. The girls were crying and the lady with a frightened expression was telling them it was all a game.

In that first charge Rudy's mules Doc and Jan were "captured." The Indians fell back to a corner of the pasture to regroup, then they formed a battle line and came charging down on us again. Doc and Jan led the charge.

This time the Indians threw themselves off their horses onto us. They were all tough and the wrestling matches had more participants than we had expected. Even Roy Brabham was in the middle of the pile.

He was laughing like a boy at a circus and throwing Indians right and left. I was thrown to the dirt several times and did some throwing myself. I remember one Indian who I grabbed by the heel and flipped over in midair as he was diving at one of our men. He landed on his back with a loud grunt.

After five minutes of melee, everyone on both sides was exhausted. We stood around laughing and puffing until we caught our breath, then the Indians rode off to hoo-rah the town.

A few minutes later George Johnson came leading his horse into camp. The horse had become excited in the charge and had thrown him off. He hit his head when he fell on the creek bank and was knocked out. He had lain there unconscious during all the fun that he had worked so hard to organize. He listened to our excited comments on the fight and got back on his horse to ride home while we went to a hotel downtown for hot showers. Most of us were covered with paint that had rubbed off the Indians' bodies onto us during the battle.

That evening I no sooner dropped off into an exhausted sleep when I was awakened by loud, angry voices. Some people had come and got Tex out of bed to complain about the wagon train going across their property without their permission. They also accused us of leaving a gate open along the way. As was to happen again, we had obtained permission from a hired hand while under the impression we were talking to the ranch owner. Tex figured that out, explained it and apologized to Mr. Thompson. Tex also explained our policy about gates. If they were open when we came to them, we left them open. If they were closed when we came to them, we closed them behind us. The gate in question had been open when we came to it.

Even after the explanations and apologies our visitor continued to complain loudly. Tex finally told him to either calm down or go file a complaint with the police. He went away muttering about us getting some bad publicity out of it and we heard no more about it.

It was too bad that we left Wyoming with that touch of ill feeling, but generally, that state was the best part of our 2,000-mile journey.

Copy of the pamphlet that was sold along the trail in 1959.

XV. From the Bear to the Snake

We came to new people in Idaho. We had met some Mormons in Wyoming, but the number was small compared to the Mormon population in Idaho's Bear River Valley. We found the Latter Day Saints especially hospitable when it came to trail finding and food giving. By the time we reached Pocatello, we were bragging about being the best guided, best fed wagon train in history. We didn't ask the religious preference of all our benefactors, but I read that over 80% of the people in that valley were Mormons. Judging from little signs like a lack of face make-up on the women and everyone's abstinence from coffee, there was a high percentage of Mormons among those who helped us.

You can usually depend on a Mormon to not drink coffee, but the beer taverns in that area manage to stay in business. I found one sure indication that a man was a Mormon was when he started talking about the number of times his grandfather "crossed the plains." In the 1840s and 50s Mormon missionaries both in the United States and Europe began proselytizing people to their faith and encouraging them to come to the Mormon Zion in what is now Utah and Idaho. The converts gathered in marshalling areas in Iowa, Illinois and Missouri. Men who had already settled in the Salt Lake area met them there. The men knew the trail and were unburdened by their own families so they could help the new immigrants.

One evening in the tavern at Border, Robbie Roberts and I were regaled with beer and stories that always began, "My grandfather crossed the plains six times." The numbers varied from five to ten, but the stories were basically the same. Each story came with a glass of beer because we were sympathetic listeners. After all, we had been there too. Mentioning the Willie Handcart Company was worth two glasses.

The Mormon Trail paralleled and sometimes was exactly on the Oregon Trail. The first Mormons came by wagons, but in 1855 the church's

Perpetual Immigration Fund was depleted and they could only afford handcarts for the pioneers. There were no oxen, but there were strong men to help push the carts. Until the Jews returned to Israel, the Mormons held the record for the greatest religious migration since Exodus.

The Mormon Trail ended in Utah and Idaho, but the Oregon Trail went on another 800 miles. In Wyoming and Idaho there were three spur trails where people turned southwest to California: the first was near present-day Farson, Wyoming, the second was at Soda Springs in eastern Idaho and the third was at the Raft River in south-central Idaho. The first of these trails went through the Salt Lake area where the immigrants could buy supplies from the Mormons. The latter two routes joined near the present Utah-Idaho border at the head of the Raft River.

The Oregon Trail in Idaho was explored by trappers beginning in 1811, then by missionaries in the 1830s. From 1843 to 1867 it was traversed by up to 500,000 immigrants. Indian uprisings in 1856 slowed the tide of people until the early 1860s. During that period only large and well-armed wagon trains could be sure of crossing Bannock and Shoshone country safely. As the Indians were pacified, Mormons and gold miners began to populate the area now known as Idaho.

The pioneers suffered various kinds of miseries in Idaho even when the Indians weren't killing them. Thirst and starvation were the major ones. Even though the trail follows the Snake River, the banks of the Snake are too high and precipitous to allow easy access to the water. The tableland bordering the river was rocky and barren except for the far-between places where springs from underground streams gush to the surface. It was usually in Idaho that the pioneers ran out of supplies and their oxen died. Things were especially bad in the dry year of 1852 when there were thousands of immigrants and no grass for the livestock.

The proprietor of Ft. Hall in eastern Idaho, Captain Richard "Johnny" Grant, made money relieving travelers of their lame livestock in exchange for grain and other foods. The proprietor at Ft. Boise, however, in western Idaho, did not fare as well. In 1852, for example, when the pioneers reached Ft. Boise most of them were poverty stricken. Their livestock had either died of thirst or exhaustion or had been killed for food. By then they had also eaten the supplies they had brought from the east or they had traded for at Ft. Hall. There was little profit in a trading post whose customers had nothing left to trade.

The members of my 1959 expedition suffered neither hunger nor thirst, but we were subjected to a searing summer sun. Paved roads preserved us from the thick dust which plagued the pioneers. Pioneer wagon trains had often moved across the plains with the wagons traveling abreast of one another rather than following one behind the other. The skirmish-line formation enabled each wagon to be out in front where it was not enveloped in the dust from the wagons ahead. Where traveling abreast of each other was not possible, the wagons would rotate positions so no one wagon was always up ahead out of the dust.

One misery we had which the pioneers didn't have was traffic. Tex and I tried but failed to find a way off Route 30 as we entered Idaho. On our exploration we got to see some original trail and hear an interesting anecdote, so the attempt wasn't entirely in vain. On the same day as our fight with the Indians at Cokeville I had phoned two men from that area, Kay Olsen and Rex Mattsen, and arranged for them to help us determine a route. We met at Border where Tex and I left the station wagon and got into Mr. Olsen's pickup truck.

The four of us drove west a few miles on Route 30 then turned north off the highway at the Roy Koontz ranch. Mr. Koontz was expecting us and was glad to help. He and I led the way in his pickup truck, while Tex, Kay and Rex came along in the other pickup.

We drove north up a canyon behind the Koontz ranch houses where a wagon train had passed years before. The canyon was named Emigration Canyon, indicating that we were on the trail. Erosion had caused deep gullies to form in it. Since it was a long, steep climb, and there was no place to camp at the top, Tex and I decided the wagon train had better stay at Route 30 rather than follow this more authentic route.

While we were driving up the canyon, Mr. Koontz told me about $40,000 in gold which had been buried on one of the hilltops. It seems that a cavalry contingent carrying that amount and escorting some immigrants was attacked by Indians there. They buried the gold during the battle and subsequently everyone was killed except for an eight- or nine-year-old boy. About 20 or 30 years later, the boy, who had by then grown into a rather close-mouthed man, returned to the nearby town of Montpelier. He stayed at a hotel for several weeks then mysteriously disappeared. Local people suspect that he either found the gold and left with it, or he found it and was then the victim of foul play.

From the top of Emigration Canyon we drove west and came to Route 30 again a few miles south of Montpelier. On our way back to Cokeville we stopped at the ranch of Mr. Mariner Jensen and got permission to camp in a meadow near his farmhouse. That would be our second stop in Idaho.

Since it rained the morning we entered Idaho, we had no inkling of the heat we were to encounter in the western half of the state. After our trek across the Wyoming desert, the rain was almost a pleasant change.

Our guides of the previous day, Kay Olsen and Rex Mattsen, were busy frying chicken at the Jensens' when the wagon train arrived that afternoon. They and other members of the Bear Lake Rangers Riding Club were showing us how to cook chickens in Dutch ovens, burying the ovens in live coals. I stood there and drooled while I learned about their cooking techniques. The method was as interesting as the chicken was delicious.

By the time we ate, other members of the riding club had arrived plus some people from Montpelier and the sizable Jensen family. The local Lion's Club trio sang songs to complete the program.

Pop Clark gave us cause for concern that day. He had recovered from the tick fever that he had come down with at the Green River, but it had left him with no strength. At the Jensen ranch the weakness had progressed until all he could do was sit by the campfire in a state of half sleep. His grandson convinced him he would have to go to a doctor again and took him to Montpelier. Bob came back later and reported that the doctor estimated Pop would be there for two weeks.

From the Jensens' our caravan moved on to a rainy weekend campsite at the Montpelier Fairgrounds. It was a comfortable camp because we had a building to sleep in. The structure was divided up inside into fair booths. Each of us took a booth where we could sleep separated like monks in cubicles.

Sunday morning a local New York Life Insurance agent came to tell us that company officials from Salt Lake City, New York and San Francisco were coming to give Tex a new Colt .45 revolver. They thought they were doing us a great honor so I didn't voice my misgivings about the idea. I knew that the gift would make the other wagoneers jealous of Tex and resentful of the firm's favoritism. I decided not to say anything because it might cost Tex the pistol. I regretted my decision a month later when the anticipated resentment cost us embarrassment and inconvenience. The three officials arrived, made their presentation, and the wagon train people grumbled. Tex realized what they were thinking and was obviously ill at ease in accepting the gift.

Thyrza cooked some terrible spaghetti for lunch. Tex and I missed it because we were exploring a route north out of Soda Springs that followed an important branch of the Oregon Trail. We were soon blocked by mud and came back feeling discouraged.

We no sooner arrived back at the Montpelier Fairgrounds when Bruce Markham of Pocatello invited us to go up in his two-engine plane and observe our route from the air. There was room for four, so we took Rod Pelling with us.

From the air we could see streaks of lighter-colored ground and darker-colored vegetation weaving across grain fields and pastures marking where the original trail had been. We could also see a perfectly straight streak where the soil had been turned over in the construction of a pipeline. The pipeline paralleled and sometimes crossed the trail. We followed the trail signs past Soda Springs and then over Lava Hot Springs. In 15 minutes we covered ground which was to take the wagon train two days to cover. Our main accomplishment on the trip was an aerial survey of the road from Soda Springs to Lava Hot Springs known as the Fish Creek Road. Besides being off Route 30, it was also shorter.

Things were quiet back in camp. Ki Roudebaugh said she wasn't feeling well because of Thyrza's spaghetti.

On Monday the wagons traveled to a campsite on the Budge Ranch just south of Soda Springs. While the caravan plodded monotonously along, June Hoyer, Ivan and I were having coffee and donuts in Soda Springs with the Daughters of the Utah Pioneers. Mrs. Barnard, the group's leader, gave us a book named <u>Toisoba</u> which was the Indian word for sparkling waters, their ancient name for that region of springs and geysers.

The first Anglo-Saxon name for the area had been "Beer Springs." It seems that the effervescence of the water had reminded the mountain men of beer. Some men even imagined they could get drunk drinking the sparkling mineral water. Joel Palmer says in his journal, "The soda water is bubbling up in every direction and sometimes rises six inches above the surface of the river. This bubbling extends for near half a mile." He was talking about "Steamboat Springs" which is now covered by the backwater of a dam. Joel Palmer was a member of the Indiana State Legislature who scouted the trail in 1845 in preparation for the wagon train he led west in 1847. He later served in the Oregon legislature and was a general in the Cayuse Indian War.

Old maps dated in the 1840s and 50s show Beer Springs as one of the trail junctions where pioneers turned south to California. Most people in 1849, some 5,000 according to one account, turned off there for California while only 200 continued on to Oregon.

The ladies in Soda Springs told us about the city cemetery one mile east of town. The first grave was dug there in 1861. The casket consisted of a wagon box which contained a man, his wife and their five children. They had been killed by Indians after the man had tried to recover his stolen horses from them. Their names were never known.

After our visit with the Daughters of the Utah Pioneers, I went about my business of finding campsites and choosing roads to follow for the next two days. I chose a campsite for Tuesday evening on Highway 34 at the junction where the Fish Creek Road turns west to go to Lava Hot Springs.

Mr. Leon Fife met me in Lava Hot Springs and showed me the town's rodeo grounds where we would camp Wednesday. Mr. Fife told me about the two Oregon Trails in the vicinity of his town. The first of these, called the "Original Oregon Trail" by local residents, goes through the town on the south side of the Portneuf River, and then crosses the river to roughly follow what is marked on the maps as the Oregon Trail Highway. The second trail is called the "Emigrant Trail" but is marked as the Sublette Trail Road. It runs slightly over a mile south of town. Mr. Fife and I drove out and looked at the still-visible ruts of the Emigrant Trail. These can be seen southwest of Lava Hot Springs where the Sublette Trail Road no longer follows the original course which was an extension of the Sublette Cutoff.

I arrived back at our new camp on the Budge Ranch just in time to shave and go back to Soda Springs with the rest of the group. The townspeople banqueted us at the Idaho Café, and then took us to where the town policeman, Dean Lloyd, turned on the Soda Springs Geyser for us. It is advertised as the world's only manmade geyser and spews a stream of 84-degree mineral water up to 125 feet in the air. We were all impressed.

There were two surprises for breakfast the next morning. First, a wonderful lady named Mrs. Walker brought us two large pans of hot biscuits, and second, as if by a signal, a herd of cattle suddenly ran up and formed a ring around camp to stare at us with big, wondrous eyes. When the wagons pulled out of the circle and snaked out towards the road, the cattle fled to the far side of the field.

That evening we were entertained by the city of Grace. They brought watermelons to our camp on Highway 34, and then gave us all rides a few miles south to see their town. On the way we again went along the Bear River which follows the course of an inverted "U" in southeastern Idaho. Our driver pointed out the dam on the river and told us how the pipelines from it were six miles long and the turbines at the end generated power for three different states. After having refreshments in Grace, we rode back to camp with a different man. Once again we heard how the pipelines from the dam were six miles long and how the turbines at the end generated power for three different states. We were doubly impressed.

Everyone at camp, including the returned Pop Clark, stood around eating watermelon. Pop grinned as the watermelon juices dripped off his chin whiskers. He had recovered in four days instead of the two weeks which had been predicted.

I drove to Pocatello the next morning while the wagon train crunched over the newly-graveled Fish Creek Road to Lava Hot Springs. Pocatello was the biggest town we would come to since leaving Casper, Wyoming, and was going to be a three-day rest for us over the Fourth of July weekend. My contacts there were the Chamber of Commerce Secretary, Al Reading, and the Chamber President, Stan Day. These men had met us in Kemmerer on the day of the shooting accident. I explained to them why I was acting so fuzzy-minded when they met me before, and they understood. In the course of working with Mr. Reading and Mr. Day for almost a week, I think I was able to convince them that ours was not really a haphazard operation. Huge, jovial, grey-haired Al Reading and his smaller, younger partner were especially friendly and helpful.

Pocatello reminded me of Douglas, Wyoming, in that it was a repeat performance at the service clubs. Ivan and I spoke to the Kiwanis Club on Tuesday, the Lions on Wednesday and the Rotary Club on Thursday. Our talks were the same as in Douglas, but we added several hundred more miles of experiences onto what we had said before.

The highway from Lava Hot Springs to Pocatello wound up the east side of the Portneuf River and seemed dangerous because of the traffic and the short turns. Al and Stan recognized the problem and agreed to show me the route up the west side of the Portneuf River on what is called the Marsh Creek Road. Stan rode with me and Al led the way in his car. The scenery was great. For some reason the rock formation running the length of the valley, the fields of newly cut hay and the meadows along the mountainside had all been either invisible or unimpressive from Route 30 across the river. Along our way I found a place for Thursday's camp on the J.R. Staley farm about two miles south of Inkom. My two guides left me off at the Lava Hot Springs camp and drove back to Pocatello where I met them again on Thursday.

Thursday was when they caught me on a coffee-cup trick. I stopped by the Chamber of Commerce office in the Bannock Hotel and Al Reading suggested we step into the restaurant for a cup of coffee. I noticed that the waitress and the customers around the counter were especially friendly, but I was made gregarious rather than suspicious by their cordiality. I ordered coffee and the smiling waitress brought it in an innocent-looking cup and saucer. I noticed people watching me, but I thought they were curious about how I managed to drink coffee with my bushy moustache.

I picked up the cup and the saucer came up with it. I thought maybe a previous customer's chewing gum had stuck things together. I held the saucer down with my free hand and tried to pick up the cup again. I gave a tug and my face fell from good cheer to puzzlement. I heard someone snicker. That's when I knew I'd been had. I looked up and the snickers turned into guffaws. There was nothing I could do but laugh too. The waitress showed me how a suction-cup device held the cup and saucer together. She brought me more coffee in an ordinary cup which I managed to drink from without dunking my moustache. From the way it was engineered, I imagine they had practiced the same trick on a few people before me.

While I was thus playing in Pocatello, the wagon train came up the Marsh Creek Road to the Staley farm. In Lava Hot Springs our people had swum in the hot mineral baths, gone on tours of the countryside and had answered the usual questions put to them by camp visitors. "How many wagons do you have? Do the wheels all have iron rims? Where are you going? Do you have horses or mules? Where do you sleep? How do you eat? When does the entertainment begin?"

In this part of our journey we were enjoying a respite from the quarrels that had marked the first two months of our trek. Old grudges were still being carried but they were kept in the background. Some were still peeved at Tex for "hogging the publicity" and for getting gifts such as the pistol at Montpelier. However, they knew he didn't seek these things out so there wasn't much that could be said or done about it. There were other small but perennial complaints that also kept us from being completely content: Pop Clark still fretted whenever he thought of someone taking a drink. Shorty Hilliard felt his horseshoeing job was thankless and never-ending, Dick Melton and others wanted Tex to sell the horse with the sore neck because it wasn't being used, and Thyrza continued to antagonize people.

The "Indian raid" at Cokeville was a great unifier. Also, we were again coming into a populated area where we were buffeted by sightseers. The camp visitors kept everyone so occupied that there wasn't time for complaints to grow into fights. Over 1,000 people visited us the evening that we camped on the Staley farm. Our resolve to get the wagon train through to Oregon, plus the short-range job of greeting guests, molded us into a fairly tight-knit and even jovial group. There would be big fights later, but for a while in southern Idaho we enjoyed some peace.

Except for our arrival in Pocatello and the big crowd greeting us, Friday was uneventful. Perhaps the most significant thing that happened was that Ivan introduced me to Mrs. Hazel Dean Hunter of Rupert, Idaho. She had driven over to talk about our arrival in that area. I was impressed by her personality, her interest in our trek and the aura of efficiency which was so much a part of her. She was later to be of great help to us.

The next morning was the Fourth of July. I awoke to find that some ill-mannered pigeons roosting in the tree above me had left calling cards on my sleeping bag. I got up grumbling about how the Pocatello Chamber of Commerce had done it to me again.

Al Reading took Ben Griffith and me out to American Falls later that morning to look over the terrain for Monday's traveling and find a place to camp Monday night. While we were having lunch in American Falls, Al told us how the Oregon Trail had gone straight north out of Soda Springs, had turned west from the east side of Pocatello around Putnam

Hill, and had gone on to Ft. Hall, about 11 miles northwest of town. From there it had turned back southwest down the Snake River to American Falls. Because of the dam which has been built at the falls, about 20 miles of the trail will forever be under water. The trail Al described was the one that Tex and I tried to follow the day Thyrza cooked spaghetti.

My mother arrived by plane that afternoon from Oregon. She was on vacation from her job as billing manager for an independent telephone company. She was what you might call an anti-camper, but she was spry enough to stand the rigors of wagon-train travel that she was subjected to on her two-week visit.

Like the early-day pioneers, she had emigrated with her family from Missouri. But they had come by train, and she was only a year old then so she remembered nothing about it. Al Reading went with me to the airport to meet her, and then I spent the rest of the afternoon helping her get acquainted with the wagon train people. She was especially glad to see Pop Clark, who was an acquaintance from her childhood in the logging town of Mills City, Oregon.

In the evening we were hosted by the city of Pocatello to T-bone steak dinners. Later we came back to the fairgrounds arena to watch their annual Fourth of July fireworks display.

During the night one of Rudy's mules somehow got out of the stable and came dashing over to camp to make sure we were still there. Our horses and mules were so accustomed to being around the wagons that they felt uncomfortable away from them. Were it not for fear of people chasing them away, we could have left them untethered and they would have stayed near camp. When we were away from towns and crowds, some of the drivers would purposely leave their animals untied so they could graze. Even on the darkest night the animals never stepped on any of us while we were sleeping on the ground.

Ivan and I drove downtown after breakfast, picked up my mother at her motel and arrived back at camp just in time for services. The local Presbyterian minister, Rev. Lininger, dressed in an 1850-style costume, gave us an interesting sermon on Jason Lee, Marcus Whitman, Jim Bridger and the perils of conformity. He told us how Dr. Whitman removed an arrow from the back of Jim Bridger. As a reward, he was able to carry on his missionary work unharmed because Jim Bridger had sworn revenge against anyone who might harm him. Mr. Bridger's word seems to have been law, because for the next 15 years Dr. Whitman enjoyed immunity in his travels among the Indians, mountain men and early settlers. Eventually he was killed by Indians, but that was far away in time and space from Jim Bridger's influences. The West was settled by people who dared to be different from their stay-at-home relatives in the East. We appreciated Rev. Lininger's point because we were daring to be different too.

A gift of horseshoes took Tex, my mother and me on a drive north to Blackfoot that afternoon. Mr. Haller, the proprietor of Boyle Hardware, gave us a box full of rubber-encased horseshoes. He had had them in stock for years with no call for them so he decided to give them to us. One of our chestnut horses, Duke, had worn a pair of the same type shoes over 1,300 miles. Most of our regular malleable iron shoes with borium welded on the bottoms lasted between three and five hundred miles. Since we had been unable to find any of the rubber-encased shoes to buy, we were delighted to receive the gift.

On the way back to Pocatello we stopped at the Ft. Hall monument 13 miles south of Blackfoot. On our Idaho state highway map this was mistakenly marked, "Site of Ft. Hall 1834." The Ft. Hall built in 1834 was actually some seven miles west of there. The map makers were most likely confused by the fact that there were three Ft. Halls: the original one built by Nathaniel Wyeth of Boston in 1834, the Ft. Hall built for the U.S. Army in 1870 some 20 air miles northeast of the original fort, and the town of Fort Hall on Highway 91 where we stopped. The town is the headquarters of the Fort Hall Indian reservation: 471,000 acres of land set aside for members of the Shoshone and Bannock tribes.

The original Ft. Hall, along with Ft. Boise, was abandoned by the Hudson's Bay Company in 1856 because of Indian wars. The original adobe walls were destroyed by floods in 1862 and the location was lost until 1916 when Ezra Meeker, then aged 91, rediscovered the site. Once an important way station for some 300,000 immigrants, the site is now rarely visited because of its isolated location. Here on July 27, 1834, Reverend Jason Lee preached the first protestant sermon west of the Rocky Mountains. The Americans owned Ft. Hall only three years before selling it to the British, but those three years had substantiated America's claim to the Idaho territory.

In Pocatello that evening we ate dinner at the Hotel Bannock, and then returned to camp for some much-needed sleep. I was no sooner into my bedroll when two carloads of Indians, most of whom seemed inebriated, drove up to camp and wanted to dance for us. We were flattered, but too tired to get up and watch a show. Pop Clark got up and convinced them that they would be welcome some other time.

XVI. THE SNAKE

Someone else was going to Oregon the slow way. Mrs. Emma Gatewood of Gallipolis, Ohio, was walking from Independence, Missouri, to Portland, Oregon, to see the Centennial Exposition. The fact that she was a 71-year-old woman made the walk bigger than it would have been for most other people. Browned by the sun and tough as leather, Mrs. Gatewood walked between 20 and 30 miles a day. At night she usually found a room, but she had to sleep on the ground under the stars in some desolate areas. Her luggage consisted of a loosely-filled duffle bag and a battered umbrella. She left Missouri on May 4, and traveling every day, she expected to arrive in Portland on August 1. She passed us while we were camped at Pocatello and we met her along the highway beyond American Falls. My mother and I brought her a bottle of soda at a roadside café, and had our pictures taken with her. From the way our route and schedule coincided, I knew I would see her some more.

At American Falls we camped at a small park near the base of the dam. Now in America's heartland, it's hard to imagine that at one time the Anglo-Americans were a minority race in that area. In the 1830s this was British territory and Americans were so scarce that the falls on the Snake River were named after one of them. The honor, however, cost him his life. An American trapping beaver with a party of French Canadians was drowned at the falls. His name was soon forgotten, but the fact that he was an American will be noted forever in the name given to the falls.

Dust bothered everyone at our camp there. The wind had changed since I chose the location so dust from an unpaved road beside the wagons blew towards rather than away from us. Those of us with initiative went uptown and escaped the dust in an air-conditioned tavern. We were admiring all the ranchers' cattle brands burned into the woodwork when the Carnines came in. Gail felt much better for his two weeks' rest.

We ate a delicious meal of young barbecued turkey served by the American Falls people, and then we met and voted to break camp at 5:00 the next morning. The weather was getting warmer and we wanted to have our traveling finished by the time the day was the hottest. When we made the decision, we didn't realize how little sleep we would get that night. Yelling teenagers in hotrods, people with spotlights on their cars, and partying visitors kept us awake.

We were up at 4:00 a.m. The wagons rolled out before breakfast because we had an invitation for that at the Massacre Rocks Café ten miles farther west.

During pioneer days Massacre Rocks were also called the Gate of Death. The trail, and later the highway, went between two huge rocks which provided Indians with a perfect ambuscade. The first known ambush there was in 1851 when a Virginian named Miller was killed and one of his daughters was wounded. The largest ambush was in 1862 when Indians attacked a large wagon train. In the day's fighting eight men and one girl were killed.

I stopped ahead of the wagon train and was served breakfast by the café proprietors, Don and Dean Whitely. They had tables and portable stoves set up outside in anticipation of the wagon train's arrival.

When I had parked my car, I noticed smoke coming from the huge rock behind the café. Near the end of my meal it occurred to me to ask one of the Whitely brothers about it.

"I noticed some smoke up on one of the rocks."

"Oh? ... must have been some Indian signals."

"There wasn't anyone planning an Indian raid or anything like that was there?"

"I dunno ... could have been."

I forced a smile. "Well, you know, our people have come a long way before breakfast and they're always grouchy when they're hungry."

The conversation trailed off while I drank the last of my coffee. I got up to leave, turned at the door and said loudly enough for everyone in the room to hear, "You might tell those Indians that we're out of blanks and might have to use live ammunition."

The Whitely brothers nodded and the other customers gave me wide-eyed stares. I don't know what happened after I left, but my people enjoyed a pleasant breakfast free from molestations by "Indians."

I drove on to the Raft River and arranged a campsite behind a settlement where the highway crosses the river. Immigrants going to Oregon crossed here and continued west along the course of the Snake. Those going to California turned south and followed the Raft River upstream. They went through the area where the present-day states of Idaho, Utah and Nevada now join, and continued southwest up the Humboldt River to the Sierras. Pioneers going to Southern Oregon over the Applegate Trail followed the same route as far as the present-day Winnemucca, Nevada, area, then veered northwest into Oregon. This trail, charted by Jesse Applegate, was used by settlers in the Rogue River Valley and the Klamath Basin.

A French Mormon woman, Lil Deschambeaux, used to have a home near this important trail junction where we were to camp. Being a good Mormon, the lady had nothing to do with coffee or tea and served all her guests only cold water. The camping spot near her home was consequently named Cold Water Camp.

For my people the place might have more aptly been named Cold Wind Camp. At suppertime the wind blew at almost gale strength. We huddled behind the kitchen truck and whatever other windbreaks we could find to eat our usual stand-up supper. Later that night it turned cold. A coyote off in the distance struck up a discordant duet with a collie dog that had strayed into camp. Between their singing and the wind blowing, it was our second consecutive poor night's sleep.

The wagons drove on to Rupert the next day and I went ahead to Twin Falls where I had lunch with the Chamber of Commerce Secretary, Bill Grange, and a local historian, Juno Schinn. Mr. Schinn gave me a map showing how the Oregon Trail passed through that area. Near the town of Murtaugh, about 15 miles east of Twin Falls, the trail has been covered by the backwater of another dam, just as at American Falls and Soda Springs. The trail near Murtaugh lies along the bottom of Dry Creek Reservoir. From the reservoir the trail parallels Route 30 and Interstate 90, crossing from the south to the north side of the highway just west of Town Falls. About 20 miles north of Buhl, at Upper Salmon Falls, the trail leaves the Snake River for some 30 miles and goes northwest to meet the river again at what was called Three Island Crossing near the present town of Glenns Ferry. This overland route was shorter because it went in more of a straight line where the river follows the course of a lazy "M."

In order to follow the original trail route as closely as possible without zigzagging around on country roads, the most logical course was to stay on Route 30 between Rupert and Twin Falls. In this, however, we were presented with the perennial traffic problems plus about 10 miles of highway construction. No one liked the idea of driving through a detour filled with dust, bulldozers, earth movers and giant dump trucks.

Back in Rupert that afternoon Tex and I asked HazelDean Hunter to help us find a route on the north side of the river away from the heavy traffic and construction. HazelDean, an attractive blond-haired lady, offered to go with me and Gail Carnine that same day. We crossed the Snake near Burley and drove through the 77,000-acre North Side Irrigation Project. The roads were good and the route to Twin Falls was no longer than traveling on the south side of the river. However, since almost every acre of ground was under cultivation, we had trouble finding a campsite for the following day. We finally found a patch of dry foxtail grass and dirt clods that was barely big enough. It looked terribly hot and dusty, but it was the only place available for miles.

Taking that route presented us with the problem of crossing the Hansen Bridge some seven miles east of Twin Falls. It was a high suspension bridge 375 feet above the water, stretching between the cliffs on both sides of the river. The bridge decking consisted of see-through steel grating. The question was, would the animals agree to cross the bridge when they looked through the grating and saw how far it was to the bottom? We inquired at a nearby grocery store and found that local people drove their horses across, so we decided to take the chance.

HazelDean Hunter arranged for us to be served breakfast at Burley the next morning. We covered the nine miles to there from our campsite in Rupert by 8:30. The wagon train was led into the fairgrounds by the Cassia County Sheriff's Posse. Miss Tamara Ashby, Miss Idaho of 1959, was there looking pretty in a rubber-tired buggy. Among the people watching us eat was a 20-voice Mormon choir which sang "Come, Come Ye Saints." The song was written by William Clayton in 1846 and was originally a marching song sung by the Mormon pioneers as they pushed their handcarts towards the Utah Territory. The rich melody and the harmonizing of the choir impressed us deeply. I thought of the inspiration the people must have received from the words of the last verse:

And should we die before the journey's through,
Happy Day! All is well!
We then are free from toil and trouble too,
With the just we shall dwell,
But if our lives are spared again
To see the Saints their rest obtain,
Oh, how we'll make this chorus swell,
All is well! All is well!

After eating and listening to the choir, the wagon train members gathered for a group picture, the only one we were to have taken during the entire trek. Local photographers had a field day because with our beards and frontier costumes, we were probably the most colorful group seen in Burley since the last circus.

My mother rode on the lead wagon with Ben Griffith that day while Tex and I attended a press conference and the Kiwanis Club luncheon in Twin Falls. We met the wagon train camped in the irrigation project and found everyone in dust up to their ankles. Besides complaining about that, they didn't like the heat and the thistles. I was glad Gail had gone with me to find the campsite because he helped take the complaints and explain why we were there. Most of the wagon trainers were reasonable-minded in spite of their discomfort. Our youngsters spent the afternoon in a large irrigation ditch near camp. The clear water was a perfect refuge from the Idaho heat and dust. The grownups' discomfort was alleviated by a group of local homesteaders who brought them dinner.

I woke up the next morning with the sun in my eyes. The cooks were making cheerful, pan-rattling noises in the kitchen truck. Rudy's mules kicked up hoof-sized puffs of dust as he led them to his wagon. Morning stillness allowed the dust to settle without blowing into our faces. The drivers harnessed their animals and fastened on feedbags full of oats. The animals cared for, they took tin wash basins from their wagons and filled them with cold water from the water truck. In a few minutes they converged on the kitchen truck with their faces washed and ruddy and their hair, beards and moustaches wet and groomed. Tres Hilliard and Val Johnson handed out paper plates heaped with eggs, hotcakes and ham. Everyone ate standing up as usual. Not even the young people moved very much because of the dust clouds kicked up at every step. Our footsteps and even our voices seemed muffled by dust. What talk there was concerned crossing the Hansen Bridge later that day.

Breakfast finished, the drivers took off the animals' feedbags and hitched their teams to the wagons. Dave Gastman went through his morning procedure of finding which driver would condone having "Burbles" and "Sore Neck" tied behind their wagons. Pop Clark, George McUne and Roy Brabham were usually the most amenable. Dave commented to me that they all seemed to be in a good mood. Ben Griffith always had "Wild Bill," the horse from Westmoreland, Kansas, tied to the back of his wagon.

The drivers hitched up, everyone climbed into the wagons, and then there was a five-minute wait for Roy. Shortly after 6:00 Tex gave a nod to Ben and the wagons uncircled in a foot-high cloud of dust. The crowded campsite became half empty. Robbie's semi-truck dwarfed the other four vehicles left in camp: the kitchen truck, our two station wagons and the water truck.

The wagon train rolled along Highway 25, then over to Highway 50. Tex rode off to the side of the wagons where he could keep an eye on everything. George's white mule, Molly, had her usual limp. It concerned us at the time, but she lived with it for the next 13 years. Duke's sore neck was running pus as he came along behind Pop Clark's wagon. "Burbles" was making her usual indiscreet noises behind George's wagon. She was so thin that Tex knew he would have to sell her. Roy's "colts" tended to fall behind as usual. On the brighter side, Tex liked to admire the mules. Ben's Buck, Brown, Red and Blue; Rudy's Doc and Jan; Shorty's Kate and Jack, and Pop's Jack and Brigham all had gained weight. They stepped out as if they had their minds intent on the business of getting to Oregon.

At 11:30 the caravan reached the Hansen Bridge and Tex signaled a halt. He dismounted, tied Reno to Ben's wagon and walked out onto the open-grate bridge decking. Meanwhile the wagon drivers chewed on things: moustache ends, lower lips, cigar butts, pipe stems and tobacco. Some took the opportunity to spit, grumble and wipe the sweat off their foreheads while they waited for Tex to finish his inspection. Tex wondered what would go through an animal's mind as he looked straight down through the grating and saw the rocks and rapids 375 feet below. He looked up at the beams and suspension cables and wondered if the animals might gain fortitude from the strength of the superstructure.

Tex walked back to Ben's wagon and got on Reno.

"What do you think, Ben?"

"I'm game if these mules are."

"Well, I think we'll go across two wagons at a time. If there's a runaway, it won't involve the whole bunch."

"Hi, Buck!" Ben shouted and gave his four reins a vigorous shake. Rudy moved out behind with his wagon. Some of the mules tried to shy off to the side of the bridge and they all walked a bit faster than normal. The iron-rimmed wheels and iron horse shoes made a horrendous noise on the steel decking. The mules pulled the wagons across with no real trouble. Dick Melton and Shorty Hilliard went across next. Shorty had to yell a lot at his mules to keep them pulling together. George McUne and Pop Clark went next with no trouble. In the end came Roy. His team of greys ambled across at their usual steady pace. The crisis was past. Tex and I were proud of our wagon train and our people were proud of themselves.

Our camp for the day was three miles farther west, at the Bruce Luloff farm. I had searched the area for nearly an hour to find a spot large enough for us that was neither under cultivation nor covered with sheep dung. I found a small pasture covered with green grass and shaded by huge poplar trees. A nearby irrigation ditch gave us water for the animals. It was like an oasis paradise compared to the previous day's dusty camp.

While the wagons came on to the Luloff farm, I drove ahead to Buhl and made arrangements for our weekend camp there. I met Pat Hamilton at a local bank and Jess Eastman, one of the authorities on the Oregon Trail in that area. The men got permission for us to camp on the grounds of the local transient worker camp.

That evening the people of Twin Falls brought us dinner. Among our visitors was another local expert on the Oregon Trail, Mr. Roy Painter. He reminded me of Paul Henderson the way he spread out his maps on the front hood of his car. Besides showing us how the trail had gone, he told us how the pioneers had crossed the Snake River at Three Island Crossing. He said that in the old days there were ripples between each of the islands and the two banks. By staying in the shallow areas and crossing over each of the islands, the wagons were able to ford the river without too much difficulty. Quite a few people were drowned trying to cross in other places.

The next day was Saturday, Pop Clark's day for church and my mother's day to fly back to Oregon. Pop went to the airport with us, then I dropped him off at his church and went downtown to meet the wagon train. Some Indians from Pendleton, Oregon, had come to give us their own special greeting. Umatilla Chiefs Art Motanic and Louis McFarland had come in full costume to warn us about how hostile they were in Oregon. Tex, Ivan, Thyrza and Lillian Gastman were in a café having coffee with the emissaries when I found them.

During our chat I embarrassed myself by misquoting the speech made by Chief Joseph of the Nez Perce tribe when he surrendered to the U.S. Army in 1877. I probably wanted to impress our Oregon visitors with my knowledge of Indian things. Somehow the opportunity came for me to recite, "From where the sun now stands I will run no more forever." But that was wrong. Louis McFarland told me loudly that it was "fight no more forever," not "run." I managed to extricate myself with an apology. My face turned red which caused my people to laugh at me. The Indians laughed too and the situation was eased.

After that jovial coffee break, Tex and I drove back to the campsite in the irrigation project where we met Robbie with the semi. I had purchased several tons of baled hay from a farmer near there so we loaded that. Next we drove back into Twin Falls and loaded two tons of rolled oats. Our work caused us to miss a nearly disastrous "Indian" raid.

The wagons had pulled into the labor camp at Buhl an hour before we met them. Everyone was talking about the surprise attack which occurred when the wagon train came through the Buhl business district. Some young men mounted on horses and dressed as Indians charged yelling and drum beating out of an alley. Dave Gastman's horse almost fell down. The mules on both Ben and Rudy's wagons panicked and ran. The two wagons were pulled in a runaway for almost two blocks. Our police escort ducked for cover and several wagon train members launched into the attackers with their best mule-skinning invectives. Later the perpetrators realized how they had endangered lives and property so they came to camp and apologized.

Mel Carter and Lee McCracken of Buhl conducted Mormon services the next morning. Mr. McCracken gave us a fascinating account of the Mormon exodus to the Utah Territory. They brought a very good choir and we got to hear "Come, Come Ye Saints" again.

XVII. HEAT AND HOT TEMPERS

Gail Carnine and I drove ahead on Sunday to choose the next week's campsites. We didn't realize that we were mapping the field for the greatest battles of our four-month trip. We drove past the ancient landmarks known as Thousand Springs and Salmon Falls and stopped at Hagerman. Our local contact, Smokey Pugmire, arranged for us to camp in the city park on Monday.

Two men from Glenns Ferry helped us find Tuesday, Wednesday and Thursday's campsites. I had contacted Con Devaney and his friend, Eldon Thompson, by telephone and they had agreed to guide us through the area from King Hill to Mountain Home. Both men were in their 30s. Con, a Union Pacific engineer, was the bigger of the two and we looked upon him as the leader. They exuded competence and friendliness without having to brag or backslap.

The four of us drove back to King Hill and chose a campsite there for Tuesday. Seeking to avoid the traffic of Route 30, we crossed to the south side of the Snake River and drove west again to Glenns Ferry on a dusty road. Since there were no campsites on that route, we decided that the wagon train should go northwest out of King Hill on the north side of the river. The caravan would follow this alternate course of the Oregon Trail and come back to Route 30 again at Mountain Home. There they would again have to face the hazards of highway travel. It was getting to be late in the day so Con and Eldon offered to come back the next day and get permission for us to camp Wednesday somewhere along the back road leading to Mountain Home. For Thursday we chose a site some five miles west of Mountain Home at Crater Station, a deserted, 1920s-style service station.

During the drive along the south side of the river between King Hill and Glenns Ferry I had a feeling of being in familiar territory. It was almost as if I had been there before and was paying a return visit. I had read about the area over and again. The terrain was only vaguely described, but the events were so traumatic that I felt I knew the area. My great-grandmother died there in 1852 where the trail came down off the tableland somewhere near Three Island Crossing. My great-aunt, Elec Owens, wrote about it in a journal which has been passed down to us:

At last we came to a place called The Salmon Falls. Most of the people crossed over at the Falls or near them, but we didn't cross. We kept on the same side. We had a desert to cross so we traveled way into the night before we camped so as to get over the desert. That night we lost our white ox. He died that night. We were completely broken up for a time.

Two of the men in the company said they were going to make a raft when they got to some timber and if we wanted to, we could go with them. So that was all we could do. We were glad of anything or any way for we had but one ox in working order. The young oxen could just walk, and a cow. We let my brother Charles go with the company and take the cattle with him. The man's name was Lyle. Lyle was to work the well ox and the others would go in the drove.

The company stopped there two nights. The men were going to leave the wagon and an old lady gave us some beans that were very hard to cook. She wanted our wagon for them so we gave her the wagon. We took most of our things that day about a mile down a hill where there was a cedar grove at the edge of the river where Towner and Howe and another man were going to help build a raft. Part of us had to sleep down the hill. The company was not agoing till morning, so mother said that she would sleep in the wagon up the hill where the company was, she and Lou.

That night she got very sick and Lou went and got young Mrs. Shepherd to do something for mother. Mrs. Shepherd gave mother an opium pill. She seemed a little easier Lou said, but as soon as it was light a man came down the hill and told us that mother was sick. We went up to see my poor dear mother. She was lying like one dead ... We were all young and hadn't any idea what to do. O, how many things rise up to my mind that we might have done! We hadn't any medicine.

My husband thought he had better go with the company instead of my brother. Mother just laid and we knew she was agoing fast. To see mother dying and knowing that my husband was going that evening; I just gave up to crying. O, if I had only known what to do instead of crying.

My great-aunt goes on to describe how her daughter died that evening of the same illness, probably cholera. She helped bury her mother and daughter together amid the same sagebrush, juniper and white dust that was there when I came through 107 years later. It was a humble death for a lady who had grown up among the courts and castles of St. Petersburg and Warsaw. The daughter of an English emissary to the Czar's court, she married Joseph Carol Uzafovage of Poland who is suspected to be the illegitimate son of Count Joseph Poniatowski. They fled to the United States in the 1830s, after Joseph Carol was on the losing side in a revolution against Russia. They brought their children, Electra, Veronica and Charles. My grandmother, Lou, was born in Louisville, Kentucky, in 1840, the same year that Joseph Carol died. The girls Electra and Veronica, known to the family as "Elec" and "Vannie," married two men who in 1852 decided their fortunes lay in Oregon. They packed up the entire family and left for the west in a wagon train or "company" as Aunt Elec called it. En route they became separated and impoverished. The survivors ended up walking into the Willamette Valley with no more possessions than the clothes they were wearing.

The morning after our trail-finding expedition, my "company" left Buhl to go to Hagerman. I drove ahead to Boise where I had decided to stay two days. It was a 120-mile drive and there were lots of plans to be made for our arrival in Idaho's capital. At the Chamber of Commerce office I meet Wiff Janssen and Kay Johnson who were in charge of greeting the wagon train. We agreed on a route through the city, had lunch together and discussed all the wagon train needs and problems. That afternoon I borrowed space in the local New York Life Insurance office and wrote to the welcoming committees in the towns in Oregon.

Tex's wife, Ludy, flew in that evening for another visit. Tex caught a ride to Boise and the two of us drove to the airport to meet her. We had dinner, and then drove out to the west edge of town looking for a campground for the wagon train. That was to no avail, but we did find a nice clover field where we unrolled our bedrolls and slept for the night.

We woke up early, ate breakfast at a truck stop and continued our search for a campsite. We soon found a place on the Strawberry Glen Road beside a deserted farmhouse. Large shade trees and a natural spring made it ideal. We inquired and found that Mr. Earl Coffey owned the property. He lived a block away near a bridge across the Boise River. Mr. Coffey was away fishing, but Mrs. Coffey invited us in for coffee and gave us permission to use the area.

We alerted the police about the traffic jam we would cause, ate lunch, then drove the 75 miles back to meet the wagon train at King Hill. During the ride Ludy regaled me with stories about past miscarriages and told me how another one seemed imminent from her "Scottsbluff pregnancy." I was terrified every time the car hit the smallest chuck hole or rise in the pavement. The ride was mercifully uneventful, but we agreed that Ludy should see a doctor as soon as possible. We called Boise from King Hill and made an appointment for the day after next.

That Wednesday morning, while the wagons followed the original trail route north of the Snake, I drove to Boise again for a press conference. From there I drove on to Nyssa, Oregon, to arrange for the welcome-back-to-Oregon celebration. It was late afternoon when I finished my business and rejoined my group. They were camped by a vacant ranch house 14 miles east of Mountain Home. Everyone was resting peacefully on the grass under some trees. Unfortunately, the peace didn't last.

After supper a sour-faced, husky old cowboy drove up to camp and demanded to know "Who in the hell let this outfit in here?" Baffled, we could only say that we thought our friend, Con Devaney, had got permission for us to camp there. The scowling rancher said that he had never heard of Con Devaney. He sat in his car and talked to his foreman while we talked it over among ourselves. Someone told us that the man's name was Jack Henley. Gail Carnine was sure that this was the place Con Devaney had pointed out to him. Con drove in at that moment and assured us that this was the ranch he had asked permission for us to camp on. He pointed to Mr. Henley's foreman and said, "Here's the man who gave us permission." The foreman, no doubt thinking of his job, denied the whole thing. Mr. Henley left saying that he was going to the State Police to have us all arrested for trespassing. While we were wondering what to do about that, we started fighting among ourselves about an entirely different matter.

Our two pinto riding horses, Geronimo, aka Burbles, and Comanche, were both too poor to be ridden. Geronimo had never recovered from distemper and Comanche was saddle sore. Tex decided to ask Ben Griffith if the wagon train could use Wild Bill, the thoroughbred that he had acquired at Westmoreland, Kansas. Ben told Tex that he could use the horse if we bought it from him. That caused an exchange of some warm words that don't bear repeating.

It was a standoff. Tex went over to the cook shack, squinted his eyes over a creamy cup of coffee, and thought about his next move. He didn't come up with a plan, but Ben thought of a way to end the argument. He sold Wild Bill to our local guide, Eldon Thompson. Tex saw Eldon leading the horse away and asked him about it. Eldon grinned, "You don't usually get a thoroughbred for what I paid for this one." That riled Tex more than ever. He decided to drive to Mountain Home and phone the headquarters in Roseburg, Oregon, about our livestock problems. I thought Tex needed to talk out his anger so I went along to be a listener.

"For two cents I'd tell Dick Smith to find himself another wagon master," Tex said on the way into town.

I mumbled something—sort of an affirmation mixed with surprise. Tex had never before even hinted at the possibility of his quitting.

"You do your best to baby those people along and all you get is crap. I'd like to get into Oregon with the same people who left Missouri. I've said that often enough. People like Ben make me not give a damn about getting there myself."

"You wouldn't quit."

"Well, I sure feel like it sometimes."

"What will you say to Dick Smith?"

"Oh, I'll probably just get his OK to buy another horse. I'll tell him something about the squabble tonight so he'll get it from me before he gets someone else's version."

We found a phone booth in Mountain Home and Tex made the call. We were quiet on the way back to camp.

The silence gave me a chance to think about everything. I thought about Ben being so cantankerous and about Tex mentioning quitting. Like anyone is inclined to do, I compared them both to myself. I had never denied anyone the use of my station wagon and it never entered my mind to quit. I felt blue because so many people were not living up to my ideals. They were not all working together to make things easier for the other wagoneers.

The most important thought I had was that we each had our own way of helping ourselves while we helped others Many so-called kind people are really just helping their own egos. A person can help others simply because it gives him a feeling of superiority. We were all individuals with our own ways of acting out our personal ideals and reacting to the needs of others. We didn't all act and react the same simply because we were members of the same wagon train. This explained our differences in behavior, but it didn't ease my discouragement over the fight between Tex and Ben.

It occurred to me that Ben wasn't being completely open with Tex. There was more to the story about Wild Bill than what Ben told us. Few of us really believed that the man in Kansas had given the horse to Ben as a gift. Contrary to the old adage, that was a gift horse that needed to be looked into. Ben's feelings about Tex may have been lack of respect, dislike, a sense of rivalry or all three of those. Whatever Ben felt, his feelings kept him from being cooperative and from telling Tex all that was on his mind. The full story about Wild Bill didn't come out until we reached Amity, Oregon.

The wagons left for Mountain Home the next morning while Tex, Ludy and I went on a horse-buying expedition. In town we bought a newspaper to look at the classified ads. An article on the front page said that a warrant had been issued for the arrest of the "wagon train manager." We immediately hailed a city policeman and he escorted us to the sheriff's office.

Elmore County Sheriff Earl Winter served the warrant. It stated that we had willfully trespassed, damaged property and left gates open. Mr. Henley came in as we read the charges. The sheriff asked him if he still felt like pressing charges. "The warrant stands," he said, and walked out scowling. A moment later Con Devaney and Eldon Thompson arrived to be witnesses for us.

The nearest Justice of the Peace was back in King Hill. The entire group of us—witnesses, lawmen, prosecutor and the accused drove back to King Hill for the arraignment. The office was a white State of Idaho truck-weighing station. The justice, dressed in Levi's and a t-shirt, sat on top of a desk and convened the court. Mr. Henley didn't show up to testify so the case was dismissed. It had been a diverting experience that had taken everyone's mind off the ruckus over Wild Bill.

Ed Bailey, the mayor of Mountain Home, along with a large group of other horseback riders escorted the caravan through their town and out to the campsite. The temperature was 110 degrees that afternoon. In order to alleviate our discomfort, the Mountain Home people brought us cold drinks and took some of our people on tours of the area. They visited the Mountain Home Air Force Base and later went to see some trail ruts left by pioneer wagons 10 miles north of where we were camped.

Tex and I took Ludy to a doctor in Boise that afternoon. He told Ludy that a miscarriage was likely, but it wasn't going to happen immediately. We drove back to camp in a more relaxed frame of mind.

While we were gone the biggest fight of the entire trip had developed. During part of the disagreement I thought the "big blow up" had indeed come and our wagon train would be dissolved in the Idaho heat. Too much drinking added to the intensity of it all. The cold drinks brought us consisted of two washtubs of beer and soft drinks packed in ice. Gail Carnine had become loud and rowdy after having had quite a few bottles of beer. His idea of fun was to fire some blanks from his pistol. Shorty Hilliard and several others thought that there were too many people around for this to have been safe. When we arrived, the wagoneers were sitting around sulking in small groups. Ben and Rudy thought there had been no harm in what Gail did so they were on his side. Shorty, Roy Brabham, Pop Clark and George McUne demanded that Gail be sent home. Shorty insisted that if Gail didn't leave then he would. Tex was no Solomon, but he managed to muddle through the dilemma.

Tex agreed with the majority and told Gail that he would have to leave. Gail refused to go. He said that even if he had to walk along behind, he was going to stick it out to the end. Ben and Rudy made it known that if Gail left, then they would go too. On the other side, Shorty was going to leave if Gail didn't.

The quarreling went on until eight o'clock the next morning. There were numerous phone calls to Dick Smith in Roseburg. Everyone told him a different side of the story. I tried to get some sleep but I was too upset to relax. Besides that, just as I dozed off a huge field mouse scampered over my sleeping bag and startled me. I kicked my legs violently but more mice came back as soon as I lay still again. Just as I was beginning to feel that I could sleep through anything, it was time to get up.

The problem was still there. We didn't like hurting anyone, but it seemed that the only solution was to force someone to go home. It wouldn't be hurting only Shorty or Gail. They each had families and friends who would be hurt too. Our efforts to reconcile them were in vain. We talked for hours and no one moved from his adamant position.

At 8:00 a.m., two hours after the wagon train should have pulled out, nothing had happened except that the Hilliards had packed their suitcases and were ready to leave. We had something else to worry about too. That day the State Highway Department was building a fence along the freeway to make it limited access. The first strand of wire was strung on the ground and ready to be stretched up along the posts. If we didn't move out soon, we would have to go back east at least a mile to get around the fence. That would add two miles on to a hot day's journey.

We knew we couldn't get along without Shorty's skill as a blacksmith. His efforts had been largely responsible for keeping us moving up to that point. In desperation Tex finally said to Shorty, "Look, Shorty, as a favor to me, will you get up in that wagon and drive it? Just for today if you want it that way."

Shorty thought a minute, "For you, Tex, I'll do it."

The crisis was averted and the dusty wagons drove over the new wire and made it onto the freeway just before the wire was stretched onto the fence posts. Their next stop was at the Hansen ranch, a campsite I had found some 20 miles west across the desert.

I took the Pelling and Carnine youngsters with me to Boise to clean up and make ready our weekend campsite. Gerry Hilliard, Shorty and Tres' 22-year-old daughter who had come for a visit, went with us. We met Mr. Coffey and worked all morning. We shoveled aside piles of cow manure, mucked out the spring, chopped down thistles and hauled away trash. The area looked like a city park when we finished.

My helpers and I made it back to the Hansen ranch just before the wagons arrived. The temperature was in the 120s and there wasn't any shade for miles. Various dignitaries and newsmen from Boise sat around in the hot sun and waited for the wagon train. I expected to see a disgruntled group suffering from sunstroke and the effects of the previous night's loss of sleep. The caravan arrived and I saw I was wrong. I marveled at everyone's ruggedness. The ride had cooled Shorty down and he decided to stay. I knew we would have more disagreements after that, but nothing would keep us from getting home as a group.

There was lots of activity in the air above us. Jet planes gave us a flyover. The mayor of Boise, Robert L. Day, arrived in a helicopter and gave us the key to his city. A small army plane dropped two supply parachutes of ice cream and lemonade.

Reno, Tex's bay horse, almost broke his halter rope in panic when one of the parachutes landed near him. A breeze carried the billowing white monster right into his face. I helped spill the wind out of it and wrapped it up before Reno had apoplexy. In a half hour he was his old feisty self again, ready to bite or kick anyone who got within range.

We all went to a rodeo in Nampa that evening then we broke camp at 6:00 a.m. the next morning to go to Boise. I was over in Oregon locating the trail out of Nyssa while half the population of Boise came to look at the wagon train. The caravan stopped in front of the capitol building and everyone was kept busy signing autographs. A special group of old people, all from pioneer families, came to greet the wagoneers. One man gave us a transcription of interviews with the oldsters telling about the settlement of the Boise Basin.

Everyone enjoyed the Coffeys' shade trees, cold-water spring and green grass. With a few palm trees and belly dancers it would have been a perfect oasis.

Sunday morning services were led by a Quaker, Walter Lee. He spoke of how we should guide our youngsters in good paths, have strength in our convictions and preserve our individuality. I especially liked the last part because of my thoughts on the fight between Tex and Ben at the Henley ranch. The wagon people didn't need any lessons on preserving their individuality.

That Sunday was the 21st of July, the anniversary of our third month "on the trail." It seemed to have become such a way of life to us by then that there was no special celebration as there had been at the end of our first and second months.

We sold Geronimo that afternoon. Shorty Hilliard explained to the prospective buyer how the horse had taken distemper back in Kansas, had gotten well, but had never put on weight again. Shorty hurried the men around the back of the horse as fast as possible so he wouldn't see the unusual conformation under his tail. We prayed that the horse wouldn't break wind and burble at that critical moment. The man walked over to Tex and paid him for it, then went back to look at it again. As he approached, Geronimo did what he was notorious for in his most alarming way. The man went back to Tex and asked, "You've never done much horse trading, have you?" Tex just laughed. The buyer was a good sport about it and laughed too.

Since the man was not going to pick up Geronimo until the middle of Monday morning, we had to tie him to a tree and leave him. He carried on pitifully as the wagon train left. His eyes filled with tears, he whinnied mournfully and stamped his feet in agitation. I felt like we were abandoning a helpless child in the wilderness. It reminded me of how we had left Rudy's horses behind in Nebraska. They had carried on the same way.

The wagons were to camp at Caldwell that day. While they were on the road, I drove into Oregon again to make final plans in Nyssa and Vale. The wagon train was lined up in the Caldwell City Park when I rejoined the group.

That afternoon a carload of us went with the local New York Life agent, Charlie Warren, and a local historian, Mrs. Ray Thomas Wells, to the site of the Ward massacre. Mrs. Wells knew the site well because she had been born there. It was about three miles northeast of Caldwell, exactly on the original Oregon Trail.

The massacre occurred on August 20, 1854, when Snake Indians ambushed a party of 20 immigrants led by Alexander Ward. Of the 20, only two badly wounded boys managed to hide and escape. The other 18 were buried there in unmarked graves. Soldiers captured some of the Indians shortly after the massacre and executed them on gallows erected over the graves. This started eight years of Indian wars which caused the closing of Ft. Boise and Ft. Hall. There is now a monument and a park at the site of the massacre.

Sightseers harassed us terribly at Caldwell. Since the wagons were in a row rather than in a circle, we had difficulty defending them. We couldn't circle up because the Caldwell people had asked us to stay on the pavement in the park and it only went in a straight line. People were dipping their fingers in axle grease and writing their names on the canvas wagon covers. Others tried cutting pieces out of the canvas covers for souvenirs. The hot weather made it hard for us to keep our tempers under control. The Indians must have wiped out the Ward party in the same heat.

En route from Caldwell to Nyssa our wagon train passed within four miles of the site of Ft. Boise. That fort's history parallels Ft. Hall's in many ways. First, both forts were established in 1834. Thomas McKay of the Hudson's Bay Company built Ft. Boise and Nathaniel Wyeth, an American from Boston, built Ft. Hall. After Wyeth sold out, the two forts served as fur-trading stations for the Hudson's Bay Company. Like Ft. Hall, Ft. Boise had several locations. McKay first built Ft. Boise eight or ten miles north of the Boise River, but for most of the fort's duration it was beside the river near where it flows into the Snake. In 1853 floods washed away the adobe walls of both forts and the walls were replaced by wooden stockades. Indian wars caused the two forts to be abandoned in 1856, and floods in 1862 washed away nearly all trace of them.

Before the white man came, beaver dams had formed natural flood control barriers on all the tributaries of the Snake River. When the beaver were trapped into extinction, the dams eventually decayed. In times of heavy runoff the rivers then flooded because there were no beaver dams left to serve as water catchments.

In eradicating the beaver the white men also caused the destruction of their own forts and farms. The few thousands of dollars' profit from beaver pelts have cost millions of dollars in flood damage and flood control projects.

Five thousand people gathered in Nyssa to welcome our wagon train to Oregon. They congregated at the Snake River Bridge on the west edge of town where a speakers' platform had been set up. Among the dignitaries there were Jack Lively and Tony Brandenthaler of the

Oregon Centennial Committee, Oregon's Secretary of State, Howell Appling, Jr., and State Senator Tony Yturri. Our boss from Roseburg, Dick Smith, had also come to see us reach that important milestone.

The greeters had stretched a logging chain across the bridge at the center. A flatbed truck served as the speakers' platform on the Oregon side of the chain. The wagons drove up to the chain and stopped while the dignitaries made speeches. The talks were mercifully short because the noonday sun was getting hotter by the minute.

The greetings were finished and Debbie Keller, the daughter of one of the Nyssa greeters, handed Tex the key to the padlock holding the chain in place. Tex unlocked it and the wagons rolled through into Oregon. The wagoneers' pride was reflected in the eyes of the onlookers.

Alan Knudtson, left, originator of the idea for the Centennial Wagon Train, visited us at our Green River Camp.

XVIII. Eastern Oregon

From 1834 when Captain B.L.E. Bonneville brought 28 wagons through South Pass to the Green River, it took nine years for the Oregon Trail to reach the Willamette Valley. Two years after Bonneville's venture the missionaries Marcus Whitman and Henry Spalding brought a two-wheeled cart to Ft. Boise. In 1840 Robert Newell and Joseph L. Meek extended the trail through what is now eastern Oregon. They and several friends drove three wagons as far as Whitman's mission at Wailatpu in what is now southeastern Washington. Marcus Whitman took news of that accomplishment east in 1842 and encouraged the "Great Migration" of 1843. It was only "great," not the greatest, but it did reach all the way to the Willamette Valley.

"Doctor" Robert Newell and "Colonel" Joe Meek first met in 1829 in St. Louis as they were setting out to become fur trappers. In 1840, still friends, they left Ft. Hall with their Indian wives and three other white men in three wagons. The trapping was almost finished in Idaho so they thought they would try farming in Oregon. They had to lighten their wagon loads because their animals grew weak pushing through the tall, thick sagebrush. By the time they reached Wailatpu, they had lightened the wagons so much that there was little left except wheels and axles. Nevertheless, they proved it could be done. They rested at the mission and went on without the wagons. The following year Doctor Newell returned for his wagon and took it to the Willamette Valley: It was the first wagon to travel the entire length of the trail.

Joe Meek later became famous in Oregon politics. With his marvelous knack for "jawboning," he was instrumental in organizing an American government in Oregon in 1843. When a division was called for, the count was only 52 to 50 in favor of a government that would eventually join the United States rather than Great Britain. Historians have given Joe Meek credit for the Americans' margin. Late in 1847 the Oregon legislature named him "Envoy Extraordinary and Minister

Plenipotentiary." The wondrous title, plus his gift for talking, plus the fact that he was President James K. Polk's cousin, all contributed towards Oregon being named a territory of the United States in 1848.

Joe Meek and Robert Newell had gone past Ft. Boise and crossed the Snake River near the mouth of the Boise River. After Ft. Boise was abandoned in 1856, the trail changed its course and crossed the Snake in several other places. Water levels and man-made accommodations along the river influenced later pioneers in their choices as to where they would cross. Settlers following the route of Newell and Meek went northwest over a range of hills and dropped down to the Malheur River. They forded it and came back to the west bank of the Snake at Farewell Bend near the present town of Huntington, Oregon.

A later crossing of the Snake was near where Ontario, Oregon, is now located, where the Malheur empties into the Snake. Another crossing was established in 1862, 23 miles north of Ontario at Old's Ferry. Seven miles north of Old's Ferry pioneers sometimes used a traditional Indian crossing. The trail routes from these crossings came together again near Farewell Bend, 30 air miles north of Nyssa.

From Nyssa our caravan followed the Newell-Meek route northwest on the road going beside Hollow Creek. The road generally follows the creek as it drops down to the Malheur River at Vale. North of Vale, Oregon State Highway 26 follows the original trail route for two miles, then the trail continues north and Highway 26 veers northwest. The trail goes through rolling, barren hills past Willow Creek, Tub Spring, Willow Spring and Birch Creek then meets the Snake again at Farewell Bend. It was here that the pioneers said farewell to the Snake River. A historical marker at the site tells how the Wilson Price Hunt expedition passed there in 1811. From Farewell Bend the early wagon trains crossed overland several miles to the Burnt River, which they followed some 20 miles north to where the town of Durkee is now located.

In his journal of 1845, Joel Palmer said of this particular part of the trail, "The road is up the Burnt River and the most difficult road we have encountered since we started. The difficulties arise from the frequent crossings of the creek, which is crooked, narrow and stony." Mr. Palmer never dreamed that someday a wagon train's main difficulty in coming up that same canyon would be in avoiding collisions with horseless carriages.

A few Indians comprised the only population in Joel Palmer's era. People of Anglo-American, Basque, Japanese and Mexican ancestry, as well as a few Indians, greeted us as we entered that territory. American ranchers brought in the trustworthy Basques to be sheepherders. As time passed, the men sent to their homes in northern Spain for their families, bought land, and are now as well-to-do as the people who brought them here. The Japanese-Americans first came during America's shameful relocation and concentration camp program in World War II. They began raising sugar beets, prospered, and now form a proud part of the local citizenry. The Americans imported Mexicans during World War II to compensate for the manpower shortage. These once-seasonal workers became citizens and landowners and brought their families up from Mexico.

The wagon train passed this multi-ethnic crowd of greeters at the Snake River Bridge and settled itself on the high school lawn in Nyssa. Besides the thousands of spectators milling around, Grandma Gatewood strolled by to see us. She chatted happily with everyone and renewed the acquaintances begun in Pocatello, Idaho. She was planning to increase her mileage per day, so we knew we were not apt to see her again.

I spent the afternoon conferring with Tex, Ivan, Dick Smith, Howell Appling and Tony Brandenthaler. Most people in camp thought we were discussing personality problems, but actually we spent all our time on such topics as finances, routes, schedules and the disposition of the wagon train when we finished our journey. The personality problems had to take care of themselves.

These problems came out in a long gripe session the next morning. Howell Appling and Dick Smith came to breakfast and Howell gave a pep talk. When Dick started to say a few words, several wagon trainers interrupted with their pet peeves. All that can be said for the complaints is that they were great for demonstrating the complainers' individuality. The philosophy I had figured out at Henley ranch helped me to be tolerant. I was embarrassed, however, that our Secretary of State had to listen to such things as, "How come Tex got a pistol and nobody else did?" or, "Why don't we leave that horse with the sore neck behind so we don't have to look at it?"

Personality differences caused us to disagree as to which problems were most important. If we did happen to agree on the problems, we couldn't agree on the solutions. These differences didn't help Tex when he tried to solve the problems in his own way. Like Christopher Columbus, whose most-used reply to the would-be mutineers was "Sail on," Tex simply said, "Well, let's keep going."

Wagon trains of the century before had had difficulties too. The subject matter may have been different, but human nature was the same. Where the pioneers contended with heat, hunger and thirst, we contended with heat, crowds and sleeplessness. Masses of people oppressed us day and night. Being under physical and nervous strain, we were inclined to magnify our grievances.

In those days I constantly felt a need for sleep. It was like being in love or in mourning, when your loved one is on your mind no matter what you are doing. It was after 11 every night before the sightseers left and I could crawl into my bedroll. Caffeine nerves, car headlights, horse and mule noises and worrisome dreams kept interrupting what sleep I had. At 4:00 a.m. it was time to get up. Dawn was breaking and the cooks were rattling around in the kitchen trailer. Our police and National Guard escorts arrived and we had to coordinate the day's travel plan.

I was fine as long as I was on my feet talking, eating or helping with the livestock, but I dozed off whenever I sat down. My head tingled like my hand does when I hit my funny bone. My eyes burned and seemed to spread a fever through my body. I functioned in spite of the drowsiness until I washed my face in cold water and had a cup of coffee. After several cups of coffee, I felt like a thin, tired, tightly stretched rubber band. In that state my duties required me to drive somewhere. Once in Ontario, Oregon, I felt myself falling asleep at the wheel so I pulled off the highway onto a tree-lined street to keep from having an accident. I switched off the engine and fell over onto the seat in a sound sleep. In about ten minutes a National Guard captain in a jeep found me and woke me up to help solve a route problem. I had to go through the pains of waking up all over again. Our system of going to bed late and getting up early caused other wagon train members to long for sleep as much as I, but it was the only way we could avoid having to travel during that time of day when the heat and traffic were at their highest.

The wagon train forded a river as it travelled from Nyssa to Vale. Except for fording a couple small creeks in Wyoming, this was our only opportunity to sample an experience which was common in pioneer days. Along the length of our trek the wagon train members had often suggested that we ford a river for the sake of authenticity. Now everyone had misgivings about the place I had chosen for fording the Malheur River near Vale. They were afraid that water would get into the wagon boxes and soak their bedrolls and baggage.

I drove Tex up to the river to prove that it could be done with no trouble. At the ford Tex took off his boots and waded across without rolling up his pants legs. He braced himself against the current and felt of the bottom to see how solid it was. We then hurried back to the wagon train where Tex stood by a wagon to show how deep the water was by the waterline on his Levi's. The wetness stopped at least eight inches below the bottoms of the wagon boxes. That satisfied everyone and we rolled on down to the river. It was a pleasant crossing. The animals playfully splashed their legs and the clear water rippled harmlessly through the wheel spokes. The spectators applauded and the participants smiled. I took some good footage with Tex's 16mm camera.

The wagons paraded through Vale then came back to a park by the river crossing and made camp. A local covered wagon pulled by a team of oxen joined them in the parade. The wagon's clean, white canvas, new red paint and neat appearance made a sharp contrast to our wagons' dusty, unkempt, weathered look. It made us realize how much our wagons had been through in order for us to have come this far.

The town of Vale, like so many other towns, went all out in their welcoming celebrations. Besides the parade and a massive picnic staged in our honor, they had an old-time cattle drive through the center of town. The mayor's horse broke a plate-glass window in a bar; otherwise it was only a mild stampede. That night there was a street dance with entertainment from young people in native costumes doing Basque, Japanese and Mexican dances.

Some local men had helped me scout the trail in this area while our wagon train was in Boise. Jim Wilson of Nyssa brought me to Vale over the original trail route. In Vale we met Jim's father, Vern Wilson, Mayor Kerr Decker and the County Road Superintendent, Carl Sperling. A local rancher and pioneer descendent, Dwight Lockett, joined us and we left Vale in a car and pickup truck to go on a scouting expedition. We wanted to see how closely the wagons could follow the original trail route north to Huntington.

We found steep hills and primitive roads. We had to carry rocks to fill the ford across Birch Creek before we could drive over it. Catering to the strength of our animals and the temperaments of our drivers, I decided we should travel several miles off the trail on what is called the Old Military Road.

Later, when the wagon train was camped at Vale, Gail Carnine and I drove out and found a place to camp the next afternoon at the Floyd McBride ranch above Jamieson. The camp was at the crossroads where the Old Military Road began. The wagons would follow this road across the deserted, dried-yellow hills until they came back to Highway 30 at Farewell Bend.

While the wagon train traveled from Jamieson to Huntington, the Hoyers and I drove ahead to Baker, Oregon. Jyme Stoner of the US National Bank loaned us facilities to mimeograph and collate a new batch of publicity kits. We were busy doing that when we received a cryptic message from Tex: we were to meet the caravan in Huntington when it arrived. During the drive south we speculated that there had been another fight. Tex would have said more in his message if it hadn't been something personal.

My stomach was in a knot until we got back to Huntington and found out what was wrong. I was relieved that it wasn't worse, but chagrined at what it was. Ben Griffith and Pop Clark the evening before had called a New York Life Insurance Company representative in Portland and complained about the non-treatment they had been getting. Ben had told them that "by George Harry" they should send someone out to talk to us the next day. The representative called Dick Smith in Roseburg to complain about the call and Tex heard of it in a telegram from Dick. Besides Ben and Pop, Gail Carnine and Rudy Roudebaugh were upset about being left out on gifts from the insurance company.

I was embarrassed because I felt that company personnel had been helpful. Local agents along the trail had served as guides and had several times loaned me office space. They had given each of us a $1,000 life insurance policy and had supplied us with a movie camera and unlimited amounts of film so they could produce a 30-minute film of our expedition. All these gratuities, however, were overshadowed by the pistol that the company gave Tex in Montpelier, Idaho. A gift of equal value should have been given to everyone or they should have given nothing at all.

The wagons made their usual circle and stopped in the school yard at Huntington. A man from a nearby café was there inviting everyone to a free lunch. Tex tied Reno to a wagon wheel and walked around telling each driver to come to a meeting as soon as the animals were cared for. The visitors, the youngsters and the apathetic were more concerned with lunch than with the meeting. Only eight men and two women gave the meeting priority over the restaurant.

We gathered in the shade of an oak tree and Tex confronted Ben with the telegram from Roseburg. "Ben, Dick Smith says here that you made a threatening phone call to the New York Life Insurance Company."

"Oh yeah? What did I threaten them with?"

"This telegram says that you said you'd get them some bad publicity if they didn't send a man out here to talk to us right away."

"Yeah, well, I called them all right. And I told them they ought to get a man out here to see us, but I didn't make any threats."

Tex's tone softened a bit. "Well what was on your mind? Why should they send someone out to see us?"

"They ought to know what's going on. Everyone is damned tired of only one man getting all the glory while the rest of us do all the work. If there are any pistols to be given away then we should all get one. If one man is taken out to eat, we should all be. And all the publicity shouldn't be centered on one man either."

Several men nodded and said they agreed with Ben.

Tex countered with the only argument he had, "Well, Ben, you know there's no way we can control all that."

Shorty Hilliard ended it all saying, "Well, let's not stand around here talking all day. I want to get myself fed so I can get new shoes on that brown mule."

Except for Ben's phone call, the meeting involved nothing new. We heard the same complaints that we had heard at Nyssa, Crater Station, Montpelier and points east. Ivan and I were miffed that we had been interrupted in our work in Baker to come back on such a trivial matter. Those who agreed with Ben and those who didn't were divided along the same lines as at Crater Station. Shorty, Tres, Ivan, Ludy, Tex and I were on one side; Ben, Pop, Rudy and Gail were on the other. Everyone else was out to lunch where we should have been.

Individually, the people in Huntington were as hospitable and generous as the café manager. As a group, however, they oppressed us. Gerry Hilliard, Cheryl Carnine and I went down to the deserted city park to escape from the multitude. The fun of being celebrities was getting tiresome. Our only company in the park was a large, friendly dog who didn't spoil the solitude by wanting to talk. Everyone else in town was down at the school looking at the wagon train. We arrived back there just as I was being called on to say a few words. I gave my usual summary of the trip, told the same old joke about the Platte River being too thick to drink and too thin to plow, and the crowd was satisfied.

That night I unrolled my bedroll under the van of Robbie's semi with "the kids." I left my sleeping bag unzipped because it was a warm night. In the morning I woke to find that I had rolled halfway out of the sleeping bag and off the ground tarp and that I was sleeping like an animal with my bare torso in the dust, stickers and weeds.

It was another short night's sleep. We got up at 3:00 a.m. and all of us went downtown for breakfast. With our visitors and new members, I counted 34 of us in the café. We had recently been joined by three Hoyer children, two more Carnine children from Gail's first marriage, and several other members' wives and relatives. Only 23 of these had been in the original group leaving Independence, Missouri. Where the pioneer wagon trains had lost members along the way, we had gained.

Back at the camp I briefed Tex, Gail and the motor vehicle drivers on the location of our camp for that Saturday and Sunday. We would be at the Skinner Kirby ranch one and a half miles north of Durkee. It was our last camp on the Burnt River which by that point had faded into a small stream some ten feet wide.

Tex took the station wagon to go horse buying, I went to Baker with Ivan to finish the publicity kits, and the wagon train left Huntington to go to Durkee.

On the way north Ivan and I stopped at Skinner Kirby's and saw that he had moved feed racks and two outhouses onto the campsite. He had cut down a weed patch by the creek, and had even made a small dam so we could water the animals easily. Our gratitude seemed meager recompense for his kindness.

While we were marveling at the facilities, Mr. Kirby came with a truckload of hay for the feed racks. He stopped to talk and the subject naturally got around to the Oregon Trail. He told us how up until a few years before, trail ruts had still been visible just east of the railroad track across the creek from where we were to camp. We had been in the same canyon, and at times on the exact trace of the trail since Farewell Bend. We were to stay that close to the original route almost all the way to Pendleton.

Ivan and I finished assembling our publicity kits in Baker and came back to camp for a peaceful Saturday evening. Tex was discouraged about finding a new draft horse for what he wanted to pay. He had been looking since Mountain Home, Idaho.

Skinner Kirby solved our horse problem the next morning. Duke, the horse with the open sore on his neck, had not been working since we came into the Bear River Valley in Eastern Idaho. Both Duke and his pulling partner, Dime, had been trailing along behind Dick Melton's wagon for weeks while he drove the sorrel mares, Buttons and Bow. Mr. Kirby loaned us a fat bay mare to pull with Dime. The two horses looked good together. Dick Melton was as proud as a new father as he hitched them up to adjust their harness and see how they pulled together. We were all delighted to see how evenly matched the two horses were in size and willingness to work. Now we could again use Buttons and Bows as riding horses and Duke wouldn't have to be traded off for another horse.

Local people arrived for a church service at 8:00 a.m. Our minister was Rev. O. Rex Lindemood, a Methodist from Baker. In his sermon he told us that our job wasn't finished now that we were in Oregon because we still needed to sell Oregon to the Oregonians; we needed to make people proud of their home state. The admonition went unheeded because the main effect of the sermon was to remind us of how much we loved Oregon.

Sunday afternoon Tex, Ludy and I drove north past Baker and North Powder to La Grande to plan our route and visits to those towns on the first three days of the coming week. Our research in La Grande showed us how the Oregon Trail had gone across the southern edge of town then up a steep hill to the Grande Ronde River about six miles west of there. The trail going up the hill had been so steep that the pioneers had hooked as many as six yoke of oxen to their wagons to get them up out of the valley. Some of the wagon wheel ruts in that area are still visible.

We had to determine if the newly built freeway over the hill was more feasible to take than to go through Union in the heart of the valley. People in Union said they were closer to the original trail than the new freeway. However, our State Highway Department map showed the trail following almost the same route as the new freeway. We surmised that the difference in opinion was due to the fact that the pioneers followed several routes. These varied according to the availability of grass, game, firewood and water. Since the new freeway was not too steep for us, and because the road through Union was seven miles longer, we decided to forego the town's hospitality.

The Grande Ronde Valley where Union is located is somewhat "round" in appearance. It once was a favorite Indian hunting ground because of the numerous elk, moose and deer. The Indians also used to gather camas roots there. Besides being good to eat, the roots were said to have medicinal value. A pioneer named Ben Brown led the first group of white settlers in the valley. The men had passed through the valley, gone over the Blue Mountains, and were camped on the banks of the Umatilla River. Compared to the dry Umatilla River country, the Grande Ronde Valley seemed like paradise. Remembering the rich grass they had seen there, they turned back to the valley and took up homesteading.

Instead of driving straight back to Durkee from La Grande, Tex, Ludy and I met the other wagoneers at a rodeo in Baker. Val Johnson had entered in the women's bull riding event and I was chosen to take pictures of her. When it was time, Val went back to the chutes and I stationed myself about 20 yards out in the arena with my big, speed-graphic news camera. A buzzer sounded and Val flew out on top of a kicking, bucking blur. The bull threw her off before I could even find her in the view lens. Having rid himself of one adversary, the bull chose me as his next target. He charged at me kicking and snorting. Still clutching the camera, I gave a demonstration of rapid, one-handed fence climbing. This amused everyone but me. I made it to the top of the fence just as that mass of flying hooves and horns smashed into the boards below my feet. Val was unharmed, but my dignity was badly damaged.

Monday morning, July 30, we left the first of our weekend campsites in Oregon. The Oregon State Police and National Guard escort helped everything go smoothly as the wagon train left for Baker.

.

The wagon train stops on the bridge across the Snake River for ceremonies welcoming the members to Oregon.

XIX. Umatilla Country

Well-fed by numerous hosts, we travelled through the same country where the Wilson Price Hunt expedition nearly starved in 1811. Those representatives of John Jacob Astor's Pacific Fur Company were traveling overland to Astoria at the mouth of the Columbia. There they would meet other company representatives who had already arrived by boat and established a fur-trading post. The Hunt party consisted of sixty men and one woman. The men were of French-Canadian, British and American backgrounds and the woman, Marie Dorion, was the wife of the French-Canadian interpreter, Pierre Dorion.

Leaving Ft. Henry in present-day eastern Idaho, they split up into three groups. Donald McKenzie took his group due west, north of the Snake's U-shaped curve through Idaho; W.P. Hunt took his group along the north bank of the river and Ramsey Crooks' group went along the south bank. Because of mixed feelings of apathy and greed, the group under Hunt nearly caused the death of Crooks' group. Hunt's party killed their last horse and made no move to share the meat with the starving group immediately across the river. Threatening violence, Ramsey Crooks forced some of the Hunt's men to send meat across the river in a canoe made from the horse's hide. One man with Crooks was too impatient and was drowned in a frantic effort to get across the river to where the meat was already cooked. The two parties came together again a few days later on the west side of the river near Farewell Bend.

They came up the Burnt River and celebrated New Year's Day in the Grande Ronde Valley. Here Marie Dorion gave birth to her third child. The baby died six days later due to the hardships of their winter trek. Friendly Walla Walla Indians aided the white men and enabled them to reach Astoria with almost their full complement. Two men had drowned in the Snake River; one had fallen behind in the Grande Ronde Valley and was never seen again. Six other stragglers, including John Day and Ramsey Crooks, eventually arrived at Astoria. The Dalles

Indians had beaten, stripped and robbed Day and Crooks. The Walla Wallas rescued them and helped them reach Astoria. Donald McKenzie's group had reached Astoria without mishap a month ahead of Hunt and Crooke.

In 1959 we suffered no harm from Indians but sightseers were a real hazard. During Saturday's traveling up the Burnt River the National Guard escort was essential in preventing disaster. The highway wound up the canyon along the river in such a way that the cars catching up with the wagon train could not see to pass. Communicating by two-way radio, the National Guard relayed word from front to rear when it was safe to drive past the caravan. Regardless of being urged to hurry, the people added to the danger of meeting oncoming cars by driving slowly and staring at the wagons in friendly fascination.

For the first seven miles out of Durkee, Highway 30 took the wagons along the exact route of the original trail. At that point the highway meandered off in a northwesterly direction and the trail continued on a course closer to due north. Fences and trees in the original trail forced us to stay on the highway. The old trail route and Highway 30 didn't coincide again until the town of North Powder, 19 miles north of Baker. The city park in Baker, our destination for the day, was five miles west of the original trail.

While the wagon train traveled to Baker my duties took me to La Grande again. I met the Chamber of Commerce Secretary, Honce Snodgrass, and we looked over a campsite at the north edge of town. I met Grandma Gatewood again while we were having lunch at the Sacajawea Hotel. She was just a day's travel time ahead of the wagon train. My advance stop in La Grande coincided with her hike through town. The suntanned old lady had lunch with us and we had a pleasant visit. She asked about everyone on the wagon train, calling them by name, and we talked about sights and landmarks along the Oregon Trail.

From the hotel I drove to the La Grande Airport. A plane was waiting there to fly me to The Dalles, where the wagon train would be in 12 more days. The Dalles was to be our last stop on the Oregon Trail. I had to arrange for a campsite, and following the example of our pioneer predecessors, arrange for a barge to take us down the Columbia and up the Willamette a few miles.

We hadn't been off the ground five minutes when air turbulence caused me to lose my lunch. As soon as I finished retching, I felt better and could enjoy the scenery. Mt. Hood stood up in the west straight ahead of us. Mt. Adams was to the north of Mt. Hood, and in the distance to the north I could see Mt. St. Helens and Mt. Rainier, at least 150 miles away. Below us I was appalled to see dirt blowing away from plowed fields. The streams of light-brown dust billowed up like smoke from forest fires. The area around Pendleton was covered by a huge dust cloud.

At The Dalles Bob Hadeen, Chamber of Commerce Secretary, along with the Mayor, the City Manager, two newspaper reporters and two radio station newsmen, met me at the airport. We drove around the town and I chose a campsite in the city park only three blocks from the pier where we were to load the wagons onto barges. Our long-deceased friend Ezra Meeker had been to the park before us and left a monument saying, "End of the Oregon Trail." I felt proud to be the first of our group to arrive. The men from The Dalles told me that in the old days what is now the downtown area of their town was swampland which had been navigable by barges. The city park where we were to camp had been an actual pioneer campsite. There the people had waited for barges to take them down the river. Thirty-foot-high cliffs south of the campsite had made it impractical to camp any farther from the river.

After meeting the barge people at the Pacific Inland Navigation Company offices, we went to a restaurant where I ate lunch again. I explained to the group how I had lost my first lunch and everyone had a good laugh. They would have laughed even harder if they could have seen me lose my second lunch on the flight back to La Grande. I felt fine until we started circling for a landing at the La Grande airport, then my queasy stomach humbled me again.

I drove 90 miles an hour from La Grande to Baker in order to not miss dinner. The Baker Cattlemen's Association had invited us all to a steak dinner at a restaurant. With no more plane rides my entire body made the steak welcome.

We slept on the lawn of the Baker city park that evening, and in the morning the women of the Baker County Historical Society gave us breakfast. Several members of the group told us how their ancestors arrived there in covered wagons in the 1840s.

The wagon train left for North Powder and I had to go to Pendleton to help with plans for our arrival there. I met Ray Calvert of Pendleton at a restaurant in La Grande where I stopped for a cup of coffee. A member of the Pendleton greeting committee, he had come to La Grande to meet us. He saw my station wagon parked in front of the restaurant and joined me inside for another cup of coffee. He briefed me on the old trail route in relation to the route of the new freeway.

The State of Oregon was just building the freeway, 80 North, out of La Grande in 1959. The freeway replaced US Highway 30 which we had generally followed since Kearney, Nebraska. The new freeway skirted La Grande on the northeast and the Oregon Trail went through the southwest part of town. The freeway and the original trail route then come together at the Grande Ronde River some six miles west of La Grande. In this part of Oregon the route west gradually turns from the northerly route of the Snake to the westerly route of the Columbia. The freeway and the route of the original trail stay close together through the Blue Mountains and descend a long, steep slope to meet the Umatilla River a mile east of Pendleton.

Ray Calvert led the way to Pendleton in his pickup truck and I followed in my station wagon. We stopped at prospective campsites along the way. We found a beautiful clearing among some evergreens at a spot called Strickland Meadows and I marked it as our camp for Thursday after we left La Grande. For Friday Mr. Calvert had obtained permission for us to camp at a mountain cabin at Emigrant Pass. From there the wagons would have an easy downhill run to our weekend camp at the Pendleton Fairgrounds. In Pendleton Mr. Calvert introduced me to members of the ex-officio wagon train welcoming committee: Ted Smith of station KUMA and Rudy Embyk, the City Centennial Chairman. We discussed weekend plans; I inspected the facilities at the fairgrounds and drove back to meet the wagons at North Powder.

We were surprised by cool weather at North Powder. We camped on the school football field where we gave our usual introduction and storytelling program for the townspeople. At bedtime I unrolled my ground tarp, army comforter and sleeping bag bedroll out on the green grass. During the night I woke up feeling chilly and unfolded my army comforter so half of it would be over me and half still under me as a mattress. At daybreak when it was time to get up I was glad that I had my clothes inside the bedroll with me so I could dress in the sleeping bag. Having to get up was tough, but having to get up in the cold and put on damp clothes would have been terrible. A sprinkler was left on all night at the other end of the football field and a circle of ice had formed where the water fell. We had been told that North Powder was the coldest spot in Oregon and seeing the ice convinced us that it was. At breakfast time it had warmed up to 34 degrees.

We shivered through the process of breaking camp and everyone was glad to get moving towards warmer territory. My advance work for the day took me to the campus of Eastern Oregon College in La Grande. I met an old friend there, Bruce Ryan from Medford, who introduced me to Dr. Al Kaiser, the author of a play we were to see at the college that evening. The play, "Doctor in Buckskin Clad," is a historical drama on the life and death of Dr. Marcus Whitman. Dr. Kaiser was well-versed on Indian history and customs so we had an interesting chat over several cups of coffee.

From the college Bruce and I went to his house where we gathered his family and several of the neighbors' children together and drove downtown to see the wagon train arrive. The parade was well organized and a large crowd lined the street. When the first wagon came past, Ben Griffith spotted me in the crowd and gave me a huge grin. He was delighted that I had arranged for the Union County Centennial Queen to ride into town with him.

I said goodbye to the Ryans and went out to our camp at Pioneer Park on the far edge of town. A policeman there told me that I would have to make another trip to the airport. A charter plane carrying 30 men from Independence, Oregon, was arriving at that moment. The men wanted to greet us and make plans for our arrival in their town in only two weeks. I and several townspeople brought them to camp from the airport. A few of the leaders sat down with Tex, Ivan and me for a long talk and the rest of the men milled around camp until it was time to leave.

One of my most bothersome experiences with a sightseer occurred later that day. I had been busy since 4:30 a.m. and felt the need for a siesta in order to stay awake during the play that evening. The problem was to find a place where sightseers wouldn't bother me. Beyond the animals' tethering line was some tall grass that looked like it might be a sanctuary for me. The horses and mules were tied to a cyclone fence that paralleled a pond. There wasn't room between the pond and the hind legs of the animals for a person to walk without being in danger of getting kicked. Going in front of the animals meant possibly being bitten. A person had to bend over until he was almost on all fours to walk between the animals' heads and the fence.

I decided that I would rather get bitten than kicked so I grabbed my bedroll, put aside my caution and crawled under the heads of the animals to get to the tall grass. The grass hid me from the world and I was asleep in two minutes. In another two minutes I felt a hard, sharp object nudging me in the ribs. I rolled over and saw a lady standing over me with a camera. She smiled down at me and asked, "Could I take your picture?" I thought some pretty violent things, but all I said was, "OK, so long as you don't ask me to move." She snapped the picture and I went back to sleep. I'm sure that somewhere today there is a photograph testifying to: A, my fatigue; B, that lady's ingenuity in finding me; and C, her gall in disturbing me with the toe of her shoe.

The production of "Doctor in Buckskin Clad" that evening was excellent in spite of its corny title. The staging was technically good and the writing left little to be desired, especially the score for the accompanying orchestra and chorus. The history of the Whitman massacre was brought alive to all of us.

After living in peace for over a decade, Dr. Whitman and his family were tragically massacred by Indians who blamed the white men for starting a measles epidemic. One of Joe Meek's daughters had been left under the care of the Whitmans and was among those killed. Indians as well as white men mourned the death of the Whitmans. Members of the Cayuse tribe under Shap-Lish, or Whirlwind, helped bring the murdering Indians to justice. Shap-Lish was a powerful medicine man who had been a good friend to Dr. Whitman.

The fact that these Indians had been Christianized made the wars of the next 30 years especially tragic. Many Indians scorned the white man for not living up to his religion and consequently renounced Christianity themselves.

Besides teaching the Indians Christianity, the missionaries taught them how to till the soil. Joel Palmer in 1845 reported in his journal that the

Indians around the Umatilla River cultivated wheat, corn, potatoes, peas and other vegetables.

Dr. Whitman greatly influenced the Umatilla, Nez Perce, Cayuse, Walla Walla and Yakima tribes. These were the tribes who, along with the Flatheads, sent representatives to St. Louis in 1831 requesting that missionaries be sent to them. As an indirect response to this plea, Dr. Whitman, his wife Narcissa, and Henry and Eliza Spalding came in 1837. Dr. Whitman set up Wailaptu Mission near present-day Walla Walla, Washington, and Dr. Spalding founded Lapwai Mission near what is now Lewiston, Idaho.

The Nez Perce tribal reservation is now headquartered at Lapwai. The descendants of the other tribes influenced by Whitman and Spalding now comprise the Confederated Tribes of the Umatilla Indian Reservation. Our wagon train would be on the Umatilla Reservation for almost the entire distance traveled Friday and Saturday.

It was midnight before we were back in camp after seeing the play at Eastern Oregon College. We had four hours' sleep before it was time to get up and be on the road again. A new nine-mile stretch of freeway was being dedicated near Mt. Emily junction, 19 miles from La Grande, at 10:00 a.m. and the officials wanted us to be there. The wagons left at 5:10 and arrived at the ceremony on time. Mr. M.C. Williams of the State Highway Department presided at the ceremony. Besides the highway officials and a few spectators, an anonymous group of funsters called the "Blue Mountain Boys" was on hand with their muzzle-loaders and demijohns. Wearing ragged bib overalls, false black beards and driving Model T Fords, they milled around, completely upsetting the decorum of the occasion. Tex cut a ribbon with his bowie knife and the wagons rolled out onto the new freeway. They traveled only a hundred yards before turning off to our campsite at Strickland Meadows.

It was a beautiful campsite. A small stream of pure water flowed through the center of the meadow where grass grew as high as our mules' knees. This had been a traditional campground for pioneers. It was surrounded by thick forest with impenetrable underbrush when we were there, but when the forest was virgin the brush was not so thick and the wagons easily passed through the trees. Our wagons were primitively picturesque as they came down the dirt road through the woods, came out into the clearing and formed their circle.

Dave Roberts, our old friend from The Cincinnati Enquirer, visited us again that day. Since our meeting on the Green River in Wyoming, he had been to Alaska, Japan, Honolulu and back to Cincinnati. We reminisced about the weekend at Green River and agreed it was a great one. The fresh, cool water, the shade trees and green grass in the center of the Wyoming desert had encouraged festivities. It was no wonder that the Mountain Men had such good times at their annual Green River Rendezvous. Mr. Roberts stayed with us for supper then traveled on in keeping with his job as travel editor.

Strickland Meadows was as peaceful as it was beautiful. We were far enough off the highway that few sightseers found us. My mattress that night was a layer of hay over a cushion of pine needles. I was in bed before dark and had the best night's sleep of any in several weeks.

On Friday the wagon train traveled to the top of Dead Man's Hill, 14 miles from Pendleton. Mr. Ed Holpuch had given us permission to camp beside his cabin and use its facilities. During the day the caravan passed Meacham, which had been an early-day stage station and was the high point in the Blue Mountains. A few miles farther on they passed Emigrant Springs State Park. The Rev. Jason Lee stopped there in 1834 and later made the springs known to other pioneers. Near our campsite was a marker commemorating a battle fought on July 13, 1878. Bannocks, Paiutes, Snakes and Umatillas were fighting against the whites. The battle ended when Chief Umpine of the Umatillas turned against the other Indians and killed Chief Egan of the Paiutes. The most hostile Indians were thus deprived of their leader and peace was made.

When our wagon train was at that battleground, I had a minor skirmish of my own. I drained my emotional energy that day in a fight over our Pendleton campsite. The Pendleton wagon train welcoming committee insisted that we camp in the middle of the fairgrounds arena. I had misgivings about the location because there was no shade during the day for our people to comfortably stay near the wagons to greet visitors and guard against vandalism. I met the wagons when they arrived at the Holpuch cabin and passed on my misgivings about the Pendleton plan.

Ben Griffith, Rudy Roudebaugh and others observed that there must be some shade somewhere around the fairgrounds and suggested that I try harder. With that support I made another sortie into the fray at Pendleton. The force at Pendleton gave some ground in offering that our people would not have to sit around in the hot sun and that guards would be provided to prevent vandalism. Otherwise they made no concessions. Tex got the word later that I had been "arrogant and obnoxious" in my arguments. It turned out later that in my battle I suffered what might be called an empty defeat. I fought for something I didn't personally care too much about, so losing didn't hurt. After all, I personally wasn't being asked to park my station wagon out in the hot sun and stand around it all day.

The wagoneers didn't really care either. Most of them were invited into private homes where they enjoyed escaping from the hot sun and the omnipresent crowds. I can't help thinking that visitors were disappointed when they came to see us. All they saw were the wagons. The other two-thirds of the wagon train, the animals and people, were being kept elsewhere.

In my preparations for the grand entry into Pendleton I made friends with Al Davis, a kindly machine shop owner who welded borium onto some horseshoes for us. He offered to lend me a horse to ride in the wagon train's parade into Pendleton the next day. We walked out to a field adjoining the machine shop and Mr. Davis called out, "Here, Sonny!" From the other side of the field a fat, sorrel gelding came trotting over to be petted and scratched behind the ears. I had never seen a horse behave so much like a friendly dog. The next morning Ted Smith of Radio Station KUMA gave me a ride from the Holpuch cabin to town where Mr. Davis had Sonny saddled and waiting for me.

I rode out with a number of local people to meet the wagons. Mr. Dave Hamley and his son, Tom, owners of the famous Hamley's western dry goods store in Pendleton, rode with me. Umatilla County Sheriff Roy Johnson and County Judge Sam Cook rode out too. We found the wagon train people in good spirits. The descent of Cabbage Hill had been hard on the wooden brakes but there was never danger of mishap. Roy Brabham led the caravan since he was driving the wagon sponsored by Pendleton. At the edge of town a drum and bugle corps met us and led the parade; Tex, Gail and I rode three abreast behind the band. Sonny, an ex-show horse, adjusted his gait to the sound of the drums and gave me a rocking chair ride through town. Pendleton was packed with people and Roy Brabham got the lion's share of applause and greetings.

At our fairgrounds camp they barbecued three beeves that day. A special crane on the back of a truck lifted each beef from over its pit of coals and onto a table for cutting. The meat served over 900 people. Several thousand people came to see us and there were special welcoming ceremonies put on by the welcoming committee.

Sunday morning after church service I was busy organizing the wagoneers into small groups to be flown in private planes to a rodeo in Joseph, 80 miles east of Pendleton. I declined the offer to go in order to do advance work for the coming week, our last one on the Oregon Trail.

The covered wagons sponsored by Hillsboro and Medford pull into the camp at Strickland Meadows in the Blue Mountains of Northeastern Oregon.

XX. The Columbia

The pioneers followed the Umatilla 18 miles west. When the river turned north, they crossed it and continued west another 75 miles before they came down to the Columbia. No one had yet used high explosives to blast a path through the basalt rocks along the south bank of the Columbia River. The going was much smoother across the plains south of there. The John Day River, the Deschutes River and numerous small creeks flowed across the pioneers' trail and provided them with water. After they came back to the Columbia, they passed the famous Indian fishing grounds at Celilo Falls then turned south onto the tableland again until they returned to the river at The Dalles. Here they waited their turn for ferries and rafts to take them down the Columbia and up the Willamette River.

S.K. Barlow, impatient with the delay at The Dalles landing, made an overland route to the Willamette Valley in 1845. He claimed, "God never made a mountain without someplace for man to go over it or under it." With this in mind he formed a party equipped with 13 wagons, 16 yoke of oxen and seven horses. Their route took them between Mt. Hood and Mt. Wilson then down into the valley near Oregon City. They succeeded in making what came to be known as the Barlow Trail, but they lost most of their equipment among the huge boulders, trees and mountains. The trail was so rough that most pioneers still preferred to wait at The Dalles for transportation by water.

The railroad and the barbed-wire fence caused the Oregon Trail and the Barlow Trail to go out of use. The railroad offered a fast, safe, and in terms of human suffering, less costly way of reaching the lush valleys of Oregon and Washington. The barbed-wire fence made it difficult for travelers to follow the shortest routes and have access to the essential sources of water, fuel and forage. Nevertheless, as late as 1910 there were still immigrant wagons following the old trail routes across the open ranges. Most of these travelers were people who couldn't afford rail fare. Some older people we met in northeastern Oregon in 1959 remembered how their fathers had plenty of help on their ranches when the immigrants passed through. The covered wagon people often needed to stop and earn money to feed their families. After the flow of immigrants finally stopped, gypsies in colorfully painted, southern-European-style wagons continued to use the old trail routes for a number of years.

Mr. Giles French, Wasco County newspaperman and historian, told us some interesting things about the origins of several local place names. The John Day River, for example, was named after that member of the W.P. Hunt expedition who was beaten and stripped near there by hostile Indians. Wasco County took its name from the Indian practice of making drinking cups from the horns of the mountain goat. The cup was called "wasco." The original name for The Dalles was "Wascopum," meaning the place where the wasco was used, or more freely, the watering place. French-Canadian voyageurs changed Wascopum to "Les Grande Dalles" or in English, the big trough, which describes the appearance of the Columbia with its deep, wide channel carved through an ancient lava flow. The Americans came and changed Les Grande Dalles to The Dalles.

Between Pendleton and The Dalles our Oregon Centennial wagon train followed the old Oregon Trail Highway which has since been replaced by Interstate 80. Most of the time there was a number of miles separating the Oregon Trail Highway from the original trail route. The highway followed along the south bank of the Columbia and the original trail was up to 15 miles south of there. When we camped at Echo on Monday, we were one mile north of the original route; Tuesday's camp at Boardman was 12 miles north and Wednesday, four miles east of Arlington, we were seven miles north. Thursday, at an archaeological diggings site west of Arlington, we were back to within five miles of the trail, and on Friday at Biggs the two routes coincided. They separated and came back together once more in the 20 miles between Biggs and The Dalles.

The first day out of Pendleton we had fun with the unexpected arrival of Thyrza Pelling's identical twin sister from California. Most people couldn't believe she wasn't Thyrza until they saw the two sisters together. Even then they couldn't be sure which Thyrza was. Jeanne Marshall, the wagon train's most tease-able girl, gave us an example of the confusion.

We had all been invited for a swim at the public pool in nearby Hermiston. I arrived with a car full of people, changed into my swimsuit and met the others in the pool. Ki Roudebaugh pointed at a lady walking along the opposite edge of the pool and asked me, "Do you know who that is?"

I shook my head no. "I can't recognize people that far away without my glasses."

"It looks like Thyrza but it's really her twin sister. Oh look, here comes Jeanne. Let's listen and see what happens."

Jeanne came walking out from the women's dressing room and we swam over to hear better.

"Hi, Thyrza. I thought we left you back at camp. You sure do get around. You're in your swimsuit already. Where did you change? I didn't see you in the dressing room."

"I'm not Thyrza."

"Oh, come on now. Things aren't that bad are they— that you'd like to pretend you're someone else?"

In the pool we all grinned at each other.

"No, everything is fine, but I'm Thyrza's twin sister."

"Gee, I didn't know she had a sister. You're kidding. When did you get here? Thyrza, is this another trick you guys are pulling on me?"

We all laughed at the way Jeanne wavered from belief to disbelief, and she started to believe.

"You guys knew it all along and let me go on didn't you?"

After our swim we were invited to attend a banquet which the local historical society held in our honor. The food was good, especially the famous Hermiston watermelon, but after the food came speeches. Besides recounting local history, the speakers extolled the glories of our wagon train. Some wagoneers discretely excused themselves and went back to camp before all the glories were extolled. We had categorized long speeches in with the other hardships of life on the Oregon Trail and did our best to avoid them.

Early the next morning the wagon train left the Irvin Mann ranch near Echo for a 24-mile trek to Boardman. This was the day the wagoneers first sighted the Columbia. They rejoiced as much as the early pioneers had done. Also that day they could see Mt. Hood rising up some 125 miles ahead of them.

The welcoming festivities in Boardman included hanging Gail Carnine for horse stealing. In the kangaroo court preceding the hanging, a sway-backed, rheumy-eyed, decrepit, jaded, 30-year-old grey nag was paraded as evidence. The judge pronounced the sentence and Gail stepped behind a black cloth that had a hangman's noose hanging down to it from a tree limb. The noose was lowered behind the cloth; an official gave a signal and a man on horseback pulled it tight. A figure rose into the air hanging from its neck and the cloth dropped. The crowd gasped because the form being jerked up into the air was dressed like Gail and was his size. In a moment the figure was motionless and everyone laughed as they saw it was only an effigy. Gail came up grinning from under the rear of the speakers' platform and the laughter became mixed with loud applause.

After the hanging there was a salmon feed and interminable dancing. The noise and lights at 1:00 a.m. woke me up from my grassy bed in a nearby field. My fatigue was greater than the disturbance, however, and I went back to sleep until we began a new day at 5:00 a.m.

Our next camp was on the George Shane ranch four miles east of Arlington. The wagon trainers had a beautiful view of the Columbia during their day's travel. The campsite was on a dry, sagebrush-covered bluff where the only blessing was a view of the river.

Thursday morning we had breakfast in Arlington where George McUne and Shorty Hilliard treated everyone to a gunfight. They had worked out the scenario in private so it was as much a show for the other wagon train members as it was for the townspeople. It started during breakfast with George yelling into the restaurant at Shorty, "You stay away from my woman!"

Shorty yelled back, "You go to hell!" It sounded so good that not everyone knew they were kidding.

They met in the street a few minutes later. Both men drew their pistols, fired at each other and George fell. Onlookers weren't sure if it was real or not. George lay there for a minute until an Arlington city policeman walked over and said something to him. He got up, his pistol was confiscated, he was handcuffed and led off to jail by the policeman. Seeing that he was not wounded the onlookers realized that the pistols had been loaded with blanks, but now they didn't know whether or not the arrest was real. Some newspapermen took pictures of George behind bars, then he was released and the wagon train rolled out of Arlington. Shorty and George, the best of friends, had a long-lasting chuckle at the perplexed expressions on the faces of the people who saw their show.

Most people were never sure whether or not the police part of the show was pre-arranged.

Camp that day was on the Roy Phillipi ranch beside the Columbia where a group of archeologists from the University of Oregon were digging. They were finding arrowheads, grinding stones, sea shells, deer bone and charcoal which testified that Indians had camped there for at least the previous 2,500 years. The thought that my choice of campsites had been a favorite place for 25 centuries gave me a sense of confidence in what I was doing. A natural cove and a good beach on the river with easy access to the water made it a logical campsite for any society.

The construction in progress on the John Day Dam prompted the archaeological activity. Archaeologists had known of the site for years but they had not done any excavating until the area was scheduled to be flooded forever by the dam's backwater. If the dam is ever destroyed, archeologists of some future age will be able to explore the site again as well as the former site of the city of Arlington a few miles upstream. The entire town had been moved to avoid the backwater. There were only a few years' time lapse between the Indian's and white man's cultures, but the artifacts would show a world of difference between their lifestyles. The Indian artifacts were small, personal items barely removed from mother earth, and the white man's were huge, impersonal, concrete floor slabs and paved streets. It causes me to believe that if a group of 20th-Century Americans were to be transported to the Garden of Eden, the first thing they would do would be to cover it with asphalt and concrete.

Leaving the diggings behind, the wagon train rolled on west to Biggs where we camped at the former site of that town. Biggs had been moved because of construction on The Dalles Dam, but the backwater had not yet reached there. The town was near the mouth of the Deschutes River where the original trail came down to the Columbia.

Word reached us that day that Roseburg, our Oregon headquarters, had been devastated by an explosion. Gail Carnine left immediately to go back for special police duty. Pam went with him but their children, Cheryl and Gary, stayed with the wagon train. The rest of the day we listened to our radios to get more details about the disaster. A boxcar full of chemicals had exploded in the railroad yard. The explosion had leveled a nine-square block area and badly damaged the rest of the town. Besides being worried about our friends there, we were concerned about our office in the Umpqua Hotel. When Gail Carnine returned two days later he told us that our desks and files were liberally sprinkled with plaster and broken glass but there was no serious damage done. Of the 11 people killed in the explosion, none of them were close friends. It was fortunate that the accident happened at night when the railroad yard and that part of town were relatively deserted. Otherwise, the death toll would have been much higher.

That evening we were invited to a restaurant in Rufus where the pioneer ranchers in the area gave a banquet in our honor. While waiting for dinner we watched a television broadcast of films taken at Roseburg. We all suffered from shock and grief at seeing such destruction in the town we knew so well. The smoke and rubble were almost beyond belief. Most of us tried to be polite and pay attention to the after-dinner speakers, but it was a sorry attempt.

A personal misfortune happened to Thyrza Pelling the next morning. She discovered that her diary was missing. She had it with her the evening before but she couldn't remember where she had left it. We looked for it all over Rufus and all over the campsite but the search turned up nothing. Everyone was disappointed at the loss because she had kept the most careful notes of any of us on the trip. Besides the record, she had addresses of many of the people who had been so kind to us along our route from Missouri. We finally had to break camp without the book. Thyrza shed quite a few tears over the loss and many of us felt almost as bad.

This was the day of our last big parade before Independence, Oregon, and officially, it was our last day "on the trail." Everything indicated that The Dalles was turning out for us en masse. The Ft. Dalles Cavalry, a group of mounted men in Civil War uniforms, was on hand to escort the wagon train past the various welcoming committees. As I drove into town ahead of the caravan, I passed several groups of Indians in full regalia waiting to give their greetings. Some of the Indians were from the Wy-am band of the Wasco tribe. Others were from various bands on the Warm Springs Reservation.

At the mouth of the Deschutes River the Indians had set up teepees. Wasco Chief Nathan Heath met the wagons there and welcomed them to the tribal territory. Farther on, at the site of Celilo Falls, Chief Henry Thompson of the Wy-ams presented Tex with some smoked salmon.

In The Dalles I talked with the police about traffic conditions then Bob Hedeen of the Chamber of Commerce took me out to the edge of the town where the parade was forming. I decided to borrow a horse from a stable near there so I could ride out to meet the wagons. The man at the stable only had one horse left: a recalcitrant muddy-colored buckskin. I was in a hurry so I didn't ask the horse's name. Lacking anything better, I named him Old Sonuvabitch. At first I didn't think of it as a name but he responded to it so well that I figured he must have been called that in the past by other riders. He responded to the reins better when I punctuated the name with my heels to his ribs.

It was a fun ride to the wagons. Along the way I met County Centennial Chairman Alf Wernmark who was a member of the Ft. Dalles Cavalry. He traded me his Union Army cap for my battered old Stetson. Later I heard that he used it to take up a collection from a crowd watching some Indians stage a dance. The Indians were about to walk away with hardly any recompense until Mr. Wernmark passed my hat around and told everyone that it was part of the wagon train. The collection went better that time.

Our parade was the largest ever held in The Dalles. Some of the rifle and pistol firing almost caused me to treat the crowd to an impromptu rodeo. Old Sonuvabitch was the jumpiest horse I'd ever ridden. The parade stopped in front of the old City Hall where we were officially welcomed by Mayor Jack Howe and more Indians.

We had trouble on the way up the hill to the park. The street was too steep and the pavement too smooth for the animals to get good footing. Every time they tried to pull, their feet would slip and they would almost fall. National Guard jeeps hooked onto the wagon tongues and pulled some of the wagons up the one-block-long steep hill. Other wagons were pushed up the hill by spectators and wagon train members. I expected some of the wagoneers to be upset about my choice of routes but they were in such a happy mood that they just laughed about it and pitched in to help. The wagons circled up among the trees, the animals were fed and tethered, and we had hamburgers for lunch.

I became wagon master that afternoon. It happened as I was downtown taking a shower. George McUne came down from camp with the news that Tex had flown to Ashland to see his family and take care of a sick horse. His last words as he left were, "Tell Dick he's wagon master this weekend." Since everything was in order with the wagon train, there was no wagon mastering to be done. My title was strictly honorary.

That evening we were invited to a salmon feed at the Inland Navigation Company dining room. We were honored by the presence of Flora Thompson, widow of the great Chief Tommy Thompson for whom she was still in mourning. She had broken mourning to come to the banquet. She was a gracious lady and we were glad to meet her. She brought her sister and her grade-school-age granddaughter, Linda Marie

George, with her. Before we ate, Mrs. Thompson said grace in her native tongue.

Cheryl Carnine was sitting on my right and Linda Marie and Mrs. Thompson sat on my left at the head table. I remembered reading how in the old days Indians had looked at some of the blond-haired pioneer children and had offered to trade Indian children for them. Seeing that Mrs. Thompson was in a good mood, I decided to recreate a similar situation.

"Mrs. Thompson, would you like to let Linda come on the wagon train with us? We'll leave Cheryl here to take her place."

Mrs. Thompson caught on immediately. She turned to Linda with smiling eyes and asked, "Would you like to go with the wagon train so the yellow-haired girl could stay with us?"

Linda thought seriously for a moment then said, "OK grandma, if you can come too."

Everyone laughed and the deal was forgotten by the adults. Mrs. Thompson gave a talk on the Christianization of the Indians. She also showed us samples of the food the Indians used to eat. Among the samples were camas plants and the dried half of a large salmon.

As we were leaving the table, Linda brought me a red-tipped ceremonial Indian feather. "Well thank you, Linda, but how do I rate that?" I asked.

Mrs. Thompson told me, "She gives you that to release her from making the trade so she will not have to go with you."

I saw that the child was serious. Knowing the importance they placed on the decorated feathers I was flattered to accept the gift. Wanting to give something in return, and feeling that money would lack lasting value, I gave the girl my pocket compass. I told her that the compass would keep her from ever being lost.

Churches in The Dalles were closed the next day in order that everyone could attend services at our camp. The August sun caused some discomfort to the minister and musicians on the bandstand, but the congregation had the benefit of the shade trees. Myron Hall, pastor of the First Methodist Church, told about the first Christian services held near there at Pulpit Rock in March, 1836. The Rev. Daniel Lee and H.W.K. Perkins had been sent there by Jason Lee, then head of the Oregon Methodist Mission. During their first winter there they baptized more than 250 Indians.

That afternoon the wagon train people rested and visited with the thousands of sightseers. The Eagles gave us dinner that evening at their club. Gail and Pam Carnine came in while we were eating and gave us a first-hand account of the damage in Roseburg.

After dinner I was chosen to thank the Eagles for the meal. As I got up to speak, someone said, "Tell us about the trip." Everyone seemed to be listening so I went ahead on the talk I had developed. It was rambling and sketchy but it always pleased the audience:

"Some of you may know how this wagon train got started. Alan Knudtson, a jeweler in Roseburg, first had the idea. He sold the idea to the Jaycees and they sold it to the State of Oregon. Now for the past four months we've been out selling the State of Oregon to the world.

"It was sort of rough sometimes. The first morning we were camped at Independence, Missouri, we rolled over in our sleeping bags and saw snow on the ground. Then it started raining. It rained for 39 of the first 40 days we were on the trail. After that there were days when it was unseasonably warm and the livestock almost gave out from the heat.

"We pretty much stayed on the roads all the way, and the roads followed the courses of the rivers just as the original trail had done. The most worrisome river was the Platte; it was a mile wide and an inch deep. We were glad we didn't have to ford it like the pioneers did. That's the river the pioneers complained so much about. They said it was too thick to drink and too thin to plow.

"Probably the most exciting part of the trip was the Indian attacks. At Chimney Rock, Nebraska, we had a battle with the Sioux. Rudy Roudebaugh's mules didn't know it was all in fun so they took off in the first charge and ended up on a ridge a half mile from the action. Then in the attack at Cokeville, Wyoming, the same mules were untied in the first charge and ended up out in front of the Indians leading the second charge. The Indian raids tapered off when I let it be known that we were out of blanks and would have to use live ammunition.

"The heat in Idaho was something else. See this twisted piece of plastic? It still writes. It's a ball-point pen I was carrying in my hip pocket out there. It was so hot that when I sat on it, it bent like taffy candy.

"The best part of the trip was the food. We are undoubtedly the best-fed wagon train in history. Every town we passed through has wanted to do something for us and usually that consisted of feeding us. The most grateful people among us are the women who don't have to put meals together in that little kitchen truck when some town is treating us like this. Anyway, we're all grateful and I want to thank you on behalf of the whole group."

Everyone applauded, including the wagoneers who had heard the same talk at least 20 times. It turned out to be the last time that I gave it.

While I talked I censored out the things I felt shouldn't be told. I didn't talk about how distemper had gone through our remuda and how pitiful it had been to leave three of our horses behind. I didn't mention the tick-picking party at South Pass and all the booze we had consumed at the Green River. Nor did I mention our fights: the one at Farson where I almost had my head twisted off with my kerchief or the two sleepless nights of squabbling around Mountain Home. Besides not mentioning how we fought each other, I kept quiet about the clashes with towns like

Fairbury, Casper and Pendleton. There are other things which after all these years are still better left untold. The loving, hating and envying caused lots of trouble, but somehow they made it all meaningful.

Coronet Films made a documentary about the Oregon Trail using our wagon train and personnel as characters and props. Pictured are: Dave Gastman, Pop Clark, Richard Carter, Bob Fineout, Robbie Roberts, George McUne, Gail Carnine, and Roy Brabham. Tex Serpa looks on from the shade.

XXI. THE WILLAMETTE

A friendly crowd watched us load the converted World War II LSM. The bow folded down to form a ramp into the 220-foot-long, 22-foot-wide hull. Captain Darrell Gutzler commanded the ocean-going tug "Frances," which was attached to the barge aft and gave it its power. We drove the water truck and kitchen truck aboard first, then we pushed the wagons on by hand. A tethering cable was stretched lengthwise down the hull and the animals were tied onto both sides of it. We worried that some of them would panic and kick one another when we got underway but they all behaved as if it were only another humdrum day. Over a thousand people waved goodbye as we backed out into the center of the wide river. Anyone who wasn't there missed a once-in-a-lifetime opportunity to see how a wagon train is loaded aboard a barge.

Our festive mood was in great contrast to Ezra Meeker's barge trip down the Columbia in 1852. Someone started singing "Home Sweet Home" and soon everyone on the barge was weeping from homesickness and fatigue. The pioneers had taken almost a week to reach Ft. Vancouver or Oregon City on their makeshift craft. Our trip was to take only ten hours.

After our departure we set out to explore the traveling accommodations. The lounge, galley, sundecks and everything else on board the Frances seemed luxurious. Most of all we enjoyed spending the day unmolested by sightseers and journalists. The best part of our accommodations was the water barrier between us and them.

There was even enough space for us to get away from one another. The anti-Tex Serpa group spent most of the day sequestered in the wagons forward in the barge. I felt vibrations of a huge sulk every time I looked at the wagons and thought of the men riding there. It was natural, however, that animosities developed among us. We could never have catered to all the different ideas as to how a wagon train should be managed. With me telling everyone what route we should take and where we should camp, and with Tex telling everyone how to harness, drive and care for the livestock, it was only natural for us to have differences of opinion. Anyone who has been around horsemen knows that each one has his own ideas on animal care. Not to be blasphemous, but I think that if Our Lord Himself had been in Tex's position, he would have incurred just as much wrath. Without strong leadership there would have been seven wagon trains consisting of one wagon each.

I can't be too critical of the sulkers because I wasn't overly social myself. I think nearly all of us felt that we had seen quite enough of each other. After touring the ship, I spent most of the day reading and enjoying the solitude. I was finally able to finish reading <u>Dr. Zhivago</u> and reexamine some of Pasternak's ideas.

At Cascade Locks another crowd of people watched as we were lowered to the new level of the river. The towns of Cascade Locks and Bonneville were arguing over which was to give us lunch. We forestalled violence by accepting an invitation on the other side of the river at Washougal, Washington. That made a total of seven states we visited in the course of our trek.

It was nearly dark when we turned up the Willamette and passed under Portland's bridges. We could have unloaded north of Portland and driven the caravan through in a grand parade, but we were still miffed at the lack of support we had received from that city six months earlier. When we reached our destination south of the city it was too dark to unload. Instead we moored up to the shore and waited for morning. Some of our members went ashore, but most of us saved our celebrating for a few days later when we reached Independence.

I saw an empty bunk in the crews' quarters and slipped into it for a poor night's sleep. My body missed the hard, irregular surface of mother earth. It was the first bed I had slept in since four months before while en route to Independence, Missouri.

From Portland the wagon train went to Hillsboro, then made stops at Dundee and Amity before reaching Independence. At Amity a man showed up to fill in some blanks in the story of Ben's extra horse, Wild Bill. Tex was walking by Ben's wagon when he heard the man ask Ben where his thoroughbred was. Tex knew then that Ben had never owned the horse; he was simply delivering it from Kansas to Oregon. Ben hadn't told the straight story for fear that someone in authority would object to him being in the horse-delivery business. Tex didn't want to eavesdrop so he missed the rest of the story. Seventeen years later Ben told me all about it. Since Wild Bill was becoming a source of trouble, Ben felt he should leave it in Idaho. Eldon Thompson hadn't bought the horse but was simply keeping it for its owner. Ben's other alternative would have been to let the wagon train use the thoroughbred, but he felt that would have been a violation of the owner's trust. The man Ben met in Amity drove to Idaho and got the horse, and time took care of the hurts.

While the wagon train traveled south through the lush fields of the Willamette Valley, I worked with the people in Independence arranging our homecoming celebrations. Chamber of Commerce Secretary John Pfaff directed the Independence people as they worked to decorate the town, plan the parade, and arrange housing and parking for all the people they expected on August 15. I set up my tent at our final campsite and tried to be as helpful as possible.

Independence overflowed with people on the day the wagon train arrived. Its normal population was 2,100, but on that Saturday the number grew to some 60,000. At least another 60,000 would have been there had it not been for the monumental traffic jams leading into town. Police reported that cars were lined up for ten miles on the two highways leading into town from Portland and Salem.

Over 100 units took part in the parade. The honorary hostess was Miss Helen Meek, great-great-granddaughter of the famous pioneer, Joe Meek. Our seven battered wagons brought up the rear as a climax to the parade. The Fifth Wyoming Volunteer Cavalry rode with the caravan. Col. Robert S. Lee and his men had driven from Cheyenne, Wyoming, to share this last good time together.

The parade ended at the Henry Hill School where carpenters had built a stockade and speakers' platform. Our current governor, Mark Hatfield, greeted each of us personally and had lunch with us. Our future governor, Tom McCall, who was then a newsman for television station KGW in Portland, interviewed many of us and recorded the event on film. Oregon's Secretary of State Howell Appling, our old friend and admirer, also joined us for lunch. Tony Brandenthaler of the Centennial Commission escorted Grandma Gatewood down from Portland to see us before she took a bus home to Ohio. Thomas Vaughan, Director of the Oregon Historical Society, received the artifacts we brought from donors along the route of the Oregon Trail. After listening to the speeches of praise and welcome, we turned over to the post office the 40,000 pieces of philatelic mail which we had brought from Missouri in Ben Griffith's wagon.

In all the fanfare only a few of us noticed the mustachioed man in the buckskin coat who stood around quietly reveling in the event. It was Alan Knudtson, the jeweler from Roseburg who first thought of having a wagon train retrace the route of the Oregon Trail from Missouri to the Willamette Valley.

Our fir-forest campground was the scene of constant celebrating for the next two days. The Fifth Wyoming Cavalry brought guitars, mandolins and fiddles and provided music. In the cavalry tent eight people fell to the ground when a portable table collapsed under their weight. Everyone was more startled than hurt and the mishap added to the hilarity.

Rudy Roudebaugh, his wife, Ki, and their daughter, Janell, wave at the crowds in Independence during the homecoming parade.

Independence, Oregon, on August 15, 1959.

More than 60,000 people were in town to watch the wagon train's homecoming parade.

XXII. SETTLING IN OREGON

Celebrating didn't stop the intra-wagon-train fighting. Most of the conflict concerned the dividing up of equipment such as harnesses and horseshoes and souvenirs such as peace pipes and plows. Those things which had been given to us as a group were being coveted by individuals. Pop Clark was one of the main contenders in the action. I accused him of misappropriating the John Deere plow which had been tied onto the side of his wagon for all but the last few days of the trip. This led to my life being threatened for the second time in the course of the journey.

"That plow is no concern of yours, Richard Carter."

"The hell it isn't. I arranged for the John Deere Company to loan it to us so our wagon train would look more authentic. It wasn't ours to give away."

"Well, it's gone and you might as well forget about it."

"Here you call yourself a Christian and you pull something like that. That's stealing, you know."

Pop pulled out his pocket knife and unfolded the blade. He waved it under my nose and said, "Don't talk to me like that, you young whelp. I'll slice you up like a piece of cheese."

The blade wasn't long enough to scare me so I held my ground. One of Pop's friends intervened and calmed him down. I never solved the mystery of the missing plow but I knew that someone's self-interest had been served at the expense of the group in general and me in particular.

That evening I had a revealing heart-to-heart talk with Ben Griffith. We were having a glass of beer at a tavern in Independence when he said to me, "You know, Richard, I figure there were three big troublemakers on that trip, and one of them was me." To me that confession cleared the way for us to be friends forever.

We had to worry about the livestock but there was no fighting involved. Individual wagon train members bought the horses and mules on liberal credit terms. Each man who wanted to buy his team or riding horse was allowed to do so. The wagons were taken to be displayed for the rest of the year at the Centennial Exposition in Portland before being returned to the towns and counties which sponsored them.

Reunions

We stopped fighting when we stopped being together so much. Perhaps the best reunion ever was at Roy Brabham's funeral in 1964. Old Roy had died in the middle of plowing a field on his son's ranch near Terrebonne, Oregon. He and the tractor kept right on going: he into eternity and the tractor into a ditch at the end of the field. Ten men from the wagon train attended the funeral as honorary pall bearers. Had Roy been able to see how we sat down together in friendship, he would have been glad that his death served that purpose.

Eventually we all became less faithful in attending the annual reunions. Some of us moved away from Oregon, others became too busy to attend, and some became too old and infirm. When we had a reunion, there was always time to remember the rain, the heat, the good times and the fights. There was also speculation concerning our accomplishment.

Accomplishments

We agreed that assembling a wagon train and taking it over 2,000 miles was not our major accomplishment, yet it was the only measureable one. Perhaps the most important thing we did was to contribute something similar to what a major league baseball team gives to its fans when it wins the World Series. Everyone who experienced our journey, even vicariously, found cause for a greater feeling of self-worth. We made Americans proud to be descended from pioneer ancestors and proud to be living in the same country with us. Although pride and self-esteem cannot be measured, any sociologist would testify that such feelings help people become more willing to work for the betterment of themselves, their community and their country.

One of our more tangible accomplishments was to attract the attention of the world to a stretch of territory that had been the scene of one of the greatest human migrations of all times. We honored the pioneers who built the western half of our nation and we let the world know that Oregon was having a birthday.

We also revived an interest in history. The arguments we caused as to whether or not we were "right on the trail," were by their occurrence testimony to our success. Four years after our journey, Rudy Roudebaugh revisited parts of the trail to see if anyone was interested in building an Oregon Trail Museum. He found that there were then over 50 such museums either being planned or being built. Before our trip, interest in such things was at a low.

From an advertising viewpoint, the amount of publicity that Oregon received was worth ten times the $46,526 which the trek cost. Besides daily articles in every large newspaper in the United States, many foreign newspapers followed our progress as well. We estimate that some three million people either saw the wagon train as it was moving or visited it at a campground. We were proud to have given the people of Oregon due value for their investment in us.

What Came Next

The wagon train experience also influenced the lives of those of us who participated. It gave all of us a taste for fame, a nutrient which has no substitute. Some members readjusted themselves into their former niches but others continued traveling. I went back to work for Bill Dawkins in Medford, but only after Tex, Thyrza and I had a four-month-long yachting adventure along the west coast of Mexico. I soon became disenchanted with the business world and left it to become a foreign language teacher.

Tex became a cross-country truck driver and continually hauled furniture all over the United States. Thyrza again took up mountain climbing and traveled all over the world pursuing those adventures. One of her excursions was to Mt. Everest. George McUne sold his welding shop and built his own pioneer village in Jacksonville, Oregon. At one time he traveled by covered wagon through Washington's Okanogan Valley into Canada and along the Applegate Trail in southern Oregon. Dave Gastman traveled from Oklahoma to California with a horse-drawn caravan on the Santa Fe Trail and also with the bicentennial wagon train which went from the state of Washington to Valley Forge, Pennsylvania.

Lessons Learned

The 1959 expedition taught me some lessons about living with myself and with others. I probably could have learned the same lessons from reading a book, but like so many lessons in life, the words are meaningless until you experience them. I learned something about getting people to work together in a group; I learned to appreciate people outside my own tribe and I learned about the danger of seeing people through a veil of preconceptions.

As far as group interaction is concerned, I decided that Pasternak was an impractical dreamer. It would be a wonderful world if we could all work together in an aura of mutual respect as long as we were dedicated to a common goal, but human nature won't let that happen. It was demonstrated to me a number of times that without a bond of friendship, self-interest will always take precedence over the goal of the group and over the well-being of the other group members. Those of us who liked Tex as a person were more inclined to work for the benefit of the entire expedition. Thyrza, for example, no matter how much she rankled others or was misunderstood, was always willing to lend a hand whenever it was needed.

At Mountain Home, Idaho, the wagon train stayed together in its greatest crisis because Shorty agreed to stay with us as a personal favor to Tex. It was always those who liked Tex who agreed to tackle such jobs as loading hay or setting up the portable latrine. Since 1959 I've seen in classrooms, offices and factories that a group will attain its goal more easily if everyone works together in friendship rather than in animosity. Simply having a common goal is not enough.

In the course of the journey I learned how to reach out of my own circle of associates and enjoy the company of many different people. I had my Russian and Spanish friends in San Francisco and my business associates in Oregon, but I had forgotten how to appreciate the loggers and farmers with whom I grew up. I had forgotten that those people had as much to give as I did. Perhaps they hadn't been to a university or hadn't traveled as much as I; the wagon train trip made me realize that their smiles, handshakes, money and election ballots were all as good as mine.

I learned in the fracas near Mountain Home, Idaho, that we shouldn't have preconceived ideas about how a person is supposed to behave simply because he is a member of a certain group. From the beginning of our trek I was shocked to see that everyone didn't behave as I thought wagon train members should. I had supposed that my group of Oregonians would be so dedicated to reaching their destination that there would be no time for quarreling and dissension. In Idaho I realized that everyone was a distinct individual, and being cast in with a tight group made each person strive harder to preserve his individuality.

Getting to know the people on the wagon train was like gaining a family. I lost the dream of finding the camaraderie which might exist in an army "Band of Brothers" or in a romantic novel. Gone from my mind were the old clichés about traveling together in harmony, forging a path through the wilderness while gazing steadfastly into the future. Instead we lived our daily lives alternately being angry and enjoying each other, like a person does at home with his family. Considering the strain we were under—lack of privacy, little sleep and bad weather—it was a wonder we didn't fight more. An original pioneer, Peter Burnett, writing his recollections near the turn of the century aptly described the conflicts on wagon trains: "There were ten thousand little vexations continually recurring, which could not be foreseen before they occurred, nor fully remembered when past, but were keenly felt while passing."

Author near The Dalles, Oregon, 1959.

Members of the Cavalcade

Dick Carter was the business manager and advance scout for the wagon train. His job was to find the route of the original trail, then find existing roads which followed as closely as possible the original route. He also chose campsites and coordinated with local authorities along the way.

Gordon R. Serpa. Known simply as "Tex," he was the wagon master. He personally chose all the members of the group. He supervised gathering supplies, and went to Missouri early to buy all the horses and mules. During the trek he rode along on his horse, "Reno," keeping an eye on the people, livestock and wagons. He kept everything moving in spite of the problems.

Ivan Hoyer was the news director for the wagon train. The 32-year-old graduated from the University of Oregon where he majored in radio production. He came from Cottage Grove, Oregon, and was a member of the Roseburg Jaycees who had conceived the idea of a wagon train.

Walter "Shorty" and Theresa Hilliard. From Myrtle Creek, Oregon, both were excellent horse handlers and had worked at fairs and stock exhibits showing horses. Shorty was our farrier, in charge of keeping all the wagon train horses and mules shod. He was also the driver of the Roseburg wagon. "Tres" was one of the volunteer cooks.

The Carnines: Gail, Pam, Cheryl, and Gary. Gail was a deputy sheriff in Douglas County, Oregon. He was the traffic control and security officer on the wagon train. Pam served as a cook. Cheryl and Gary were with the wagon train from the beginning.

The two Robbie Roberts, Sr. and II. Robbie Sr. drove the semi which was our hay and supply storage facility. The truck was loaned to us by the Oregon Truckers' Association. Robbie II, then a fifth grader, grew up to work 25 years as a police officer and also rose to the rank of captain in the U.S. Coast Guard.

Dave Gastman was a former boxer and mountain guide who helped with traffic control and was the official wrangler for the wagon train. He and his wife, Lillian, were from Cottage Grove, Oregon.

The Roudebaughs: Rudy, Ki, and Janell. Rudy, an Oregon logger, was originally from the Oregon Trail town of Lexington, Nebraska. Ki was named after a landmark on the Oregon Coast, Kiwanda Point. Although Janell was still in school, she was also with the wagon train from Independence, Missouri.

Ben Griffith drove the four mules pulling the Independence wagon. His was the lead wagon and carried souvenir mail from Independence, Missouri. After retiring from farming, and before volunteering with the wagon train, he had been a real estate agent in Salem, Oregon.

George McUne drove two white mules pulling the Jackson County wagon. He owned an auto repair shop in Medford and had a collection of horse-drawn wagons. He was an avid hunter and fisherman.

Jeanne Marshall's home was in Roseburg where she worked as a secretary in the Douglas County Juvenile Department. She and her family had been on many camping and hunting trips. Jeanne drove the kitchen truck when it was her turn to be on cook duty.

Weaver "Pop" Clark. At age 66 Pop Clark was the oldest member of the wagon train. From Hillsboro, Oregon, he had worked most of his life in the mining and lumbering business. He built the wagon which he drove in the caravan.

Bob Fineout was the grandson of Pop Clark and the relief driver of the Hillsboro wagon. His main job was to drive the water truck. He supplied water for the livestock and people at the campsites where generally no other water was available.

Dick Melton was another wagon driver. His grandparents had been among the founders of Roseburg. He had been working on a horse ranch in Azalea, Oregon, before joining the wagon train.

Roy Brabham was the builder of six of the seven wagons in the wagon train. Patient and fun loving, Roy worked faithfully at greasing all 28 wheels. He greased wheels and Shorty Hilliard shod the animals every evening.

Thyrza, Rodney, and Trevor Pelling. The two boys joined the wagon train when their school year finished. The Pellings moved to Portland from Europe in 1946. They had once travelled 1500 miles of the Oregon Trail by car. Thyrza was one of the drivers of the kitchen truck.

Valoyce Johnson. Val, from Hubbard, Oregon, was working for an insurance claims adjuster when she left there to join the wagon train. She had spent much time on farms and ranches, handling everything from skillets to branding irons. Val was one of the three drivers of the kitchen truck.

Lowell and Edna Blair (not pictured)

Because of differences of opinion as to how the livestock should be cared for, the Blairs went home to Oregon when the caravan was in Wyoming. Lowell had been one of the drivers and Edna was a cook.

Oregon Cavalcade Itinerary

This itinerary as well as the photos of the members on the preceding pages of this appendix appeared in the pamphet that was sold along the trail during the expedition.

Itinerary

Starting Point . . .

Independence Mo., April 19, 1959

Will Arrive at . . .

Kansas City, Kansas	April 19
Olathe, Kansas	April 20
Gardner, Kansas	April 21
Lawrence, Kansas	April 22
Topeka, Kansas	April 24
St. Marys, Kansas	April 25
Westmoreland, Kansas	April 28
Marysville, Kansas	April 30
Fairbury, Nebraska	May 2
Hebron, Nebraska	May 4
Kearney, Nebraska	May 11
Lexington, Nebraska	May 13
Cozad, Nebraska	May 14
Gothenburg, Nebraska	May 15
North Platte, Nebraska	May 16
Ogallala, Nebraska	May 20
Bayard, Nebraska	May 25
Scottsbluff, Nebraska	May 27
Torrington, Wyoming	May 29
Casper, Wyoming	June 7
Independence Rock, Wyoming	June 11

Three Forks, Wyoming	June 13
South Pass City, Wyoming	June 19
Farson, Wyoming	June 22
Kemmerer, Wyoming	June 26
Border, Wyoming	June 29
Pocatello, Idaho	July 4
Rupert, Idaho	July 9
Burley, Idaho	July 9
Twin Falls, Idaho	July 11
Boise, Idaho	July 17
Caldwell, Idaho	July 19
Nyssa, Oregon	July 21
Vale, Oregon	July 22
Baker, Oregon	July 27
La Grande, Oregon	July 29
Pendleton, Oregon	August 1
Boardman, Oregon	August 4
The Dalles, Oregon	August 8
Hillsboro, Oregon	August 11
Dundee, Oregon	August 13
5 mi. north of Salem, Oregon	August 14
Independence, Oregon	August 15

OREGON CAVALCADE MAP

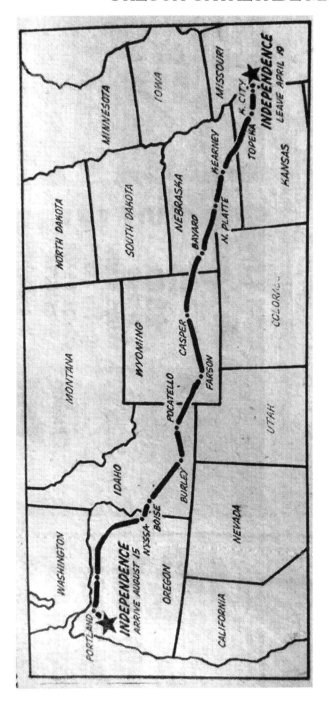

Map tracing the route of the Cavalcade expedition printed in the Medford Mail Tribune.

REFERENCES

Ox-Team Days on the Oregon Trail by Ezra Meeker.

The Oregon Trail by Francis Parkman.

Covered Wagon Women, Vol. 5 by Kenneth L. Holmes and David C. Duniway.

Aunt Elec's Journal by Alexandra Uzafovage Owen. Available for in-library use at the Oregon Historical Society Museum, Portland, Oregon.

Umatilla chieftains Art Montanic. (left)
and Louis McFarland (right) welcome
Tex Serpa and the wagon train to
Umatilla territory in Oregon.

Acknowledgements

Thanks to:

My wife, Jane, for having faith in me while working on this project.

Ivan Hoyer and the Portland <u>Oregonian</u> for giving me the photos.

William Dawkins for sending me on this expedition.

The Oregon Centennial Commission, Tony Brandenthaler, Chairman, for allowing me to stay with the wagon train after my boss, William Dawkins, resigned the account.

My great aunt Elec (Alexandra Uzafovage Owen) for leaving us the journal of her 1852 crossing of The Oregon Trail.

Karen Robinson of Buenos Aires for putting the manuscript into digital format.

Kristin Carroccino for being my publishing advisor and developmental editor.

The Jaycees of Roseburg, Oregon, and of Independence, Missouri, for initiating the idea of the wagon train and helping it get started.

Proofreaders Penny Reid and Beth Cockrel for their invaluable help.

Jeanne Marshall VanMeter for sharing her memories.

And especially all the historians, civic leaders and authorities who aided us along our way over the route of The Oregon Trail. I mentioned as many of them as possible in the text.

ABOUT THE AUTHOR

Richard Carter was born in Klamath Falls, Oregon, to parents who were lifelong Oregonians. He grew up on a small farm in the Rogue River Valley, and then served three years in the U.S. Army where he became a high-speed radio intercept operator and an expert in Soviet and Chinese codes.

Since 1959 Richard's interests have taken him to entirely different places. He always had an interest in foreign languages, especially Spanish and Russian. This interest led him to earn master's degrees in the teaching of the Spanish and Russian languages, and ultimately to become a high school foreign language teacher. It also led him to make 17 trips to Russia as a tour guide and interpreter, and at least 10 trips to various Spanish-speaking countries. In 2008 he and his wife, Jane, walked the 500-mile Camino de Santiago pilgrimage across northern Spain. They have returned to Spain each year since to serve as innkeepers in some of the hostels along the pilgrimage route. They live in Seattle and have two grown children and two grandsons. For permissions and ordering inquiries, please contact Richard at dcart29@comcast.net.

Richard and Jane Carter in Sotilla de la Adrada, Spain, June 2015.

Made in the USA
San Bernardino, CA
05 May 2017